A Surgeon in Combat

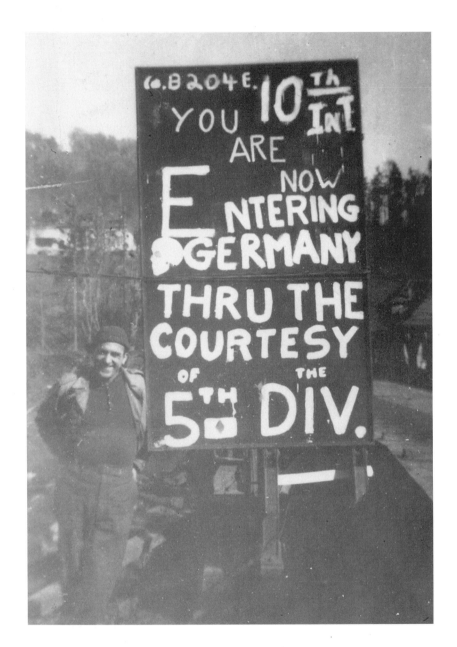

Crossing the Kyll River near the German-
Luxembourg border, February, 1945

A SURGEON IN COMBAT

European Theatre – World War II

OMAHA BEACH TO EBENSEE

1943 – 1945

William V. McDermott, M.D.

WILLIAM L. BAUHAN, PUBLISHER

DUBLIN, NEW HAMPSHIRE

1997

BOOKS BY WILLIAM V. McDERMOTT

Surgery of the Liver and Portal Circulation
An Atlas of General Surgery
Surgery of the Liver
History of Surgery at New England Deaconess Hospital
A Surgeon in Combat

LIBRARY OF CONGRESS CATALOGING IN PUBLICATION DATA

McDermott, William V., 1917-
A Surgeon in Combat: Omaha Beach to Ebensee: Europe. World War II, 1943-1945
by William V. McDermott.
    p.   cm.
Includes bibliographical references and index.
ISBN 0-87233-120-2
1. McDermott, William, V., 1917-,   2. World War, 1939-1945—Medical care—United
States.   3. World War, 1939-1945—Personal narratives, American   4. World War, 1939-
1945—Campaigns—Western Front.   5. United States, Army—Biography.   6. Surgeons—United States—Biography.   I. Title
D807.U6M38 1997
940.54'7573—DC21   97-3025
                                                            CIP

William L. Bauhan, Inc., Publisher
Old County Road
Dublin, New Hampshire 03444

Printed in the United States of America

To the Memory of

EDWARD D. CHURCHILL, M.D.

Surgeon, Scholar, Mentor

John Homans Professor of Surgery, Harvard

&

Chief, West Surgical Service, Massachusetts General Hospital

About This Book

A few years ago, my daughter, Janie, and I came upon a huge box of correspondence in a back closet of my house in Dedham, Massachusetts—a collection of more than seven hundred letters I had written her mother during World War II. I was about to throw them out, but Janie was so infuriated at the idea, I had to promise that I would not dispose of the letters without recording the gist of most of them for her and the rest of the family.

The editing process eliminated at least one half of them I considered too personal for general interest. The remainder was transcribed with commentaries inserted appropriately, since censorship had prevented including many of the details essential to understanding events. At that point, several individuals who read through the rough draft thought it might be of considerable general interest, so I revised the text with that in mind.

Dick Wolfe, the curator at the Countway Library at the Harvard Medical School, and other readers thought that the manuscript would be more accessible if it were transformed into a narrative style, using most of the material in the original letters and maintaining their general flow. The resulting manuscript therefore is in narrative form based on the letters as well as memories they generated, information that might not have survived military censorship.

In the long process of rereading, editing and reediting these
letters to Blanche, a number of thoughts occurred to me. I found
myself surprised at many of my reactions and often, my lack of
perception over many events and circumstances of the era.

My anti-German reactions, which were expressed so often, were
hardly praiseworthy but perhaps understandable at that time,
when all the brutalities and horrors of the Nazi philosophy and
programs were so evident. Less understandable was my lack of
reaction to the obvious fact that our combat forces were comprised
almost entirely of male white Americans—very few African-Ameri-
cans, Hispanics, Asians, or other obvious minorities. The blacks
who were drafted were, in general, assigned to ordnance and supply depots and to driving trucks that delivered supplies and equipment. I know that Colonel Benjamin Davis led a squadron of Af-
rican-American pilots in Italy and there was a Japanese-American
regiment, also in Italy, which I believe was the most highly decorated unit in the army, but that was about the limit of integration.
Why this discrepancy was not obvious escapes me, since from
youth, I had been anti-Nazi, antifascist, interventionist, and pro-
Roosevelt, and certainly against anti-Semitism or racism in any
form.

Why the concentration camps were such a shock also puzzles
me. During a visit to Germany in 1938, I certainly knew about
Dachau, but had a vague concept that it was only a prison for political opponents of the Nazis. Even the knowledge of Bettelheim's
experiences, the history of our S-2 officer (Franz Siegel and his
family), and the knowledge of the anti-Semitism that was rife in
Germany somehow did not prepare me for the horrors of the concentration camp at Ebensee.

We were no better in our analysis of Stalinism. Certainly, there
were redbaiters at home but many of us felt that they represented
only reactionary anticommunism. We were not knowledgeable

about the Katyn massacre of Polish officers by the Russians or about the millions of executions perpetrated during Stalin's rule. I seemed, in my letters, to excuse and overlook the brutalities of the Russians while venting anger on the Germans—probably because the Red Army was such a vital ally during the war.

All of which underscores how much more clearly we view events in retrospect. On the other hand, I think that much of the discussion in the letters may be surprising to subsequent generations.

For better and worse, here we are more than a half century after December 7, 1941, the date which Franklin Roosevelt referred to as "the day which will live in infamy." Since then there have been decades of incredible events. Perhaps we have reached a point in history when wars such as this and later conflicts will not recur. The events of the past few years in Russia certainly would lend support to this hope, as we enter a new and perhaps less brutal century, although the persisting ethnicity in the Balkans, the horrors of Somalia and Rwanda, the virulent religious fanaticism in India and elsewhere, and continuing evidence of racism in the world make it clear that we still have a long way to go. Somehow, I feel that we will reach the goal of "malice towards none; with charity for all; with firmness in the right" that Lincoln expressed in his second inaugural address—a beacon we can follow with hope and direction, and "achieve and cherish a just and lasting peace among ourselves and with all nations."

Acknowledgments

Before completing these remarks, I would like to acknowledge the contributions to this text of a number of individuals. Obviously, since these events are based on our correspondence while

I was overseas, the presence of my wife, Blanche (who died suddenly in 1969 of acute pulmonary edema), runs throughout the book. Readers will find my letters to her, transcribed exactly as written and set off in different type, interspersed through the narrative.

In addition Richard Wolfe, curator of rare books at Countway Library, who has been of inestimable help as the writing progressed, and my publisher, William L. Bauhan; I am indebted for the secretarial help of Joan Long as well as Kerry Jones and Scott Phillips, that was essential as was the continuous editing and revision carried out by Anne Lunt and Patricia Storey. Members of the 550th AAA (AW) Battalion and the 1st Auxiliary Surgical Unit of the 30th Field Hospital, are all a part of this tale—if not always by name, certainly by collective input. Although I did not encounter any friends who were in the same general area, direct or second-hand commentaries—from or about George Starkey, Gene Lewis, Ted Robie, Jim Kreisle, Mel Osborne, and Joe Patterson—added to the general background. And so—on to the tale itself!

Contents

List of Illustrations

Maps

Chronology

1943

January	Casablanca Conference
February 2	Stalingrad
May 13	Fall of Tunisia to Allies
July 9-10	Invasion of Sicily
July 25	Fall of Mussolini
September 19 (to May 1944)	Third major series of U-Boat attacks on convoy routes (Wolf Packs)
September-December	Invasion of Italy

1944

January	Anzio
June 6	Overlord—Normandy
June-August	Marianas, Guam, Saipan
July (to June 1945)	Battle for Burma (ended May 2)
August 16	Landings in Southern France
October 22-24	Leyte Gulf
December 1944-January 1945	Battle of the Bulge

1945

February	Yalta Conference
March	Phillipines conquered
March 7	Remagen bridgehead
March 27	Rhine Crossing (3rd Army)
April 12	Death of Roosevelt
April 25	Death of Mussolini
April 29	Death of Hitler
May 2	German surrender in Italy
May 7-9	V-E Day
July 17	Atomic bomb explosion in New Mexico
July 21-23	Truman, Churchill, Stalin in Potsdam
August 6	Hiroshima
August 10	VJ Day
September 2	Formal surrender

Prologue

World War II broke out in Europe while I was still a student at Harvard Medical School, which I had entered after finishing Harvard College with the Class of 1938. The events described in these letters began in the spring of 1941. The war was going badly for England, and in my view, for America as well. Americans of that era fell into two strongly opposing political camps about which most students rallied. The "isolationists" felt that the United States should stay out of any European wars. The "interventionists" (of whom Archibald MacLeish was the ultimate protagonist), believed strongly that we should be involved actively in the support of England, as soon and as much as possible. President Roosevelt, an interventionist, was faced with very strong opposition by people like Ambassador Joseph Kennedy and Senators Robert Taft, William Borah, and others, and had to move more circumspectly than he might have if left to his own devices.

In the spring of 1941, the students of Harvard Medical School gathered in one of the amphitheaters to hear on successive days a plea from the Surgeons General of the army and the navy to medical students to sign up with the armed services. The objective was to give us inactive commissions, allow us to continue with medical school and one year of hospital training, and call us to active duty if the occasion warranted. Both men predicted that we would be at war before the year was out, and stated bluntly how completely unprepared we would be for conflict. Both the army and the navy had very small, limited medical support services and without a draft there was no way they could bring any of us into service. If we accepted inactive commissions, they would at least have a backlog of reserve officers on whom they could call after a sufficient training period. Following these impassioned pleas, a number of us rushed off and signed up for commissions. I became a second lieutenant, Medical Administrative Corps Reserve—a peculiar rank related to the fact that I could not have any kind of a commission in the Medical Corps since I did not yet have a doctoral degree.

Life went on and Pearl Harbor did come. The Medical School offered to speed up the curriculum for anyone who wished to graduate early and thus be more rapidly available to the armed services. A number of us signed up with this new curriculum, which meant that we would graduate from medical school in February 1942 instead of June, start our internships and residencies several months earlier, and complete a year's training prior to induction.

In December 1942 I met Blanche. Because of gas rationing we courted mostly by travel on street cars back and forth between Brookline and the Ritz and other spots in town. We became engaged in February, and married three months later on May 15, 1943, after I had finished a year of surgical residency. Shortly after a brief wedding trip to Florida I received my orders to proceed to Camp Edwards, where I was to become a battalion surgeon ultimately assigned to the 574th AAA-AW (SP Battalion)—a mobile armored half-track unit that carried multiple machine-gun mounts. The presumed role of these units and similar 40mm Bofors gun battalions was to serve with the infantry armored divisions and provide mobile antiaircraft protection against low-flying planes; a secondary use was to provide light covering fire during operations such as river crossings.

Blanche came with me to Camp Edwards, where we were for-

tunate enough to find a garage apartment on Eel River Road in
Wianno—a wonderful spot owned by a Mrs. Sicard, who hadn't
intended to rent the apartment but took pity on us. So there we
were ensconced happily for the summer.

The enthusiasm of this volunteer army was not matched by skill
and experience, and the efforts of the small minority of regular
army and National Guard officers to turn us into a functioning
military unit were initially ludicrous, to say the least. The concept of moving a mass of almost a thousand men in the appropriate direction by a combination of such commands as "By the right
flank—March!" "Route step," "Parade rest," and other totally unfamiliar expressions led to occasional chaos. Even the battalion
surgeon had to take his turn in leading formal "parade."

By dint of constant drills, classes, texts we gradually improved.
The Medical Field Manual was totally outmoded and one had to
adapt a limited basic medical knowledge to a hazy projection of
what might actually occur in combat—a situation that few of us
had ever experienced except for my staff sergeant, George Koca,
who had served in the Aleutians along with scattered officers and
enlisted men.

Rather suddenly, in September, I received secret orders that
because of an injury to the battalion surgeon I was assigned to go
overseas almost immediately with an activated unit (the 550 AAA-
AW). When I moved under sealed orders, Blanche and I separated "for the duration," and she returned to Brookline.

After being issued our gear and listening to all the rumors as to
where we might or might not be going, we left the staging area and
proceeded directly by train to board troopships in Boston Harbor. Our ship was a small Cuban-American passenger liner called
the *Borinquen*. My bunk was in a small stateroom with five other
officers. Since the medical detachment brought up the end of the
line in all movements, I got the last bunk, the top of the inside

three, with just about enough room to turn over without hitting the ceiling.

Before boarding, we milled about on the docks for some time, drinking coffee provided by the Red Cross volunteers. One of them, Marky Pierce, was an old friend. When she spotted me (unbeknownst to me) she rushed down to Marblehead Neck, where Blanche was staying with her family, and told her where I was. Thanks to Marky, Blanche was able to watch the troopships leaving Boston Harbor from the lawn of her family summer home.

From where I was on the troopship, I felt that the war was going so badly that it would take ten years before we got home from wherever we were going. It seemed likely that we would be heading for the European Theater of Operations, but it would still be some time before we could be fairly certain. Everything was carried out in as much secrecy as the armed services could achieve.

1

Convoy to England

After periods of frantic preparations alternating with interminable waiting, we were finally alerted for overseas duty—destination unknown! A pre-dawn breakfast, grotesque contortions involved in climbing into full field pack and harness, an uneventful trip by train, and we arrived at the port of Boston. There, we were herded about by transportation officials, fed coffee and doughnuts by the Red Cross, and finally struggled up the gangplank of the *Borinquen*, a Cuban-American cruise ship. Obviously, as a troopship she carried more passengers than in her cruise days, but the whole setup was remarkably pleasant. Six of us shared a stateroom on one of the upper decks—a considerably better arrangement than most of our ancestors experienced in arriving in America, from the *Mayflower* on.

We sailed in the late afternoon of October 23, 1943 and at dawn saw the faint outlines of America fading on the horizon. Much later, when letters from home reached me, I learned that Blanche and the family had gathered on the lawn of our summer home to watch our convoy move slowly out of Boston Harbor.

It gives one a peculiar sense of timelessness not to know when the return trip will take place; I was certain that I would be gone for a number of years. The ocean was flat all day and broken only by the wakes of the grey transports and warships. Not a pitch or a roll, but obviously that was only a transient lull. Breakfast was the best meal of the day and was announced by a steward going around with a gong. Any resemblance to a Mediterranean cruise ended at that point. We were required to stay in our clothes constantly, asleep or awake, and wear two-piece heavy woolen underwear in case we should be precipitated into the frigid North Atlantic waters.

No one talked much about home. In fact, I can't remember any conversation at all about it after we left. There seemed to be a sort of tacit agreement to say nothing at all about what we had left behind. On the whole, it was a good idea.

The general feeling of nervousness and tension that had been noticeable prior to and during embarkation seemed to disappear once the men had a chance to see for themselves the magnificent protection given the troop convoys. This particular convoy, the largest (an estimated forty thousand troops) to leave the United States since the war began, was composed of a number of troopships from Boston and New York which had a rendezvous far out into the Atlantic with twelve destroyers and the battleship *Texas*. The destroyers were well out on the periphery of the convoy, the ships of which were clustered together in the middle of the circle. The whole arrangement was obviously structured to ward off U-boat attacks. The Germans had devised a system of "Wolf Packs" and troop convoys were prime targets. It was quiet and peaceful for a good part of the time but every so often several destroyers would race through the convoy at top speed and join others in the far side of the circle in beating off or sinking a U-boat or two. All we could see of this activity were the fountains of water following the depth charges that they dropped out on the horizon. Curiously, this repeated sequence did not engender fear in any of its physical symptoms. These came later but this seemed to be a distant abstraction without much threat or relevance to oneself.

The *Texas* was one of the old battleships and was not used in major combat in the Pacific; her only role was to be there in case the *Bismarck* came out to attack the convoy. In that event, the *Texas* was to head directly to the *Bismarck* with all guns blazing while the convoy turned tail to escape—a suicide mission. Fortunately, the old ship never had to commit suicide to protect a convoy. In fact, she went on to provide heavy covering fire for our landings in Normandy.

On the second day, we ran into a heavy ground swell and got our first taste of seasickness. Of course, most of these kids had never been on a ship before and had been waiting to be sick since they first set foot on board. Crowded quarters didn't help. Some of the high-priced help were a little under the weather too, since even majors and colonels slept four to a room. I was used to the sea and open water from early life, and since I didn't roll out of my eyrie in the night, I survived without problems.

The one thing we really missed, in addition to having room to move around, was a good hot shower. In all transports, fresh water was rationed and except for drinking fonts, was turned on only a few minutes twice a day for shaving. We were permitted one salt-water shower a day; not much of a substitute for the home product. In salt water, soap takes on the consistency of putty and the adhesiveness of glue. Our salt specials gave us the feeling of having played the lead role in a "tar and feathers" lynching.

The only entertainment outside of reading and writing was a continuous poker game. This trip alone should have provided enough to last the rest of my life. The sea chopped up again and as a result there were a lot of sad sacks in sick call who ran through all shades of green. If it is true that an army travels on its stomach, this one looked as if it wouldn't get much farther than the port where we docked.

Another occupation of battalion officers was censorship of mail. The officers' mail was spot-censored outside the battalion, but we were required to go through the mail of our various units and detachments. Since there was very little for the men to do but write, the job was tedious but at times amusing, since some of them often forgot that we were censoring the mail and wrote long discussions about us. Others, who apparently had the censors firmly in mind, added little plugs about how hard they were working and how much they deserved another stripe.

Another aspect of the tedium was the fact that the ships and transports of the navy were bone dry. We didn't have as much as a glass of beer after we left camp. A small carpet that would buzz me ashore, pick up my wife, and deposit us at Eel River Road in front of a fire with two fat old-fashioneds would have been mighty handy.

We occasionally had a little excitement from submarines in the morning but on the whole, the monotony of a trip like this was appalling after the first few days. But we really got a blast toward the end of the first week. The ship was rolling and pitching but it was truly magnificent on deck. A huge expanse of angry sea rose up with every pitch, spraying the deck and then falling off endlessly as the bow rose in another crest.

Our constant zigzagging made it impossible to analyze our route. It was only after we landed that I was able to untangle where we had been. Apparently, after the convoy formed, we went south almost as far as the Azores in an attempt to distract the Wolf Packs, then turned north. By October 30, we came in sight of land to starboard, apparently the west coast of Ireland, and then turned the northern tip to head south.

On November 4, twelve days out of Boston, we eased into the port of Swansea in Wales. By the time we entered the Irish Sea, we were apparently out of the high danger zone, and could strip down and sleep between sheets—quite an event when you've been sleeping fully dressed for days on end.

We debarked to board a troop train and headed north to Liverpool. The most impressive thing to me during our comfortable ride through the countryside was the spirit of the British. People collected at windows and doorways, all waving, holding their fingers up in Churchill's V gesture or with their thumbs up. Little groups of moppets gathered on their way from school and jumped up and down cheering. Some of the towns showed obvious scars of indiscriminate bombings. We came into the Liverpool station at night and since Great Britain had a complete blackout (entirely different from our dim-outs), we really walked blind as we marched through the suburbs, following the white street markings and the dim blue lights of the unit ahead of us. We would hear people talking to us, cheering and singing, but couldn't see a thing although they were in doorways on the sidewalk only a few feet away. It was truly an emotional experience when we thought of what they had been through for four years.

When we awoke, the setup at camp was very pleasant—stone barracks, excellent mess equipment, and a very attractive countryside which we hadn't had much chance to explore. We stayed in these barracks some days to draw combat equipment and then moved to a somewhat more permanent position.

2

England at War

LIVERPOOL TO CATTISTOCK, DORSET
November 5, 1943 – January 17, 1944

The name of our temporary barracks, "Blue Bell Lane," was a little euphemistic but the quarters were an improvement over the *Borinquen*. A lieutenant commander in His Majesty's Navy, at present inactive because of a wound, briefed us on the area, the possibility of air raids, and entertainment services in Liverpool. After he left, I explored the mysteries of the English electrical system, which was based on 250 volts. Since all our American equipment, specifically our radio or "wireless," was built for 125 volts, we had to set up a system so that we could plug it in. For hours we argued about resistance coils and transformers and I filled several sheets of paper with formulas and calculations without accomplishing much except deciding that the most sensible thing to do would be to find some experts before we burned the camp down.

We were surprisingly comfortable. Of course, the food had fallen back to normal army standards after a short interval of navy food, but the luxury of a hot shower every day more than made up for that. We even had a regular laundry building, with rows of tubs

[26]

and washboards and a large drawing room. I don't mean to imply that I was ever impressed with laundering either as vocation or avocation, but as long as I had to do it, an efficient setup was certainly better than a 2x4 basin or a flat rock with cold water. I gradually improved my technique to the extent where things came out a pale grey. There's no question that one acquires a number of new talents in the army. I even did a short stretch of not-too-strenuous sewing.

The men, all quite young, reacted to this environment much as one would expect in a boarding school. Sometimes I felt like a proctor, involved in settling very minor but intensive personal disputes, which frequently seemed to be at the kindergarten level. On the other hand, the men were extraordinarily loyal and would do anything for the unit (usually without being asked), to say nothing of the spontaneous favors they did for me. I never entirely figured this out since I cannot recall that I did anything for them in particular and promotions were nonexistent. Motivations were puzzling but their kindness was very agreeable and gave me a lot of faith in the human race.

England undoubtedly has its good points but I'd like to go on record with the unqualified statement that climate is not one of them. Even the most violent references I'd heard to the English climate had been distinct understatements. The sun came out for two days between 3:30 and 3:45 but otherwise the British Isles were an extinct part of the universe as far as I was concerned. An almost continuous feeble drizzle seeped under collars, up trousers and leggings, and down into boots. In retrospect, it was a particularly uninteresting stretch with very few subjects of conversation except discussions of the weather, leading to the conclusion that the English drink tea because, under the climatic circumstances, hot tea is practically essential to maintain life. There were other inevitable comments about the drab aspects of army camp. We were always torn between a desire to get on with the "invasion" and a natural gnawing fear of what it would be like.

The training program was not too vigorous and we were able to visit the countryside. I wrote to Blanche describing a magnificent old Norman abbey, built originally by Hugh Lupus shortly after the Norman invasion, where St. Anselm was one of the early leading lights. This information should have been censored, since anyone with any sense could find out where the abbey was and thereby trace the exact location of our battalion. By repeating the same exercise on thousands of other units and millions of letters, one could, in theory, document exactly where the entire American army was quartered throughout Great Britain. That, however, would be an impressive statistical operation and I doubt if even the Germans were methodological enough to pursue it.

On November 10, 1943, we were finally told that we could mention towns and cities we visited on leave as long as we didn't give away our specific location. This was checked by our S-2 so I supposed it was accurate but, as it turned out, all names of cities and towns were cut out by the base censor. Apparently he did not get the same instructions that we did.

Silver lining department, London division: Local papers said on November 11 Lloyd's was quoting 3–2 odds that the war would be over by late spring. Very cheery but to us not very realistic. As Damon Runyon wrote, "The race is not always to the swift nor the battle to the strong but don't bet on it!"

It was difficult to report news of much interest. We did have a two-star brass hat and a few other attending high-priced help wandering around at inspection one morning but nothing very dramatic happened and we occupied ourselves with drills, forced marches, and other fascinating occupations.

By our tenth day, I was the proud possessor of a pair of mutilated lower extremities, since early that morning, we went pounding across the English countryside and pounded back through a driving rain on a twenty-five-mile full-pack march. It was the first long march we had had since leaving the United States so everyone was fairly soft. Just after we got back and I had gently hauled my bleeding stumps onto the bed, I realized we had a sick call, the only encouraging feature of which was to find that most of the troops seemed to be in worse shape than I was.

Except for occasional trips to the city for concerts or the theatre, life was dull. I recall the comment of one of our officers who, after many days of this drabness, was sitting glumly when someone started prodding him about what he was going to do post bellum. "Head for Switzerland," he said. "Why Switzerland?" "To stay the hell out of the next war!" This was a fairly characteristic expression of the griping that went on constantly.

The local Kiwanis Club gave a party for the officers and since someone had to stay on as duty officer and I was still hacking from bronchitis, I volunteered to stay behind. From the reports, it was just as well. The party turned out to be nothing but a surging mob packed into a main room in one of the local inns with some of the local talent providing intermittent entertainment. There was a raffle auction every few minutes. At any rate, it was for me a very quiet, peaceful evening. After a little work and a few issues of *War Medicine* I got started on a Russian prize novel, *Rainbow*, by Wanda Wasilewska, which was the story of a Ukraine village during the German Occupation.

There was little one could write about. Although my letters ran to five or six pages, they were mostly about books, thoughts, and general events of the world, plus extensive personal communications about people. There were descriptions of the local scene and the various forms of entertainment at the Philharmonic and local theatres in Liverpool, combined with vague descriptions of the dull life in the army camp with nothing but ordinary drills and marches. We had not picked up guns or large heavy equipment or trucks, jeeps, and tracks, so there was little we could do except sit and wait. In one letter, describing the local scene, I quoted Cornelia Otis Skinner about English train whistles: "a shrill, nervous shriek like the whoop of an elderly spinster who had just been pinched."

There was one day of excitement when we encountered a louse infestation, which required that all personnel strip down, burn their ticks and matting, take showers, shave all body hair, and start with fresh clothing and bedding. Insecticides were not yet available so delousing a battalion was a major project, but at least it provided some excitement and activity.

On Thanksgiving Day, after our usual 5:00 P.M. evening meal—which on this occasion was turkey instead of cold cuts or Spam—we headed into Liverpool for a combination reception and concert given for American troops. The colonel gave me two box seats, since he didn't feel well, so Captain Joe Krimsky and I found ourselves in the mezzanine with American and British colonels and assorted admirals in boxes on each side, with a first lieutenant and a captain in the middle. A member of Parliament and his wife shared our box and more or less took care of us during the evening. The concert itself was terrible (a combination of hymns and martial music) and the speeches consisted mainly of the usual platitudes. Following an hour and a half of this, our box companions led us out to a reception by the Lord Mayor—much glitter and brass! Unfortunately, I didn't have any knee breeches and silk stockings but no one seemed to notice. We had tea and crumpets and later on, some very flat beer for the young set. Soon I wormed my way to the rear and escaped, and Joe and I wandered about and ate and drank at leisure with our friends from London. A memorable Thanksgiving!

When not in combat, the battalion surgeon holds sick call every morning, where he disposes of numerous minor and occasional major problems either by treatment within the battalion area or by referral to a nearby larger medical unit. Occasional emergencies also crop up for diagnosis and management. Regular daily inspections are held to maintain sanitary facilities in good shape and a report on these and the health record of the unit is submitted monthly. Components of a standard training program for medical corpsmen were presented daily to our own personnel and occasionally in lectures to the entire battalion on the management of battle injuries.

Two interesting cases turned up: one man was jaundiced (probably acute hepatitis), and the other had an unusual hernia of a section of the peroneal muscle (outer calf) through its fascia. I had to decide whether to operate on the hernia there or send him on to a general hospital. I don't think even minor elective surgery should be done with the minimal mobile equipment that goes with a battalion aid station, but the temptation was strong in a fairly simple case like that. Certainly, the experience was a far cry from any of the days in the residency program at the Massachusetts General Hospital.

One day, after a jaunt into the country to follow up two men whom I had sent off to the nearest station hospital a few days before, I dropped in on a weekly staff conference to hear the music of medical and surgical talk again. It was pleasant enough but somewhat disappointing. It certainly did not represent Thursday morning Grand Rounds at the MGH, where pearls used to fall from the lips of the high and mighty in showers and where, in my early days, I used to tremble before the front row of the great gods. Nor was it like the Wednesday afternoon meetings of the West Surgical Service where, under the benign eyes of Doctors Churchill, McKittrick, and others, the house staff used to argue about their cases in critical and interesting detail. At any rate, it was a brief return to the medical world, which is rare for an isolated battalion surgeon. I began to feel less detached from medicine than I had most of the time up to that point.

It was in late November of 1943 that the so-called "Patton episode" of slapping a soldier who was undergoing treatment for "shell shock" took place. The incident resulted in disciplinary action which temporarily removed Patton from command, and received a great deal of attention in the British press regarding the relationship between line officers and medical corps officers and the areas of responsibilities of each. Little did we know that after the invasion we would join Patton's Third Army in Normandy.

One of my corporals had a brother in the Irish Guards and returned from a short compassionate leave with him full of wild and lurid stories of the activities of the Guards division, which gave us a somewhat chilling picture of what actual combat would be like.

Eventually, we had drawn all our guns, vehicles, and equipment. On December 5, before dawn, we began our long trek south, pounding across the country in convoy on a frigid ride in what to all intents and purposes was the middle of the night. Starting off the day with a long drive in a blackout isn't entirely a satisfactory way to live. The jeep may be a marvelous invention in terms of utility and combat but it certainly is one of the more miserable forms of transportation ever devised. In this area, the sun gets warm enough at noon so the frost melts and all the mechanized vehicles and tracks tear up the ground until it is a tremendous sea of muddy ruts. A few hours later, everything freezes solid again so that any sort of travel by vehicle gives you the sensation of being hooked up to an automatic milk shaker. I finally settled down to a miserable cold, rainy night in a tent during which I had a call to go out to see one of the men in the forward battery; fortunately, there was nothing seriously wrong so I was able to trudge my way back.

Our destination was the small town of Cattistock in Dorset,

W. V. McD, on first arrival in England, 1943

Camp in Cattistock, Southern England 1943
l-r: Perlo, Akulonis, Krimsky, McDermott

where pre-Invasion maneuvers and training were to be held. Battalion and medical headquarters were located in large stone manor house, complete with gardens and walks, and the men were settled in tents without flooring, which made for miserable living conditions and endless numbers of upper respiratory infections appearing on sick call. I complained bitterly about this in successive reports to headquarters but all I received in return were memoranda requesting that I "reply by endorsement as to what had been done to correct the described unsanitary conditions." After that I learned to check off as "excellent" the section in the monthly medical report inquiring about health of troops and living conditions. Even slow learners like myself eventually adapted to the practicalities of army routine.

Eventually, I did hunt down an Engineer Company, who cheerily agreed to put wooden flooring under the tents. At that point, the arrangements represented to our men the ultimate in luxury.

As the New Year approached, the colonel suggested that we arrange a party for the men and the townspeople. Unfortunately, the officers who were making the plans concerned themselves only with collecting nurses and local dollies. In some mysterious way, Captain John Miles and I were suddenly saddled with all the details of arranging the location, the music, the bar—very ironic since we had both been outspoken in the small ranks of opposition to this marvelous plan and had been in favor of having our own officers' party in the club and drinking our own liquor ration or part thereof in peace. When all this descended on us I had to collect the detail and tramp down to the local church hall, which also served as a theatre, auditorium, and what have you for this little section of the country, while John scraped together an orchestra and scoured the area for instruments. The hall was in a terrible state from disuse, so I had the men scrubbing, dusting, carpentering, bringing in trees, hanging up wreathes, cleaning the one latrine, and replacing the installations therein with a GI portable model, which at least was clean. The lighting didn't work, the central heating didn't work, the furniture was broken—in fact, it was a helluva mess all around. But labor is no problem in the army and in about four hours we had the hall fixed up with a dance floor surrounded by tables, a very respectable bar built in one corner, and the place decorated with local vegetation and flora. It was hardly the Ritz but for the purpose, a reasonable facsimile thereof. John then appeared with a four-piece band, bartenders, liquor, and two hatcheck girls (the term "girls" by courtesy as they must have aggregated well over one hundred years between the two of them). We then retired to the "Joint" (our name for the local officers' quarters in the bleak grey manor house) and collapsed in front of my fire over a tall drink.

After dinner, we climbed into "blouse and pinks" to see what fruit had come of our labors. It turned out to be a pretty good party, with the products of the grape and grain flowing freely and the place itself looking much better at night than in the daylight. Even the orchestra sounded fairly good after a few drinks. The New Year had a reasonably royal welcome, after which we repaired en masse to the officers' mess for eggs and coffee and a few songs. Since the party was the battalion's first general exposure in weeks and months to any consecutive series of drinks, a number of men got extremely crocked, but there were no real problems and everything was very genial. An elderly retired British general had a wonderful time and said that he made a great mistake in his youth by going to Sandhurst instead of West Point. He turned out to be the older brother of Sir Bertram Ramsay, chief of British Naval Operations.

For many days we worked like beavers to establish the battalion in some reasonable degree of permanency. Although some units were still living in pyramidal tents, most of them now had wooden floors and the rest of the men were quartered in evacuated houses in and around the town. Major Foster, the executive officer, had assigned all of the officers to various billets and Vogt, Miles, Siegel, and I lived right above the bar in the officers' mess. Downstairs we had a large room for the officers' club and bar and another large room for the mess, with kitchens and scattered rooms for some of the enlisted men in the back. We could now draw liquor rations, which were pooled in the bar and paid for on a basis similar to some clubs in the South. I wouldn't say there was enough to develop a serious case of cirrhosis, but compared to the dry season we'd been through, it looked stupendous. With some creative scavenging, a little carpentry, some local holly, a few pictures, and additions here and there, life was more like *living* than before. We established a regular dinner hour, for which all officers dressed and during which all the little army formalities took place, reminding us that we were still civilized human beings in spite of the fact that we grubbed around all day in mud and field clothes, leggings, and boots and often spent days in a row on maneuvers.

The main drawback was, of course, the bathroom. The entire house contained just one "closet" on the second floor (and a damn small one at that), and one very ugly bathtub and basin in a dingy, cold room on the first floor. Far from viewing a room for bathing as a seat of carnal luxuriousness, the English seem to regard it as a necessary, somewhat unpleasant ritual to be dispensed with as quickly as possible. So the old dream of a hot bath in a big beautiful warm room was once again deferred.

Some of the other officers were quartered in the home of General Ramsay, who had every intention of remaining there and enjoying every bit of it. He liked nothing better than to corner one or all of them at any time and as often as possible and talk endlessly about battles, campaigns, strategy, and tactics of every military leader from Hannibal to the present. A typical Colonel Blimp if I ever saw one.

Despite the increasing pace of military activities, we still had time on an occasional evening for poker, my major vice. This particular talent, if one can call it that, added remarkably to the allotment Blanche received regularly, courtesy of the United States Army.

I received regular permission to go to the nearby station hospital for conferences, which outside of a few journals was about my only contact with the world of medicine. I stayed for dinner with the staff afterward and drove back in the blackout. One evening my driver and I decided to save a little time by trying a shortcut we discovered on the map. All the road signs had been taken down after Dunkirk, when the British were awaiting a possible invasion, and there are very few distinguishing features between one English road and another—all are the same width and all wind through innumerable tiny villages. After we had gone on for some miles without running into the large town with the statue of Thomas Hardy that was our only recognizable landmark, we were finally forced to admit we were lost. Then began the infuriating process of asking local people for directions. The first local pointed out usefully that we could go either way and get back to Cattistock where our headquarters were. The next man pointed off an entirely different direction which led over the hills and where there was *no* road at all. The next person we encountered was a very nice lady who pointed out that you couldn't get to Cattistock from where we were and the best thing to do was to go to another town and get directions from there. Several other people gave us fantastic directions all ending in circles and esses, until I began to wonder if we had gotten on the grounds of a lunatic asylum and were driving around inside the fence. Eventually, however, we ran into an American MP and got straightened out. This and a few other similar experiences made me wonder what would have happened if the Germans had managed to cross the Channel and begin an invasion of England. I pictured two Panzer divisions en-

countering each other going in opposite directions on a small
English country road with neither having the slightest idea where
they had come from or where they were going.

Despite the landings in Italy, there seemed no prospect of an
early end to the war, but both Blanche and I tried to keep up our
spirits. She was working at the Red Cross Blood Donor Center
but outside of the immediate family and friends had little social
life of any kind. Everyone cheered at the new Russian offensive,
which seemed to be a turning point in the war on the Eastern
Front, and we all knew that the increasing pace of our maneuvers
was pointing toward an invasion in the West. It would be hard to
say that there were many officers and men in the American army
enthusiastic about combat itself, but the recognition that this was
the only way of getting rid of the horrors of the Nazi regime and
returning home made everyone anxious to get moving and engendered an atmosphere of restlessness.

There was much subdued talk after Roosevelt's remarks on the
fact that we could anticipate only a very partial demobilization
after Germany was defeated. For the men who had been in service well over three years, it must have seemed like just another
hill before the end of a long road. After a first wave of disappointment on everyone's part, I was not so sure that any demobilization would be such a good idea. I would have felt a little guilty to
resume suits and tweeds while friends were out in the Pacific.

One evening, the local station master called the aid station. An
English soldier going home on leave had slipped and fallen while
waiting a change of trains. I took him down to the aid station and,
as he had an obvious Colles fracture of the left wrist, splinted it
and gave him a little morphine and the aid men drove him to the
nearest English hospital, where it could be reduced and immobi-
lized. He had fought with the 8th Army for three years without a

scratch and then cracked himself up when he was practically on his own doorstep. Ironic.

During January and February, we became increasingly involved in maneuvers on the Salisbury Plain, which were geared to an invasion of the continent. Knowing what these maneuvers were like, I didn't even make the gesture of taking along pen and paper to write home. While England was continually wet, it seldom really poured rain, but Pluvius apparently had a keen and watchful eye on the 550th just as he does on those who plan picnics, a day in the country, a hunting or fishing trip, etc. No English mist accompanied us on this latest little jaunt into the field, but just good old-fashioned rain—continuously, miserably, steadily, and unremittingly from the time we left until our return to Cattistock several days later. All this was accompanied off the beaches by real ocean fog which rolled in like a smoke screen in thick, heavy, billowing waves. Of course, with all this wet, the trucks, guns, jeeps, tracks, and men turned the bivouac area and the entire maneuver site into an endless sea of mud in which we walked, talked, slept, and ate with some form of wetness seeping in steadily through every crack and crevice. It gave us a picture of what extended field operations were like, particularly in the winter months, and made us more cognizant of the realities behind the historical descriptions of such periods in history such as Napoleon's retreat from Moscow. It did feel wonderful to get back to a semblance of a hot tub, which was still available to us in headquarters.

On our return from the first few days of maneuvers, there were a number of letters with information about various friends, such as Oley Paul, Brad Millett, Larry Rainsford, Crocker Wight, and many others. Perry Johnson was killed in the Pacific when he went down with the destroyer *DeHaven*, off Savo Island. Angus MacDonnell went down over Europe in the B-17 he was piloting and I was sure that we were losing other friends every day and

every week. One of my letters concerned a clipping which Brad
sent regarding George Starkey's marriage to a "McMurray girl"
from Maryland. Various information was exchanged about people
like Benson Roe, Oscar Hills, and others.

In the Pacific, the Battle of Midway in 1942 had stopped the
apparently invincible Japanese fleet and in retrospect proved to
be the turning point of the war in that theater of operations. In
Russia, the Germans had reached Stalingrad and almost seemed
invincible until the surrender of Von Paulus and his Sixth Army
stopped what had appeared to be a total disaster. The allied landings in North Africa and the subsequent invasion of Sicily in 1943
brightened our lives.

In the fall and winter of 1943, however, the German and Japanese forces still presented formidable obstacles, to say the least.
The end of the war seemed years away, even to congenital opti-
mists like myself.

The beginning of maneuvers, on land and on the beaches, with
various top-flight divisions including the First Infantry (known as
the "Big Red One"), made it obvious that the Invasion was at least
in the offing. How soon? None of us could hazard a guess, but it
was obvious that there were many more weeks or months of preparation ahead of us.

As an example of the naïveté of the green soldier, I recall being
distressed by the constant bitching in the First Division and wondered if Eisenhower realized that the men's morale was shot! After we had been exposed to combat and shared the comradeship
of danger, we recognized that constant grousing is characteristic
of a tough, experienced, and effective unit, but that certainly escaped me at the time. Certainly, this division was one of the few
units, if not the only one, that would have taken and held Omaha
Beach during the nightmare of D-Day in that particular segment
of the Normandy coast.

3

Pre-Invasion Maneuvers

CORNWALL AND THE SALISBURY PLAIN

January 18–March 6, 1944

The upper crust in Dorset and Devon society is deeply involved with riding and hunting ("the unspeakable in full pursuit of the inedible"). I did some riding, but as for hunting—I was fairly safe on that score, not only because of an inherent reticence and distaste for breaking my neck but also because the hunts were on Wednesday mornings, automatically eliminating me as a member of the working class. Sunday was often an abbreviated work day but more often than not something turned up or it rained fiercely. All in all, I was unlikely to return home a solidly established member of the horsy set.

Maneuvers and training filled most of our days, however. The 550th AAA-AW Battalion was a light completely mobile anti-aircraft unit with four individual batteries of either multiple four mounts of 50-caliber machine guns on a half-track (a lightly armored vehicle with tank tracks in the rear and wheels in front) or rapid-firing 40-mm Bofors guns drawn on a flat platform on wheels. Such battalions were "corps troops," which meant that they were basically under a corps (a unit comprising two or more divisions) and could be temporarily assigned to any division depending on combat needs. The primary roles of light AA battalions were to protect division troops in convoy against strafing fighter planes and to provide light covering fire for a river crossing or other assault and temporary protection of a particularly important bridge, road, or encampment against low-level bombing.

During maneuvers, we were under the First Army and functioned primarily with the First Infantry Division, the unit that ultimately provided the first wave of troops for the assault on Omaha Beach on D-Day. Its identifying shoulder patch gave the First Infantry its nickname of the Big Red One.

Our periods of extended field operations that rainy winter made us appreciate what the men in the mountains of Italy were going through. War hardly fits into the magazine-ad picture of tanks, guns, half-tracks, and men in clean ODs with spotless leggings roaring across sunny fields and rolling green slopes. It mainly boils down to a lot of dirt, sweat, rain, and mud and endless hours of training for short periods of action before you finally return home to try to think up some glamorous tales to tell your grandchildren. Whether or not maneuvers were more popular with the infantry, as opposed to those in jeeps, tracks, or tanks, is open to question. The beating my rear end took from the seat of the jeep and the measures of protection I tried engendered an inevitable force of attention that became almost exclusive. Detailed memoirs of history of the 550th could be written under such titles as "Across Europe with Pad and Powder" or "Around the World on a Cotton Horse."

I have mentioned the pleasure of coming in after one or two days in the field and having a hot bath. A good part of the time, however, this proved to be rather an illusory thought. A hot bath was always a doubtful quantity in our "mansion" since there were an incredible number of places where things could go wrong between the point where water entered the house cold and emerged from the bathroom faucet hot—and they usually did go wrong. The house seemed to fit perfectly into Noel Coward's little ditty "Stately Homes of England."

> *The pipes to the bath are ready to burst*
> *In the lavatory you fear the worst*
> *Although it was used by Charles the First*
> *Quite informally*
> *On his journey North and by George the Fourth.*

From Cattistock, we were ordered to Cornwall, near Land's End, for firing practice and other activities.

What a shock! After contemplating heading into some sort of wilderness and primitive life, I found myself in the lap of luxury (practically) for the next several days in a British camp—hot showers, officers' mess with white tablecloths and ATs (corresponding to WAACs), serving as waitresses, officers' lounge and bar, a movie theater—in fact, if my room hadn't been so cold, I would have thought that I was practically a civilian again. Joe and I valiantly tried to start a fire in one of these minute stoves that the English like to think will heat a room in no time at all. No paper or fuel to start with, we were definite flops; we thought of rubbing a couple of Boy Scouts together but there were none of those around either. I'm sure that coke will burn but it takes an incredible level of heat to accomplish this. Eventually I became proficient at the great and ancient art of fire making.

The trip in convoy to Cornwall from Dorset was pleasant and unhurried—we stopped overnight on the way so that we arrived in time to pick up the rest of the battalion, who had come on by train. We roared in and out of innumerable small villages almost before we realized they were there, and passed neat farms utilizing every available foot of space and dividing the countryside into geometric patterns with inevitable hedgerows separating the pastures. At times, these fertile areas faded out into endless stretches of desolate rolling brown moors, the only sign of life being an occasional tin mine in the distance shown by a pair of conical heaps of slag rising up through the mist like breasts of supine giantesses. Time and miles rolled by pleasantly enough, particularly since I had sense enough to pass up riding in my jeep in favor of the cab of a truck, where it was reasonably warm and comfortable. The main trouble in traveling in convoy is regulating your bladder to fit in with the few stops. It's impossible, of course, to stop at any but the prescribed times, so that if you get overconfident at one stop and pass up your chance or drank too much coffee at breakfast, life can be very unhappy for a time.

The camp was very close to the far western tip of England at Penzance, where the battalion had extended firing practice off the cliffs in collaboration with British instructors. Our activities were varied and interspersed with lectures, several of them on camouflage in the field. One of the instructors was a little mousy but professional-looking English officer who brightened us up by surprisingly interposing illustrative little anecdotes that completely belied his prim appearance. One concerned the vicar who, on meeting his curate on his return from a honeymoon, inquired about the trip—"And how did you find it?" "Oh, quite all right, sir," replied the curate, "but it *is* remarkably well concealed, isn't it?" A reasonable analogy!

I was reminded of a good line from a movie about a young American couple off on their honeymoon who were saddled at the same time with a secret service mission for the English government. "It's best for you not to know too much or to appear to know too much," a Foreign Office official cautioned the pair. The young bride promptly replied, "That's what my mother told me when I came out in Boston."

Censorship restrictions were particularly strict during this trip to Cornwall. I presumed that army headquarters did not wish to give an impression of any extensive activity suggesting an impending invasion, although we still had a long time to wait.

It soon became obvious that I had entirely the wrong training and preparation for the life and activities of a battalion surgeon. If any more rabbits came in for surgery, I intended to put in for a transfer to the veterinary corps. Whether the boys were actually finding these rabbits hobbling around aimlessly, as they said, or were illegally removing them from the local traps made no difference from the medical point of view—but a pair of three-legged bunnies that survived presented a grave problem since the two were satisfactorily differentiated in terms of sex. Even my meager knowledge of the tribal habits and reproductive capacity of the genus cottontail told me that by the time we reached Berlin, all the transportation facilities and rations would be absorbed by rabbits—even starting with six legs instead of the usual eight.

I took time out to write Blanche:

Sunday, February 5, 1944

Another somewhat anomalous Sunday in Cornwall without any distinguishing features to differentiate it from any other day of the week or any other Sunday of the year! A few English officers of the permanent staff who maintain order in the establishment in between the rapid turnover of transients like ourselves present an interesting picture of the structured life. They eat breakfast at nine, have cocoa at 11, lunch at 12:30, tea at 4:15 on, wash and dress for dinner at 7. Then a whiskey, a game of snooker and off to bed at the end of another hard day. Of course, the London Times comes in after lunch for an hour or so and various light novels are lying around for the insomniacs. . . . One gray-haired captain made quite a picture—riding breeches, carefully shined boots, one hand in the pocket and the other with a glass of port, rocking back and forth on his heels discussing the progress of the war. He stood out like a fragile relic of antiquity surrounded by Visigoths in the afternoons when the officers come in from the field in leggings spattered with mud or wet from the beaches and obviously with a rather barbaric attitude towards fighting a war. He really was a very nice and pleasant chap but obviously troubled and very futile, but was hanging on as a last Roman. A few of the British officers were very helpful. One captain in particular was commissioned from the ranks after spending some time in the Far East and India as a youthful Sergeant Major. He was an invaluable instructor with extraordinary extensive knowledge of the guns, tactics, battalion, regimental, divisional, and even Army strategy. . . . These descriptive commentaries on the British mess and associated perquisites have probably given a full picture of how we regard these luxuries—table cloths, reasonable food, hot baths and comfortable beds—particularly after a period of physical exercise associated with field maneuvers. As Mae West commented—"Too much of a good thing is just right!" . . . We will not only leave here and the pleasantries of the British mess but we will also leave our headquarters in that particular stately home of England with its cockroaches, bad plumbing, huge cold rooms, long drafty halls and pleasant grounds—all this will tomorrow be a thing of the past and we will move into new quarters on the Salisbury Plain. It is not far away, but it's just as much of a nuisance moving the battalion as if it were across the continent.

Once again, we went through the process of packing, pounding over the highway in a convoy, and then unpacking and getting resettled—and all for a fairly short period of maneuvers in the Salisbury Plain, which clearly were based on invasion tactics. We were based at a large American camp that we of the soft Western Civilization have come to look on as essentials of everyday life. The barracks were moderately warm; we could have a daily hot shower in a reasonably warm room in the same building; there were even mirrors and hot and cold running water. And if by chance an extra beer before retiring prompted a call of the wild at 2:00 A.M., one did not have to race across an open field battling an icy gale but could casually saunter a few steps down a warm hall and go through the routine without the gnawing fear of a disabling genital frostbite—that would be a sad way to come home!

Following lectures and instructions on terrain maps, each officer in the unit was taken far out into the country with compass, flashlight, and map as his only means of finding his way back to headquarters. By this time, everyone was familiar with one of my foibles—an almost total absence of a sense of direction. As one of my colleagues put it, "He would have trouble getting from his front door to the back door without rehearsals." The battalion surgeon was not exempt from this exercise, though, so inevitably my turn came and there I was in the middle of the night, alone in the wilds of Dorset and the Salisbury Plain, dependent solely on compass, terrain map, and flashlight. As I pointed out earlier, because of the fear of a German invasion, all street signs and highway markers had been removed; and as we were all well aware, the winding and tortuous lanes through field and over stream were not designed by a sane and logical planner.

Before my departure, a pool was organized relative to my time of reappearance. The intervals between departure and return ranged as high as a week. I regretted that I had never signed up for a Boy Scout course in astronomy, path finding, or something in that general area. I can still recall how cold it was that night. Each time I took off my gloves to hold a light on the terrain map, I thought that my fingers would drop off. With the possibility of a prolonged and wandering trip, I had considered taking with me a bow, some arrows, and flint and steel. If the army left England for the Continent without me, I trusted that someone would organize an expedition to scour the wilds of England. But all the worry was for naught! A miracle happened and I was the first one of my group to return to base. Perhaps the motivating force was the announcement before we departed that mail delivery would be made for the first time in days.

One of our lieutenants had a chronic draining ear for several weeks, and I decided to take him over to the Fifth General Hospital for an ENT consultation. The Fifth General was one of the Harvard units—the one from the Brigham, which had left while I was still in my last year of medical school, a lifetime before. The consultation gave me a chance to immerse myself in the medical world again. I enjoyed sitting through Major Bart Quigley's orthopedic clinic and had a long pleasant time with Bob White—a wonderful guy who had been chief resident at the Children's Hospital when I took an elective course there early in my fourth year. I always liked him and I was grateful to him, as he had written a magnificent recommendation for me while I was applying for an appointment at the MGH and other places. I also saw Richard Warren, one of the younger visiting surgeons at the MGH who left with the Brigham unit.

Life was not that much more interesting at a general hospital. I learned that the diseases that a group of young healthy males contracts are apt to be dull except for an occasional appendix, a rare gall bladder, a mass of convalescents from flu, pneumonia, grippe, etc. and the usual traumatic cases (herniated intervertebral discs, slipped cartilages in knees, fractures and dislocations, and of course the regular parade of venereal disease). All in all, a drab collection with which to maintain intellectual interest over a long period of time. In fact, the Medical Corps seemed to be very much like the rest of the army; they all wanted to be doing something other than what they were doing or going someplace other than where they were. The hospital man wanted to get out with the field forces and see something of the war and those from combat units liked to visit the hospitals and see something of medicine.

After various consultations on some of my problems with the

officers and men in the battalion, I made arrangements to have some of our medical detachment sent in for training in the blood bank with a view to developing their skills with plasma infusions, which we might need in combat.

Friday, February 24, 1944

A new doctor arrived in the division today to take up an assignment. He had been in a station hospital and felt so bored with absolutely nothing to do that he requested a transfer to the combat forces to see a little of the war. I'm afraid that he'll be disillusioned in no time if he gets more than the few mild whiffs we've had. Constant and increasing restlessness is a hard thing to fight—I think that after these four months, if I was still single and unattached, I would probably try to transfer to an airborne unit but that would probably be almost as dull and routine at this point as anything else. . . . At the moment . . . we are sitting here eating shrimp and drinking Port. Smitty opened up a package from home and found three cans of shrimp so I cracked a bottle of Port to go with them. Wonderful! I have developed quite an attachment for Port in the past few months—not a deep or lasting affection though due mainly to the absence of bourbon, the scarcity of scotch, the rarity of good red or white wine—but it's there nonetheless so I'll probably come home wearing a Purple Heart from having contracted gout in England.

We had a long cold day out in the field. It was good fun despite the temperature although I'm not at all sorry that we are not sleeping out in this particular maneuver. Don't let anyone try to tell you the Army gets inured to the point of enjoying sleeping on frozen ground and eating lukewarm C-rations out of a tin plate because they don't. Since I can't go into specifics of place or function, I can only tell you that I did find a wonderful spot for a picnic which we should share someday. It was hardly much of a picnic but this seemed so much made to order with only two things lacking—Blanche and a warm spring day—right in the middle of a wide area of slopes covered with hedges and bracken with a high wooded knoll which overlooked the countryside for miles. For some reason or other, I turned the jeep in closer to investigate and found a narrow natural roadway cut under the side

of the steep slopes of the knoll which was almost invisible except at
one angle and which would up to the top. It was hollowed out
almost like a miniature volcano and formed a small cup at the peak.
The whole surface of the cavity was covered with thick, short,
bright green grass—the kind I've seen only in England—which felt
like a springy Oriental rug under foot. A small spring bubbled up
in the center and ran off as a tiny rivulet at the entrance. Except for
the narrow cleft at the entrance, the sides rose sharply to the
wooded sides of the hill in which the depression was carved, so
that it was completely shielded from the wind but not from the sun.
From the ridge above the hollow, you can see the tallest spire in
England rising into the sky in the distance. Wonderful! Some
time I'll take you here (if I can remember how to find it) on a
bright summer day or we can think back lazily of these to-be-
forgotten days.

By this point, we had completed a lot of the training of pre-
Invasion maneuvers and were more or less in a holding pattern in
a fairly large army camp in Colchester. We still had training missions on a daily basis, but were clearly marking time and awaiting
further orders.

At the end of February, we took off on another three-day stretch
on maneuvers—hardly a "few days in the country" as we used to
know it but, on the whole, not too unpleasant. We were fortunate
in that we had no snow and only an occasional drizzle of rain,
something to be thankful for if one has to spend as many hours as
we did in eating, sleeping, and slogging through mud with rain
dripping down our necks and into every available crack and crevice in our clothes. Two of the nights were bitterly cold, but a sleeping bag can be comfortable as long as you're dry and keep your
nose and ears covered. It was a little rough, however, to get a march
order at 2:00 A.M. and crawl out of a warm sleeping bag to dress
and push off in an open jeep into a biting wind. My face and lips
were burned to a crisp from the odd combination of frostbite and
sun. On the brighter side, we did see a lot of the countryside,

learned a lot about rural life from bivouacking in and about farms, cow pastures, chicken yards, etc., got mixed up with a fox hunt, and on the whole, had a pretty good time. On return, I felt healthy and hungry but very tired, sleepy, and dirty. After some food and a bath, I hit the sack for a few hours. Since we were on the move most of the time, I only managed to snatch a snooze here and there. It was wonderful, however, to see the post loom up in the distance just as dawn was breaking and to conjure up visions of a hot breakfast, a bath, and a warm bed.

After clearing out the final minor problems form the aid station which were the result of various trauma on maneuvers, I had just relaxed when we received the news that the 550th gypsies would be off again on Sunday, March 3, having finished the mobile training at his post. New assignment meant another change in A.P.O., which we had to send home as soon as it was definite. We were heading for East Anglia to various airfields, not very exciting but at least we would be through with some of those training schedules for a while, which meant that I would probably have more time for reading during the quiet stretches—medical journals and references, which I had sadly neglected, as well as some of the lighter stuff that Blanche and others sent regularly. This also meant a chance for a leave, although I could not plan on it. I would have liked very much to go to Oxford or Cambridge for a week, where Americans could live at the universities and sit in on the lectures, use the libraries, and in general function as temporary students. It certainly would have been a change and sounded interesting but the openings were few and assigned in order of application so they were entirely taken up far in advance by SOS officers (Service of Supply—i.e., quartermaster, ordnance officer, and headquarters personnel), who had much more permanent assignments and stable futures than the units in the field forces. The way we had been hopping around, it had been impossible to plan on anything. Another move meant the usual packing preparations so I had to race around to the various hospitals in the vicinity and obtain the release of as many of our men as possible who were recovering from various and sundry problems and were reasonably fit for duty. Then came the usual headaches of the actual packing of the aid station and personal equipment since the convoy was pulling out very early on a Sunday. Living in and out of a pack, footlocker, and duffel bag without knowing how long you would be settled anywhere was a bloody nuisance. The amount of stuff required (aside from any such luxuries as books, pictures, writing equipment, etc.) was incredible, for a unit isolated in combat actually had to be, in theory at least, temporarily self-supporting.

The training maneuvers which we had just completed were competitive in the sense that all units were given ratings by field inspectors on their performances. We ranked second among the light AA units, which was a little disappointing. On further thought, however, it was obvious that we would not be among the first troops on the beachhead, which left us with mixed feelings of relief and disappointment. As it turned out, the casualties in the unit which was given top ranking were horrendous as was true of all the troops in the initial landings on Omaha Beach, although not among those debarking on the other American, British, and Canadian beaches.

That time was still far off.

4

The Long Wait

EAST ANGLIA

March 7–May 8, 1944

We completed mobile training and maneuvers in a cloud of glory with excellent commendations (though not the top ranking). It was bitterly cold as we headed out into the blackness early Sunday morning, with a thin blanket of snow over everything. For the first few miles, I huddled in the jeep in as small a ball as I could, wearing as many layers as possible—the sides were always open and we drove with the top down in convoy in order to be able to see the columns, pass signals back and forth, etc. Gradually, it became lighter and we were driving into a magnificent sunrise, which made life warmer and pleasanter. As we proceeded to the north of London and headed east, the winding narrow country roads widened into highways, the rolling green hills lined with hedgerows gradually and imperceptibly flattened out, and the picturesque tiny villages in stone and thatched-roof houses became real suburbs with rows of ugly attempts at "modern" housing, billboards, dumps, and flat brownish fields scattered between various settlements. Although they were much better dressed, the people seemed less cheerful and friendly than those in the rural areas—less lively and responsive. This part of the trip, through the fringes of mass civilization, was drab, and I began to feel nostalgic for the slow, quiet, friendly England I had known to date. I missed seeing miles of valley and farmland and small villages dotting the roads. I missed the large country houses, and the people living in them—I even missed cursing at a hunt when a pack of hounds held up our convoy.

Convoys travel slowly and we slept out one night. Eventually, we arrived at our new quarters at an airfield near Bishop's Stortford, where I lined up a bed in a warm hut. A late breakfast and then down to the usual business of getting settled and organized. We had a pretty good setup, with local headquarters, the aid station, and officers' quarters and mess all in a wing of one building, but the various units of the medical detachment working under my aegis were split up among airfields over a broad area. I had to do a lot of racing around.

After a short stretch in the officers' quarters, we moved to a large evacuated English house that was in a very convenient position relative to the scattered units of the battalion and hence housed the battery command post, the aid station, and our living quarters and mess. Its convenience began and ended solely with its location, however. There was one tiny boiler for bath water (about enough for one bath per day—for a child) and the damn thing often didn't work, although we repeatedly attempted to get it into some sort of running order. Our only other choice was to trudge out some distance to one of the field showers set up in tents. When you live in the fields, you more or less expect to face problems connected with washing, eating, and sleeping. When you move into a large house you might expect to find *one* bath that worked! I wondered what the English did in ordinary life. Apparently no one counted on bathing while living in the country.

The mutterings in my letters about bathing facilities in England reminded me of an experience some years after the war when I had been invited to participate in a symposium organized by the newly appointed professor of surgery at Cambridge University, Roy Calne. After arrival and settling in to Trinity College, I went to dinner at the faculty dining room and sat beside a very elderly and delightful don with whom I discussed the bathing and toilet facilities of the college. He told the story of many years before when he was a very young member of the university and the subject of installing modern showers and bathtubs at Trinity came up for discussion at a faculty meeting. Apparently one of the older dons declared that he saw nothing wrong with the existing, very primitive equipment, clinching his argument with the statement: "After all, the term is only eight weeks long!" So much for the American way of life.

March 12, 1944

I was listening to a few GIs in the Aid Station discussing the soldier's vote about which there has been so much political footballing and boondoggling in Washington. Finally one of them was asked by another if he'd vote for Roosevelt to which he replied, "Damn right—he got me over here and it's up to him to get me back again." Very concise political philosophy, I thought! . . . We have acquired a few bicycles so in leisure moments I have been using one on local trips to various sites, getting into reasonable physical condition. I have to admit, however, that, because of my advancing age, I still fall back in the jeep for any longer jaunts such as to the outlying batteries for which I'm still responsible. The jeep may be a fine institution although I am afraid that the present popular enthusiasm in America for buying them for civilian use will wane after a few trips on bumpy roads on cold nights. They are practical for our purposes, but I doubt if I'll have much desire to ride in one once I've climbed out of olive drab for good.

We were assigned to defend the airfields in the area of Bishop's Stortford, but not much defense was necessary, as most of the German air force that arrived over England now seemed to concentrate on London. Since we were scattered over such a wide area, it was more expedient for me to make rounds like a country doctor, going from one airfield to another where we had mini-aid stations set up, than to have the troops come in to battalion headquarters.

I tried to do some shopping in Bishop's Stortford one day for something to send to Blanche, but was consistently foiled by the peculiar British custom of closing all the stores from noon to three while everyone took off for lunch. None of the merchants or shopkeepers worried much about losing customers—none of them had very much to sell anyway, and there were always triple the number of customers for the goods available. As a result, they all had a somewhat bored attitude, knowing that if you didn't buy some particular thing, someone else would. I found one bookshop open, however, so out of an extensive and assorted collection of junk I picked up a novel by Goethe. One of the battery officers had come along with me and we lunched together, enjoying the novelty of having a meal served on a white tablecloth, seeing a few people dressed in something besides olive drab, and having a quick hoot before lunch. This "civilized" lunch was somewhat different from the highly sophisticated atmosphere of New York. I had sometimes wondered if the same sort of nonsensical conversation was flying around the restaurants in England or if the war had knocked most of it out.

One afternoon I was out at one of the gun sections talking to some of the officers when a small English moppet wandered up, apparently from one of the nearby villages. After standing in the group with his arms folded for a while, he pointed into the sky at some sort of cub-trainer that was flying around and said, "I say, isn't that an early Fairchild?" We were supposed to recognize planes from our training so we all blinked a few times and replied, "Yes, of course." He told us that his uncle had gone to the States sometime early in the war "to teach the Americans how to fly." Lucius Thompson allowed that this was very nice of him, where-upon the youngster replied, "I don't think he wanted to go, the army sent him." He then wandered over and watched a GI who was doing a little carpentry and after restraining himself admirably for a few moments said, "Wouldn't it be more satisfactory to drive those nails obliquely?" and walked off, leaving the GI with his mouth open. He stayed around for quite a time entering into learned discussion on guns, the war, in fact just about anything at all with great self-expression and with a very wise, serious little face. He turned out to be twelve, although he didn't look an hour past his ninth birthday—a precocious but very attractive little man. We thought of signing him up as a plane spotter—he never missed one the whole time he was with us.

I ended up that day by going to some movies in the officers' lounge—a few local combat films on the air force and another one in a series of army orientation films, *Why We Fight*. All the ones of this series that I saw were excellent. Together they formed a pan-orama of the whole era beginning with the events leading up to Munich, eventually to the war, and carrying through the various aspects of the war itself—the invasion of France and the low countries, the Battle of Britain, the war on Russia, etc., entirely composed of films taken by correspondents, army photographers, and film captured from the enemy—all very well edited and documented with maps and running commentary. These films were very popular in London theaters. The main film was on Russia but being a military photographic account of the war, it was more or less free of political propaganda.

The Russian people in the army had done a magnificent job, I thought. I doubted that any of us can entirely appreciate what a comeback they had made and what suffering, heartaches, and courage it took to accomplish that. On the other hand, I could understand those who evinced suspicion and skepticism towards a totalitarian government that was so diametrically opposed to everything we believed in. Nonetheless, at that time, winning the war as quickly as possible was more important to me than any long-range political theorizing. Until the war was won, or until the Kremlin gave direct evidence to the contrary, I was perfectly willing to accept them completely as allies. I did not think, however, that we or the English should put up with a lot of nonsense from *Pravda*. As long as we ourselves were open and aboveboard, concentrated on winning the war, and made it quite clear to the Kremlin that we expected them to do the same, I doubted that there would be any trouble. Looked at objectively, I do not think that we ourselves were entirely free from some political chicanery. All the continuing appeasement (Darlan in North Africa, the handling of Spain and Argentina, the Badoglio government in Italy) might have been justified on the grounds of immediate necessity, but I doubted it. It all smacked too much of the old British attitude in the Chamberlain era.

I finally got leave to visit London, for pleasure but also on minor official business.

March 19, 1944

Since I'm allowed to say when we are in London, you can tell from the heading on this letter alone that I am on a brief junket via a short train ride on semiofficial business. It certainly is nostalgic to traverse the area which was familiar to both of us, although separately. I had a long walk along Picadilly, the Mall and the Strand, browsed around various bookshops and stores and eventually ended up at the theatre which, you probably realize, starts very early because of the night air raids on the city. . . .

I came in with Captain Davis without room reservations but fortunately was directed by the Strand Palace to a small crowded hotel in Regent Park where we got a double room and took off immediately since it was already mid-afternoon. Davey felt like counting the number of bars in London so I left him peacefully ensconced in the Red Cross Officer's Club awaiting the opening gong and took off to find something I could send you. Shopping in London, however, was extremely disappointing. I really didn't find anything that I thought you might even faintly enjoy. I had picked up a ticket for *There Shall Be No Night* at the Red Cross so about that time, I wandered down toward the Aldwich Theatre. As I mentioned, the evening performances now start between 5 and 6 so the people can get home before the blitz begins. En route, I met another one of our officers, Joe Alkalonis, and headed him in the general direction of where I thought Davey might be. As there was a few minutes before curtain, I stopped in for some tea at the Waldorf next door which I had with a very genuine New Zealander. The play was magnificent, I thought, but then I've always liked Lunt and Fontanne. A scotch whiskey between acts warded off hunger pangs. During the intermission, a very distinguished-looking middle-aged couple came over and somewhat hesitatingly started to chat about the play. It was a very pleasant, if short, conversation and just as the bell rang, they asked me if I would like to come to have dinner and spend the night with them. I was somewhat overwhelmed by all of this and assured them that there was nothing I would like more if I didn't have to meet a friend for dinner. We parted at that point after he pressed his card on me and made me promise to take a raincheck (not the expression he used). In addition to being surprised, I was very much moved. They were both extremely charming attractive people and in addition had the most kindly faces I've seen in a long time. She was in semi-mourning so I inferred, perhaps incorrectly, they had lost a son in the war. Maybe I looked lonely although I didn't feel so but it was genuine kindness of heart, something you don't find often and I'm sorry I couldn't accept. . . .

London is an amazing place now. I'm not sure you would even recognize it except for the immutable objects like Buckingham, Westminster, etc. From your descriptions of New York with its

bejewelled refugees, I think London is the reverse and has probably more Americans than British at the present time. It would
seem that three quarters of the people you pass in hotels, on the
street, or in stores are in uniform and the great majority are
Americans. Refugees are of a somewhat different ilk—Poles,
Czechs, French, Belgians—all in uniform! It brings home the
phrase, "United Nations" very directly—united, I hope, in something besides just the war.

Another innovation which I can't recall in prewar London is the
"Picadilly Commandos." It is a real battle for a lone male to fight
his way through the Circus after dark. It makes the tales of Paris
read like nursery rhymes.

You have read and seen all the pictures of the results of the
bombings so I do not need to embellish those with verbal descriptions. The city runs along quite normally in the day but as the
skies darken, it becomes only too evident that a much more tragic
and brutal aspect of the war still exists.

The following evening, I resumed my regular rotation as O.D.
(Officer of the Day) for the entire base. Each tour of duty as O.D.
turned out to be quiet but very luxurious inasmuch as the medical officer on duty had a *heated* room with adjoining bath (*hot*
water). There were also sheets on a very comfortable bed—not a
cot. I reveled in my brief span of luxury. Perhaps the best part
was the complete solitude—a whole night to take an unhurried
bath and stretch out comfortably in bed to read in a totally quiet
environment after sleeping in the same room or tent continuously
with several men—eating with dozens and working with hundreds
day in and day out. Solitude is a rare thing in the army and something to be snatched at when the occasion presents itself. This is
particularly true, I suspect, of the battalion surgeon, since every
time you try to read, write, or do anything someone always appears with a stomachache or wants to borrow some soap, play
cards, or discuss some problem, or is just plain garrulous.

Towards the end of March, we had a beautiful day, really beautiful, with the first real whiff of spring in the air, warm sun. Everything seemed to become a shade greener. Spring is a marvelous thing anywhere and given a decent break by the weather, the countryside of England is lovely. "O to be in England now that April's here" took on new meaning. Everything seemed to come to life and, for a time at least, to lose that dull grey sheen that had hung over the country since my arrival five months earlier.

Miles and Krimsky, flushed out by the spring air from their hibernation, came down for lunch decked out in blouse, pinks, and our new somewhat garish shoulder patches of the Ninth Air Force. Following lunch, the three of us took off for Bishop's Stortford, where we embarked on some attempted shopping. I began to wonder how any of the shops (except for food, clothing and department stores) stayed open at all—empty showcases, empty shelves, a few large, hideous odds and ends, cheap secondhand jewelry, drawers full of secondhand bric-a-brac. After intensive cultural and shopping efforts, we were obviously in need of restoration and found ourselves in a hotel having tea and waiting for the bar to open—which it did, and we recuperated satisfactorily over the three consecutive whiskeys.

The weather continued to be glorious and we began to forget we were in England. It was really magnificent. Anyone who has been through an English winter can probably appreciate how we felt with two consecutive warm, bright sunny days. I gathered from an English officer that it doesn't pay to get too enthusiastic about it. When I made the obvious comment about the day, he replied somewhat dourly that it was indeed pleasant but they had often had snow in May. A happy thought!

I had a rush call that day from one of the battery commanders. The only message I received was that he had been in a bicycle accident. On the way down in the jeep, I speculated at length as to what sort of injury he might have had. He was quite a stoic, so

I knew he wouldn't have called for the ordinary scrapes and bruises. To my surprise he met me himself, ambulatory and apparently intact except for a furrowed brow and worried expression. The mystery cleared after I learned how the accident occurred. He had come down very hard astride the crossbar and sustained a painful but hardly serious injury to the crotch. Tales from some of the junior officers, however, about the *terrible* consequences that they heard ensued from blows in that particular region upset him to the point where he pictured himself as a withered and senile old man at thirty. I examined him with a straight face (a difficult job), assured him that he would remain a healthy and virile young man, and fixed him up with a suspensory to carry him through the next few days. He was much more disturbed than if he had had a chunk of shrapnel in his head, but I left him smiling and happy.

March 30, 1944

As I described after my previous visit London is really a madhouse with surging crowds, uniforms of almost any nation you could imagine, hotels jammed, underground and buses packed, taxis hard to find, restaurants crowded and theaters booked up weeks ahead. This week was worse than usual because it had been designated as "Salute the Soldier" and these were exhibits of tanks, artillery, AA guns, etc. all over the city, much parading and speech making, appearances of the King and Queen and so on. Fortunately, when Sawicki and I arrived on our partly business–mostly pleasure trip, we had no trouble getting a room because I headed directly for Regent Park where Davis and I had stayed the last time. I had had a long conversation with Mrs. Smalley, the owner, during that visit and she promised me a room at any time if it was at all possible. She is really very nice—I would guess an impoverished aristo who has turned her home into a private hotel, catering mainly to a crew of English Colonels, but very attractive and inexpensive. We left our things, and on Mrs. Smalley's recommendation, went to lunch at the Hungaria—excellent food, very much a

New York atmosphere and good wine—then there was a hectic
afternoon, cleaning up a few details here and there, and before I
knew, it was after five and time for the theatre. I picked up a couple
of tickets to *A Lisbon Story* at the Red Cross in the course of the
afternoon—that Red Cross is really a godsend, because otherwise
you could never get tickets for any of the popular things which are
sold out completely for weeks ahead. They do a wonderful job
and it is one organization to which I firmly intend to contribute
regularly for the rest of my life—they find rooms, suggest restaurants, get tickets of any kind, give directions and information, have
inexpensive billets for the men, run entertainments, arrange loans
and care in case there is sickness at home, solve problems and so
on and on. This letter was not intended to be a paean of praise of
the Red Cross but I've been very much impressed with what they
have done particularly for the men. The theatre was excellent—
one of the best musicals I've ever seen although that may be
because I've been away from anything like that of so long. Patricia
Bark was marvelous—I'm enclosing a program and a copy of one
particularly good song which I bought to send you. We had a good
dinner after the theatre at the Reindeer (Officer's Club) but after
that I was about ready for home and fireside after all the trotting
around which the afternoon involved so we both decided to head
for Regent Park. The underground at this time of night is a tragic
and pitiful sight since all the platforms are lined with tiers of bunks
for families who come down to avoid the air raids—sleeping
children, babies, old women, all huddled together in dismal
stations deep in the earth. It hardly seems worthwhile if you sit
down and mathematically calculate your chances in these days of
comparatively ineffective London raids, but I suppose after so many
years of it, you react purely on the instincts of self-preservation.

While we could refer to London when we went there either on
leave or on official business, we were still limited by censorship in
what we could write. For example, I could not refer to an air-raid
on London that took place that night. After returning to our hotel, the mournful wail of the air-raid sirens began. I should have
headed for a shelter, but it was obvious that the area beyond Hyde
Park in Regent Park had not been the target of any recent bomb-

ing so I stood on the small balcony of my room and watched. One almost forgets the tragedies and destruction associated with any air attack because of the spectacular visual scenes of bombs crashing, searchlights criss-crossing the sky, anti-aircraft tracers streaking up at all angles, fires burning below and the occasional plane going down in flames. The raids were almost entirely concentrated on the City of London and the dock areas along the Thames, so standing on the balcony was not as foolhardy as it may have seemed. The nearest bomb must have fallen at least a half a mile from my balcony.

Religion in the armed services has its vagaries; everyone noticed that there was nothing like danger to drive the G.I. to a religious service. Coming over on the convoy, one would have thought that we were carrying an entire coterie of potential saints—and of course, once we were involved in the Invasion, religious pressure built up again and there was a recurrence of saintliness.

As I had prophesied somewhat gloomily, Easter brought an end to our days of spring and the climate reverted to type, with leaden skies, drizzles off and on, and a damp cold wind.

The nightly ordeal of censoring mail had become practically like an after-dinner coffee—as soon as we got up from dinner, all the officers headed up the stairs, sat down in a circle about a huge stack of letters, and began the procedure of reading, signing, reading, signing, until the pile disappeared. A very dull task on the whole! The average human (including myself) is far from a litterateur, but occasionally there was something that brightened up the half hour. One boy invariably ended up a tender message to his wife "with oceans and oceans of love and millions and millions of kisses, your husband, Private Homer J. Smith." We often wondered if they had been formally introduced or married by proxy through a Lonely Hearts Club. Such formality seemed very impressive in this younger generation.

This problem of self-censorship by the officers was complicated by the vagaries of the instructions we received. We were not allowed to mention the name of the air base where we were stationed or the nearby towns but apparently we could say anything we chose about London—where we were, what we did, where we went, what we saw, etc. I could even describe an air raid as long as it was in London and as long as I didn't mention any objectives. There was hardly any point in going into much detail however— particularly since I slept right through one of the London air raids, so could hardly be called an eye witness to that one.

Throughout April there was little of interest to recount except the trips to London. Places like Simpson's, Quo Vadis, the Embassy, and the Florida had not changed since my prewar stay. Claridge's probably harbored all the high-priced help at lunch time and was an amusing observation post. From time to time, we were awakened by JU-88s droning overhead, but were never directly attacked.

The daily ritual seemed to go on and on. My letters home are a succession of discussions of family items, personal feelings, and reactions to news stories. Each officer had a small room at headquarters, which after a few weeks was completely filled with a bed, chair, table, and piles of books and magazines not to mention a duffel bag, valpack, and footlocker with clothes, equipment, etc. I was reminded of a poem by Burgess:

> *I wish that my room had a floor*
> *I don't so much care for a door*
> *But this walking around*
> *Without touching the ground*
> *Is getting to be somewhat a bore.*

One break in the monotony was the time when we were given short leave to attend a symposium at a nearby general hospital. A group of us from my station took off after lunch on a balmy spring day. A regular receiving line met us at the hospital and then we headed to the ward where the cases were to be presented. Well over 150 English and American doctors were present, several of whom I already knew. Two of my instructors from med school were down from the City Hospital unit. The clinic was interesting, well organized, and well presented, with the usual violent discussions over controversial subjects like the local use of sulfanilamides (always good for a battle) and others of similar ilk that raised blood pressures on both sides—treatment of burns was of course a standby for an apoplectic surgeon to demonstrate his individuality. All were instructive and a lot of fun. The "informal assembly" consisted of nothing more inspiring than a hoot before dinner—which at that point I did consider inspiring. Dinner itself was excellent under the circumstances—tomato juice, roast beef, potatoes, asparagus (unheard of), salad, and ice cream (another rarity). When we came in to dinner, we found that the nurses had been distributed among the tables to afford the gay lilt of feminine chatter. I sat between a gibbering two-ton truck and a lean and hungry soul who I suspected had parked her broom outside. Across from me was a very pink-cheeked, very stupid English major. Gastronomically, if not intellectually, it was a treat, and I was perfectly happy to concentrate on roast beef and ice cream with a minimum of conversational effort.

The "illustrated lecture" by Hamilton Bailey, the author of a simple but widely accepted short book on war surgery, was fairly typical, I thought, of English surgeons. Somehow or other, they (the good ones) seemed to accumulate an enormous number of cases; specialization was nowhere near as precise, or as widespread, as in the United States. Their information and knowledge was sound but tended to be empirical, without the more scholarly background of the study of basic psychological principles characteristic of American surgical training environments. Bailey's was a potpourri of suggestions of diagnosis and treatment, a description of various gadgets he had devised, his method of urethroplasty (which sounded good), without any particular central theme. However, there was a lot that could be gleaned.

Following the lecture, we repaired to the officers' club, where we met the first disappointment of the day. We shot to the bar immediately, fought our way to the source of supply, and found fruit juice! Considering the size of the crowd and the scarcity of liquor, that was only to be expected. We recovered from the shock and I stood around with a glass of this stuff and reminisced about Harvard and Boston with Ellis and Mansfield. We were finally inspired to move out to the dance floor but after pushing a chubby disciple of Florence Nightingale around for one number, it seemed an appropriate time to head home.

On the basis of an invitation to visit the House of Commons with G. Russell Strauss, a member of Parliament I'd met on an earlier visit, I had another short leave in London. It was a wonderful day. I went in with Emil Roos and we spent most of the morning on business, but I found myself with a little time before lunch and headed up Picadilly to find #134, where Blanche had lived for a year. I found it but there was no longer any permanent aura about it—nothing frilly in the windows—in fact, it was very cold and austere-looking, the site of the Czech Ministry of National Defense. From there I turned up Downing Street to look for the Farm Street Church, which was as lovely as Blanche had described in her letters. Unfortunately, it was damaged in the Blitz, and very little of its stained glass remained. All the beautiful little chapels around the sides were intact, however. As I wandered around the church, a wizened old lady who was working there came up and started to talk to me. I don't suppose it was very common to find an American officer in that particular church,

which is somewhat off the beaten path, has no particular historical interest, and is not a traditional parish church. At any rate, she
chatted on and on about the church, which was clearly her whole
life. She was eighty-five years old and had worked there sixty years,
as her mother had before her. She knew everything about it—
historically, architecturally, and ecclesiastically—and having found
a willing audience was perfectly willing to talk on indefinitely. She
claimed to remember Blanche, but wasn't sure. I think she just
liked to feel that she remembered everyone who had ever set foot
in *her* church. However, she was a very sweet little old lady and
was going to say a prayer for all of us.

I headed downhill again to the Berkeley Buttery for lunch with
Roos—an attractive place, with a good bartender, good food, and
all the nonsense and chatter of the smart set packed into a room
for a drink and a meal. The English smart set were a little handi-
capped by almost five years of war and clothes rationing. Otherwise, it might have been the Stork, 21, or the Ritz, with fewer silver
fox jackets and complicated-looking hats and a more varied collection of uniforms. After lunch I went to Dunhill's—which also
had been bombed. The firm was functioning in a much smaller
space and the cellars where the tobacco and the cigars of the
world's elect used to be stored in special air-conditioned cabinets
were no more. They used to have a record of the tobacco blend
they had mixed for me many years ago, but that went with the
Blitz. They had only a few pipes coming in now and then on rare
occasions, and these were always sold shortly after the doors
opened. All in all, it was very sad. Before the war they had
such a magnificent assortment of briars (French and English),
Meerschaums, etc., that you could easily spend a day just looking at pipes.

I went out to Kensington Palace Gardens, where Mrs. Strauss
had asked me to have coffee before meeting her husband at Parlia-

ment. They had a fascinating house—one of the large rambling, weatherbeaten, solid architectural horrors of the section, entirely done over inside on modernistic lines. Very airy, efficient, functional and neat—more the setting for a cocktail party or a liberal salon than home. It was a beautiful day and we stretched out in the sun on the terrace, which looked over their own gardens and farther onto Kensington Palace, where all the broken-down royal relations were collected. The Strausses were very hospitable, interesting people—she did feature stories for the *Herald Tribune* and had an office in the house where she did most of her work.

At about four we left to meet Mr. Strauss at Parliament. He was, I think, in the Conservative party, although his politics were very liberal, but then, that is possible in the English system. He joined us in the lobby and ushered us through the series of guards—like getting into the vaults of the Bank of England. The House of Commons had been completely demolished by a direct bomb hit, so the Commons met in the House of Lords—very plush and ornate—while the Lords met in a side room somewhere else. He had two seats for Mrs. Strauss and me on the floor, where we sat through a great deal of rhetoric being bounced around on the budget, which had just been read by Sir John Anderson. After about an hour of this masochism we went out for tea. I was relieved that my future career carried no indications of being immersed in parliamentary proceedings or politics in any form. The Strausses had asked me back later in the evening (rationing precluded dinner invitations, particularly in London), but I had to decline, thanked them very much, and left to join Emil Roos for dinner at Meurice's (Quaglino's)—excellent soup and lobster, a couple of quick drinks, music, and then back to the railroad station. Thus went the day and my financial reserve—but we were paid in a few days and there was a poker game in the interim, so I was able to recoup.

Late April brought really magnificent spring days—the kind of days on which England can more than make up for the miserable winter days she doles out so endlessly, Even though so much of the country had, of wartime necessity, been converted from flowers to vegetables, it still was rapidly becoming one vast garden. In spite of the placid loveliness of everything, however, the eternally green fields and the living poetry of the rural districts, I knew I could never live there. Beyond question it could very easily lull you into a hazy state of comfortable somnolence and gracious living—but that would always be my violent objection. There was no longer any grandeur, no feeling of any underlying power, no real zest for living, nothing overwhelming either in man and all his works or in nature. With all her faults, her youth, gaucheness, and exuberance, America had never given me the sense of stagnation that I felt in England. I missed everything I knew about America—the fine woods, lakes, mountains, and trout streams of New Hampshire, the flat sandy Cape which would always be beautiful to me as Blanche's and my first summer home, the long beaches and the semitropical surroundings of Florida and the Caribbean (again the rosy glow and the prejudice), the roar and soaring heights of New York that make you want to both get in and get out, the stately, quiet loveliness of Chestnut Street in Salem (where I grew up) or Beacon Hill. It would undoubtedly be pleasant to have a flat in London, an office on Harley Street, and a house in the country where it is green year round and you can ride placidly along lanes or gallop frantically over hedges and walls, climb up the hills, and browse around in tweeds and pipe discussing local and national politics—but I might very shortly come to hate it. It could be too enervating—like spending your life in a lukewarm bath.

April 30, 1944

How the people of Germany, for instance, at least half of whom
must have had some recollections of the last war could have
willingly set a course which so obviously would result in war
becomes harder and harder to understand. All the obvious
explanations, psychological (Prussianism, mass inferiority complex, revenge), geopolitical (Lebensraum, lack of self sufficiency,
Drang nach Osten), economic (abnormal import-export balance,
reparations, shaky currency standards, depression, etc.), and any
others that you could go on dragging in indefinitely don't seem to
me at this point to hold much water. Admittedly to most male
youngsters, there is a certain element of glamour and virility in
uniforms, marching music, drums and marching men, but that
couldn't account for more than a small part of the whole picture.
I'm not speaking so much of revolutions or civil wars which have
undoubtedly planted the seeds of and nourished some ideals of a
fumbling humanity and which have contributed to progress and
humanism; what I am referring to are the wars between peoples,
races and nations germinated entirely by nationalism, territorial or
material aggrandizement or dynastic ambitions. Even the few
aspects of modern war which can still be somewhat colored and
glamorized to people at home, none of that appears to the men
involved. It's incredible; it really is! When I was sitting comfortably at home, at least I could rattle off some of the more obvious of
the so-called "explanations" along the lines of Fay's Origins of the
World War and even think that I had some understanding of the
course of events but now they are just well-propounded and
organized thoughts of some men trying to understand themselves
and explain to others that for which there is no explanation. This
is no pacifist mumbling, Blanchie—I was an interventionist long
ago and even if Pearl Harbor hadn't made it so obvious, I would
still feel that we had no other choice on any grounds—defensive
ideals, honor or just plain self-preservation. All I am trying to do is
battle out with myself to find some reason beyond all this—which I
can't do.

By early May, it was clear that we were in a holding pattern.
Everyone felt the invasion was becoming increasingly imminent

and we were under stricter guidelines and censorship.

> Just finished a fascinating article in JAMA by Bettelheim, a German
> psychologist on the reactions of the human mind to conditions and
> life in concentration camps. He escaped from Germany after long
> stretches in both the Dachau and Buchenwald concentration
> camps and his whole psychological study of his fellow prisoners
> was excellent—portraying how gradually over a long period of
> time, all but the strongest minds will break down eventually, come
> to accept the Gestapo's standards instead of their own. It is not an
> active and enthusiastic acceptance but rather the dulled and
> sluggish sensorium adapting itself to initial torture and horror,
> followed by a routine, substandard living filled with insidious
> propaganda which unnoticed, slowly eats away the higher levels of
> thought and eventually reduces the weaker mind to the level of
> their captors. The concept of men, tortured and imprisoned
> because of violent anti-Nazi principles, coming slowly to the point
> of accepting their captor's standards, is almost incomprehensible
> but his description of the slow, almost imperceptible changes in
> their principles is excellent, if a little disheartening. Very interest-
> ing! You know, the Army itself makes an interesting psychological
> study. It may be a difficult job for our society to re-absorb the
> millions of men who, for a number of years, had been adapting
> themselves to the standards and discipline of an Army which of
> necessity stamps out individuality and almost puts a premium need
> on mediocrity. It is not so much the fact that men come to recog-
> nize and accept the fact that advancement depends, not so much
> on ability as on time, place and circumstances—as it is that there is
> such a common and widespread tendency to voluntarily partially
> anesthetize oneself. In other words, as a kind of false armor, men
> stop reading or thinking about cause and effect, the future, political
> or religious philosophy, civilian or economic problems—almost
> anything that doesn't have a direct bearing on their everyday life. It
> is easy to see why. They know that their fate and disposition is
> almost entirely out of their hands and to protect themselves against
> disillusionment with its resultant psychological upsets and against
> the fear of looking into the future, they wall themselves in with a
> protective shell of automaticity and non-thinking acceptance of
> events as inevitable. This is obviously a mentally stupefying

process and the antidote is for man to realize his importance as an individual and that the whole Army is made up of individuals without whom it could not function. The average man, however, realizes that this antidote is potentially hazardous in that it opens chinks in his armor through which he can be emotionally hurt.

These comments on Bettelheim's article emphasize the progression in brutality in the concentration camps from my initial, peripheral contact and references to Dachau in 1938, through the descriptions of Bettelheim to the tales which began to filter to us as we crossed the Rhine and on to the direct exposure and to the ultimate horror of the concentration camp at Ebensee. I felt from that day that no human beings, even the SS, could be suddenly degraded to that level of atrocity and the process of degradation of the Germans *must* have taken time.

Subsequent letters from Bishop's Stortford are of little interest. We were in a "holding pattern" with the batteries spread out around several airfields in East Anglia. Obviously, the Luftwaffe had been considerably weakened by this time and there were only occasional and sporadic attacks on the airfields, although London was still undergoing intermittent night bombing, as I saw during my brief three visits.

In general, one day ran into another, with regular inspections and sick call at the batteries, nightly poker games, reading, and various organized or casual exercise and sports.

One of our persistent and disrupting problems was venereal disease. Obviously, if you take thousands of young men out of their ordinary, probably somewhat restrictive environments and transplant them to an area where the percentage of young women far exceeds the male population (most of whom were fighting the war overseas), one could anticipate the results—a breakdown of ordinary restraints and widespread promiscuity. The standard British comment was that "the Yanks were overpaid, oversexed,

and over here!" Be that as it may, all the medical units faced a sig-
nificant number of sexually transmitted diseases—some syphilis
but mostly gonorrhea and nonspecific urethritis. Unfortunately,
we did not have satisfactory antibiotics available (and would not
have until we were first issued penicillin in Normandy) and the
standard treatment was both uncomfortable and somewhat unsatisfactory. We issued condoms regularly, provided lectures, and
circulated warnings, but it was obvious that these measures met
with only limited success.

Finally, in late May, we received march orders to leave East Anglia
and proceed to the marshalling and staging areas near the ports of
embarkation in southern England. The long-awaited day of the
Invasion was drawing closer; the "Long Wait" was nearly over.

5

Marshalling and Staging Areas

SOUTHERN ENGLAND

May 19–June 5, 1944

After packing up essential gear and checking out all the guns, equipment, and vehicles, we began our trek southwest by winding our way through the countryside north of London and moving into the crowded Nissen huts of the marshalling area in southern England, where the 1st and 29th Infantry as well as several armored divisions were located.

Endless columns of troops were now streaming into marshalling areas. Although the weather was deteriorating alarmingly, it was obvious that D-Day was not far off. Fortunately for the ordinary soldier, life in the army presents such a constant series of problems concerned with eating, sleeping, shaving, washing, keeping dry and relatively warm, and such mundane matters that one does not become overly concerned with the overall strategic problems. Those were left to Eisenhower and such detached figures. Boredom had given way to excitement, and some degree of suppressed apprehension. At least we were moving in the right direction. All of our letters written in May and early June were held in local post offices in the United States so that on D-Day, our families were inundated with mail after a month-long drought.

May 23, 1944

This mad-house presents a real problem in writing, what with the racket, confusion, radio blaring, constant interruptions with nervous medical questions, etc. Just now, our friends on the other side of the channel are barking away on the radio with their usual propaganda line. The German and the German-inspired stations in occupied Europe are quite popular. They have excellent musical programs of both modern and classical pieces, obviously chosen to attract the American troops. Obviously, their little chats from Calais Cassie and others, and their "news" summaries are quite amusing (although not intended that way) but tonight someone had become quite carried away with himself while on an anti-Semitic barrage and hence has just been turned off in favor of another station. We really appreciate the efforts to which they go in propaganda since it makes for good listening but sometimes, as in this case, it is extraordinarily crass, inept and inefficient. The human mind works in interesting ways and I am sure that if troops

Nissen hut, Cattistock, 1943

l-r:John Miles, W.V.McD.,Joe Akulonis, Joe Krimsky

were suddenly forbidden to listen to German programs, their effectiveness would be increased a thousand-fold.

Having just finished disporting myself in the delights of an open-air shower, I was thinking how easy we will be to please once we return to civilization. We will arrive home like an army of children at the circus raving about food, reveling in hot baths, luxuriating on soft beds and mattresses—all of which should simplify the domestic lives of thousands of wives. There is very little to do now except to read and wait except for interminable inspections.

At this point we were, geographically speaking, back together as a battalion, and were settled into Nissen huts, inspecting and organizing equipment, reviewing much of the material from maneuvers many weeks ago and in general crammed into tight quarters. The weather was improving and I could bask in the hot sun, stretch out on the grass, and read or write for long periods. Hot water was available from field showers and everyone's spirits were good.

May 26, 1944

It's appalling to stop and think of the tremendous waste of time in war. Here I am with more free time than I'll ever see again for years, and little or no chance or opportunity to spend it in an interesting or constructive way.

This is hardly a very dramatic day—a little work on minor ailments with the troops, a little reading, a little sun, a cold shower, which is fine on days like this, and lazy periods of daydreaming. This doesn't sound much like a war, but then even if it did, I couldn't very well write you about it. You can probably tell more from speculations and facts in the newspapers and magazines at home than you can derive from my letters. At any rate, here we are with very little to do and a great deal of time in which to do it.

You seemed puzzled by our "Financial Status" so this seems to be a good point at which to provide details.

"Financial Status"

$ 166.67	Base Pay Monthly (First Lieutenant)
75.00	Dependent (BO'R McD)
42.00	Board (For me and dependent)
16.67	10% of Base Pay for Overseas Duty
$ 300.34	TOTAL
-200.00	Allotment
$ 100.34	
-18.75	War Bond
$ 81.59	
-6.75	Insurance
$ 74.84	
25.00	Average cost of my food monthly
$ 49.84	My net monthly income (minus various expenses of equipment, officer's mess, etc. but plus poker winnings which come by quite consistently and which you receive in these various money orders which I send on).

By May 28, the clouds had cleared and it was magnificent in the country with the top and the windshield of the jeep down (as required in combat conditions), the sun blazing from an absolutely clear blue sky and enough breeze from the speed of the vehicle to keep one cool. Weather reports for the following day left something to be desired, however, and as we learned later Eisenhower was forced to alter the Invasion schedule somewhat.

The next step to actual embarkation was the staging area, which meant a roadside existence for the thousands of men packed into the available routes to the docks of Southampton.

Joe Krimsky and W.V. McD. in Staging area, May 1944

May 30, 1944

This certainly is a return to the primeval lifestyle, what with pitching pup tents, shaving, bathing, and washing out of helmets full of water, getting dressed inside a pup tent when it's raining out as it was this morning—all of this involves a remarkable amount of gymnastics and acrobatics. It's sort of a rocking motion whereby you lurch forward, pull something over your head, then roll over and back to pull something on from below. Repeated four times, these maneuvers result in draping yourself with t-shirt, shorts, OD shirt and trousers. Socks, boots and leggings require a somewhat specialized form of the old-fashioned bicycle exercise with frequent rest periods. Once all this is completed, you burrow around in the equipment, which takes up all the space not occupied by a

sleeping bag, find and wriggle into a raincoat (best accomplished in
the prone position through a series of flapping motions resembling
the flight of an elderly and decrepit seagull). At this point, with
what little remaining strength you can muster, you worm your way
out into the drizzle for powdered eggs and coffee. Shaving and
washing involves a choice between the outside of the tent where it's
raining or the inside where it's dry but where the range of motion
is so limited that the gyrations essential to the time-honored
routine of shaving are impossible. However, on the positive side, it
must be said that in warm weather, it is a helluva lot better sleeping
out in the air than in the crowded huts, barracks or houses. This
continuum does make one wonder a little about the appeal of the
"back-to-woods communing with nature" idea! I suppose there
may be differences in the Canadian Rockies, for example, where
you could inhale the freshness of the morning dew, bathe in idyllic
mountain pools, gambol over flower-blanketed slopes, chase
butterflies, feed the chipmunks, etc. I'm not sure, however, how
much of a wood nymph or child of nature you basically would be.
If the idea of a forest idyll as a second honeymoon does not appeal
to you, however, I would be more than happy to forgo the idea and
limit ourselves to someplace like Sea Island. I really cannot
develop a very clear picture of Blanche living in a tent but one
never knows. There may be more of Thoreau in you then I had
realized!

It is now dusk and the constant noise of thousands of men
crowded into a small area has abated, and the night is quiet except
for the buglers blowing taps, first nearby and then fainter like
echoes as the call is taken up along the line. Very lovely but silent
and lonely particularly when the last note fades away and the deep
silence falls again, so silent that it's almost tangible.

Early in June, another officer and I had to take off unexpectedly
on a jeep jaunt for supplies. Before I finally dragged my heels into
my sleeping bag, I had covered what felt like a considerable part
of the United Kingdom. In essence, the trip consisted in driving
all afternoon, which was pleasant enough since the country was
lovely and the weather fair. After a stop at the hospital and a two-

Marshalling area: postcard home

hour stop at a supply base, we drove on until 5:00 A.M. The huge supply depots were astounding—acres and acres of buildings, railroad tracks, guns, tanks, equipment of all sorts stretching as far as the eye could see. It was in operation night and day without letup. We covered only a minute section of the whole plant, but it gave us an inkling of the enormous resources and men and equipment that were behind the drive towards D-Day and invasion.

The return drive was hardly pleasant. We hadn't planned on any night driving and very foolishly had no flashlights, forcing us to crawl through the blackout reading maps by a cigarette lighter. Any illusions we might have had about June nights were rapidly dispelled—it was very cold and wet, and by the time we arrived at our next stop, a British camp, at 5:00 A.M., we were a bedraggled, haggard, sleepy, hungry, wet, and thoroughly miserable pair. The rest of the ride back was a nightmare. The two consolations of the trip were a fried egg and the sight of my own sleeping bag just after noon. That damn thing never looked quite so good. Within about thirty seconds of pulling up at the unit, I was sound asleep with all my clothes in a heap and never moved until dinnertime.

The tent life was really very healthy at that time of year. Since I could not write or read once darkness set in, there was no choice but to crawl into a sleeping bag and pound out a good eight hours. I must have very little of the blood of Irish kings despite descent from Diarmid, for stones and mounds beneath the sleeping bag passed almost unnoticed. Roots and rocks under my head and butt never prevented my giving a remarkably good imitation of a log within a few seconds of flattening out.

A baby woodpecker adopted me and rode around on my shoulders, apparently thriving on a mushy diet of powdered eggs and milk, which he took through an eye dropper. Not a very varied diet, but then neither was ours! Six meals in a row consisted of canned corned beef, canned peas, canned peaches, and coffee.

Shortly before the Invasion, a lieutenant in the Tank Corps arrived at Battalion Headquarters with orders for four officers and six enlisted men to come with him on detached duty. Our colonel was extremely irritated because he was not told why we were going, where we were going, or under what circumstances we might return. The orders were valid, however—he checked—so off we went through the English countryside in a two-and-a-half-ton truck. Because of the absence of any signs and because we had no maps of the area available, I had no idea where we were going, nor did I have any idea where we were when we arrived after several hours at our destination. We unloaded our gear and ourselves and were ushered into a large stone country house. The grounds were guarded by smartly dressed MPs who checked us off as we came in the front door as if we were arriving at a plush hotel. Our rooms had hot water and we had time for a short rest and a shave and bath before coming down to the main floor, where a rather impressive meal was served in a huge dining room. A number of other officers and men from other battalions were present, but none of us had the slightest idea where we were or why.

After dinner, we were ushered into a large library, which was set up like a schoolroom with individual desks. After an MP seated us and then stood guard at the closed door, the lieutenant from the Tank Corps introduced himself as an officer of Army Intelligence. We would be with him for two to three days on detached service, learning a special code. Before he went any further, we had a solemn ceremony in which we all swore that we would reveal nothing of what went on in the castle to anyone at any time. We were to learn a difficult box code that was in successful use from prisoner-of-war camps, the lieutenant explained. The Germans allowed POWs one or two brief V-mail letters per month and the trick was to include in a very short letter any salient bits of information of value that could be garnered and transmitted. If any of us was taken prisoner, he was to go to the commanding officer of the prisoners in the camp, introduce himself by name, rank, serial number, unit, etc., and state that there were a number of men captured with him who could verify his identity. The commanding officer would establish his own authenticity by giving the names of various prisoners who were members of his unit and could verify his rank and position. (Any general officer who claimed to be the sole prisoner from his unit was almost certainly a plant, we were told, as it was extremely unusual for anyone over the rank of major to be captured alone.) Once mutual authenticity was verified, the newly arrived prisoner would reveal that he had a way of getting information from the Stalag to the screening center in London. All of this was fascinating, of course, and some of the tales that were reported of the importance of information transmitted through this box code stimulated us to work diligently at the project. We worked two days at the code with regular and continued examination and critiques of our competence and were returned to the battalion just before the Invasion.

Years after the war ended, I came across an intriguing and obviously relevant reference to this espionage network in an interview with First Lieutenant Brewster Morgan by Robert Popp ("Yank in the RAF," *Military History*, June 1991):

Popp: When did you reach the infamous Stalag Luft III?

Morgan: It was June 1943. Stalag Luft III was in Sagen, a town in Silesia, half-way between Berlin and Breslau. Upon my arrival, I was brought before Squadron Leader Harvey Melville Arbuthnot "Wings" Day, the camp senior officer. He was to determine whether I was a German plant, and, if not, what useful intelligence I had picked up on the way to Sagen. I told him that I saw what I believed to be a Focke-Wulf factory from the train and its approximate location. Shortly thereafter, it was bombed. Only then did I realize the unique coded message system that existed between the prisoners and the people back in England.

Obviously, this refers to the same secret coded system above described and illustrates the effectiveness of the system.

Immediately after our return I began to receive warm personal letters from a lieutenant in the WAF (Woman's Air Force of Great Britain) whom I had never met or even heard of. I was completely mystified until it occurred to me that I should search this letter for a coded message, and there it was! I had to reply in kind with an answer of sorts both to the cheerful and frivolous letter *and,* in code, to the coded message. Clearly this was intended as a form of continued "practice" in the use of the code and the correspondence continued for some time even after our landings in Normandy. The Germans never discovered this code and it continued to be useful throughout the war.

After our expedition to learn the secret code, we returned to our rather primitive lifestyle awaiting the Invasion. We knew that we would be actively involved because we had been in training and in maneuvers with units of the First Army, including for a time the First Infantry Division, but rumor had it that we were considered only the second-best battalion of our type (AAA-AW battalions) and therefore another unit would probably precede us in terms of the various waves entering France. A certain bizarre kind of pride left a disappointment that we had not won out in the competition, but reality would make it clear to any dolt that being in a somewhat later wave in the Invasion would be safer than the initial beach landing. In any case, it was all out of our hands, and there was little we could do except sit and wait until we were loaded on the cross-Channel ships.

6

Invasion of Normandy

OMAHA BEACH TO ISIGNY

June 6–July 24, 1944

Tuesday, June 6, 1944, D-DAY!

This is the first step on the road home, dearest one—the day we've been waiting for, hoping for, training for and biting my tongue to avoid mentioning or discussing too much in letters. It is not particularly dramatic or histrionic here. There is just an immense feeling of relief, of admiration for the boys who have just left for the first landing, of quiet confidence in them and in the whole mass of men who will follow them, of prayer and of faith. Obviously, there is no point in talking further about it since there is so little that I would be permitted to say but perhaps I can tell you more in a later letter from France.

After we had been thoroughly cleared for boarding, the engines of all the vehicles were covered with a thick coating of cosmoline, and pipes were installed in the intake of the carburetors and in the output through the exhaust pipes in such a way that they stood several feet above the level of the vehicle itself. This bit of engineering permitted the vehicles to be driven under water for a short period in case an LST (Landing Ship Tank) was unable, for one reason or another, to reach dry ground. After these preparations we then drove slowly in directed order onto a designated LST and huddled in our vehicles awaiting departure. Eventually and tediously, we pulled away from the harbor and began the trip across the channel to Normandy. Miserable weather and rough seas! Half of the battalion were seasick or soaked or both.

While plowing through the heavy waves, I was sought out in my jeep by a navy corpsman who asked me to follow him to the compact ship's quarters where two young navy doctors greeted me and gave me the best breakfast I'd had in months (in the next war, I intend to join the navy). They were just out of a nine-month internship and we had lots of common ground and mutual acquaintances. After leaving us on the beachhead, they would take care of casualties who were boarded for the return trip to England.

Being with them certainly made for a pleasanter crossing, plus an excellent view from their quarters of the crossing and the arrival at the beach in Normandy. An added reason for enthusiasm was the fact that they opened up a reserve of brandy, practically the first alcohol I'd had except scotch and an occasional pint of mild and bitter. We enjoyed a quiet, congenial evening despite the rough crossing. Even though the English had given us a cordial welcome and even more enthusiastic sendoff on the trip to port and to the boats, and were very friendly and hospitable during our brief stay, no one regretted leaving the land of the chilblain, lakes, hedgerows, mild and bitter, coal grates, and perpetual bleakness. Not that I had any illusions that France was going to be any better, but at least I wouldn't be marking time—and every kilometer would be a step on the way home, albeit a little roundabout. We thought at one time that we'd be in earlier than we were (June 12), but then we hardly had much to say about the conduct of the war or the disposition of the troops.

Towards dawn, we could see the bluffs of Normandy rising out of the mist and smoke. As we headed towards the beach, we passed the battleship *Texas,* our companion and support in our convoy to England two months earlier. She was now engaged in providing heavy fire cover for the landings from her 16-inch guns. The officers and senior noncoms had been given area maps and it was obvious that we were to disembark on Omaha Beach, which we had heard was the scene of the most vicious resistance by the Germans. All the other beachheads had moved well inshore and the American troops on Utah and the British and Canadian troops on Gold, Sword, and Juno beaches initially had fairly easy going, except for sporadic air attacks and shelling. Information was still very confused in getting to us. While our own particular landing site was supposed to be on the Dog-Easy section of Omaha Beach, we somehow or other headed into Fox-Green—little matter, since the whole area was a shambles anyway. Fortunately, the LST came close and the tide was such that when the ramps went down, our vehicles all came directly on to dry land as far as I could see.

From a distance, the cliffs had looked somewhat formidable, but as the ramp dropped, we could see lines of armored vehicles of various sizes and descriptions working their way slowly up various rough pathways. The LST on which we arrived was already loading wounded for the return trip to England. A number of people were rather vaguely directing traffic—if one could call the chaos by such an orderly term—but most of us seemed to be more or less on our own in terms of getting out of the hot corner and up and over the bluffs. My own jeep followed a short line of half-tracks that were maneuvering up a dirt roadway—more of a lane than a road that eventually reached the fields and road heading towards Vierville, just inland from the beach.* Fortunately, most of the pillboxes and emplacements had been deactivated on the first day of the Invasion.

---

* In 1988, when I returned with Dave Dunn and my children to Normandy for the first time since the war, I was able to locate the same lane leading up over the cliffs from Omaha Beach into the flat lands of Normandy.

Looking towards Normandy, D-Day, June 1944

As headquarters battalion became somewhat organized, we had a quick, somewhat nervously administered briefing, the sum and substance of which was that we were to "dig in" near Vierville and should be prepared for counterattacks on the ground or for air attacks on the beach that we had just left. All the battery commanders were warned to be extremely careful about air identification, since the American Air Force had control of the skies during the daytime and it was relatively rare for a Luftwaffe plane to break through to reach any of the troops coming on to the beaches or already beyond in the fields and hedgerows of Normandy. Maneuvering through the wreckage off the beaches and through the lanes cleared of mines and obstacles by the engineers was somewhat nerveracking, but except for the confusion as to our exact landing site, everything went remarkably smoothly. Although artillery shelling was going on in the vicinity of Vierville, there was not even a "near miss" from artillery or from the air.

Beyond the occasional bombings in East Anglia or in London this was the first exposure of most of our battalion to any form of active warfare. It is difficult to recall and describe the feelings associated with embarkation and arrival at the beaches. Certainly, the sweating and the dry mouth were universal, but otherwise everyone seemed either unusually jocular or excessively quiet. The whole experience of our initial exposure to the actual war was relatively traumatic—although this is not intended to minimize the nightmare that the first wave of the 1st Division had faced for some hours until the beachhead was reasonably secured.

We were given revised censorship rules and told that we could now say that we were in France, but should avoid mentioning specific geography.

June 16-20, 1944, Vierville, Normandy

C'est La Belle France on whose good earth I have already left the imprint of my grimy puss. I never knew it was possible to get quite so dirty in one day but I should guess that it might very well be a chronic state from now on. One could, I suppose, mark the days of the invasion by the layers of accumulated dirt, similar to the way one defines the age of a tree. The tramp of thousands of feet and the roll of thousands of wheels over France's dirt roads keep the air filled constantly with a fine penetrating dust. Fortunately, the landing did not entail getting soaked through or I would be plastered with a thick layer of mud instead of just dirt. I don't know how well this is being described in the papers at home, but even from the wildest yellow journals, I don't think you could obtain an adequate description of the magnitude of the whole operation. It's beyond belief—the number of ships, planes, men and equipment involved, pouring ashore in a massive never-ending torrent. Except for those few obvious remarks, you can probably pick up more from the papers than I would ever be allowed to write. Anyway, the term "successful landings" does meager justice to the courage of the men who first cracked the beaches a few days ago—it was no pushover, I assure you. The devastated villages and

W.V. McD. in dug-in aid station off the beach
in Normandy. Note comforts of home! June 1944

fortifications stand as mute testimony to the struggle which they
had to establish beach-heads for those of us who were to follow. So
far, I can't give you much of an impression—it's a lovely country
and even the ravages of war have destroyed little of the pictur-
esqueness of the winding, rural roads heavily shaded by carefully
spaced trees, the famous apple orchards (without the apple
blossoms at this time of the year) and the neat French farms. As we
rolled inland, we have seen little of the local population—a few
somewhat apathetic people seemingly still dazed by the destruction but friendly and hospitable. The tricolor waves again from
homes, some of which are intact, some shattered, and then, behind
the advancing lines, the farmers are beginning to try to pick up
some threads of their life and work. It has been a long, fairly hard
day and I'm somewhat bushed at present. Digging a foxhole in
which to unroll your bag and blankets for the night is no picnic at
the end of the day and I doubt if any sort of racket could keep me

awake tonight.

My foxhole is impressive with a roof of shelter-halves beneath which there is almost enough room to stand upright, pegs on the wall to hang equipment and clothes, small cupboards dug out of the sides, in fact everything except electricity, central heating and hot and cold running water—or chambermaids. Since we may settle at this spot for a short time at least, I'll probably add further improvements tomorrow if I have time. One distinct advantage to manual labor is that even the C&K rations on which we have been subsisting taste fairly good. This must be a fascinating letter—a detailed recital of domestic life. I guess one develops a very narrow worm's eye (or mole's eye) point of view after a short period of this type of existence. You spend so much time on the essentials—eating, digging, keeping comparatively warm and dry, and sleeping—that there doesn't seem to be much time left for the ethereal things of life. I can't recall how much local color I gave you yesterday. This is really a lovely country, very green, lightly wooded and while worn and torn by all the works of man, nature herself absorbs the scars so well that they are hardly noticeable. I shouldn't have said, "all the works of man" because the peculiar thing about war is the odd way in which it strikes. Right in the midst of a completely destroyed area, you may find a house, a church, or a farm standing untouched. On the beach, for instance, I remember noting one villa without a scar while everything else over a long stretch was charred and shattered.

My God, I'm dirty—I've got my eye on a cow trough for tomorrow if it's warm enough and quiet enough to consider standing in it and sloshing water over me. I doubt very much if I'll make the acquaintance of a tub or a shower for some time.

A few of the towns and villages in the areas occupied so far are said to be practically intact with hotels functioning and shops opened, but it probably won't be our luck to hit any of them. Right now, the cow trough seems to offer the closest approximation to civilized bathing that I've seen in this general area. This business of burrowing, digging and in general maintaining a close affinity with the good earth makes you unrecognizable within a short time.

Now that we're completely underground (Aid Station, individual foxholes, etc.), life is taking on a more civilized aspect—at least to the point of having light to read by at night since we can completely black out both the command post and the casualty area. It's very luxurious to have light again, even a gasoline lantern. The discouraging thing is, I am sure, that as soon as we get everything completed to the limit of possibilities, we'll move out. The outfits that come in later and follow in our footsteps should have a very soft life indeed with all the digging done, comforts of home installed and the table practically set for dinner. One advantage of being forced to rely on the sun as the source of all but emergency lighting is that I'm getting plenty of sleep, even with the inevitable interruptions during the night by the JU88's.

This has been a very interesting experience. I have often wondered just how men would react when they hit their first campaign. I remember someone somewhere described it aptly by saying you feel like a June bride—you know what will happen but you don't know how it will feel—which sums up everything pretty well. In confirmation of the theory of almost infinite adaptability, within a remarkably short time, the routine noise and racket doesn't even interrupt sleep and with everyone bitching about food, hot water, and spreading the usual rumors and scuttlebutt, it's just the same Army life in another country under somewhat more realistic conditions than maneuvers.

The major gripe which we all have is the understandable but nonetheless disappointing absence of mail for days. I understand that they have so-called "mulberries" *[floating docks that were towed from England and "fixed" on the beaches to expedite debarkation of larger vehicles and equipment]* built as a harbor so that perhaps we will begin to get mail delivery some time in the near future.

I have enclosed a sample of the money we are using or rather have but are not using. It looks like a cigar coupon. If I save enough, I may be able to get an electric train which might be useful someday to our children, a subject and a process to which I obviously have given considerable thought, albeit a little round-about.

Omaha Beach was the responsibility of the V Corps and the assault was led by the 1st (Big Red One) and 29th divisions, as well as the 2nd Ranger Battalion, which accomplished the remarkable feat of scaling and capturing Pointe du Hoe, a promontory on a sheer cliff projecting in such a way that German guns in the pillbox could command most of Omaha Beach. The 1st Division sustained heavy casualties and the whole operation seemed headed for disaster until a few spirited and courageous souls, led, driven, and encouraged by Brigadier General Norman Cota and other individual officers and men, worked their way out of the melange of riflemen, engineers, navy beach-masters, tanks, and other vehicles up the heights and gradually eliminated the German pill-boxes and strong-points.

By 11:00 A.M., Vierville was in American hands, and by night-fall, the Americans controlled a perimeter a mile deep beyond Omaha Beach. The contributions of the 82nd and 101st Airborne divisions, which landed in Normandy well before H-hour of D-Day, cannot be overstated.

Part of the problem encountered by those landing on Omaha Beach related to topography, and part, at least, was due to the unexpected presence of the German 352nd Division, which arrived behind Omaha Beach shortly before D-Day for routine maneuvers, without any suspicion of the imminent landings. Despite enormous casualties sustained by the first wave and despite the confusion and terror of many of the green troops, sufficient men reached the seawall alive and by steadily eliminating German strong-points provided pathways for succeeding waves to move off the beach and onto high ground. Surprisingly, a concerted German counterattack never developed.

The landings at the beach after D-Day proceeded smoothly and efficiently. With relatively few casualties, the units landed and moved off the beaches and by evening we had strong lines established several miles inland. In fact, with the early disastrous reports from Omaha and only 197 casualties on D-Day at Utah, it has been said that the Command Center in London was consid-

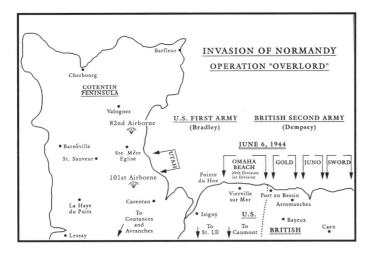

ering diverting future waves to the more successful landing area, but this did not prove to be necessary.

The British and Canadian landings on Gold, Sword, and Juno beaches were also very successful, although great difficulties were encountered later involving the inland battles for Caen and other German strong-points.

After some days of foxhole living, the beachhead was considerably enlarged, units from Omaha and Utah had joined to form a solid front, and we were moved inland and laterally to Isigny. There the batteries were redeployed with some of the Bofors guns in protection of the newly installed Airstrip No. 1, where P-51s (Mustangs) began to operate in support of ground troops slogging their way slowly and painfully through the hedgerows.

In the latter part of June, a terrific unexpected gale from the north hit the Cotentin Peninsula and really made a mess of things for a time. In the five days or so it lasted the storm wrecked the artificial sea wall and breakwater that the engineers had built, damaged the "mulberries" that were used as docks, held up all supplies and reinforcements, and in general raised hell with the whole invasion plan. Day after day, the storm whistled and roared across the peninsula at almost hurricane velocity, as if it would never stop. We were grateful that the first days of the Invasion had not coincided with the storm, because by the time it did hit, there were more than enough men ashore to hold the beach. If all of this *had* occurred a few days earlier, there might well have been a cataclysmic disaster.

The second phase of the Battle of Normandy came a month later with the grinding battles preceding the breakthrough. Our battalion moved from Vierville to Isigny on June 25 ("D plus 19," in the terminology of the time). Cherbourg was captured on June 27 by units under Major General Collins and a line was established across Normandy running from the west coast near Lessay short of St. Lô and swinging down the east coast at Omaha Beach to a junction with the British and Canadian forces, who had moved inland from Gold, Sword, and Juno beaches to the Bayeaux-Caen area. There we were stalemated for the better part of a month with spasmodic bursts of activity as the infantry moved through the *bocage*—the hedgerows that encompassed all the fields with a think fence of earth, tangled shrubs, vines, and saplings. On July 3, Middleton's VIII Corps attacked south towards Coutances-St. Lô and Caumont, but the operation ground painfully to a halt. As General Bradley wrote, "Thus, my break-out and dreams of a blitz to Avranches faded badly."

June 25-30, 1944, Isigny, Normandy

We are now civilized again, at least temporarily, since some of us now have rooms in a stone chateau, a very beaten and battered chateau admittedly, but it still has rooms and a roof and at least, we are not sleeping on the ground which is a considerable advantage. Ordinarily, we wouldn't use local buildings for quarters but this was apparently a real feudal fortress and the walls and roof are constructed of huge stone blocks which seem to us to be at least as satisfactory as a foxhole. In the past era, this must have been extraordinarily picturesque. It is quite large, constructed in the form of an open rectangle around a large courtyard. The open end of the courtyard faces on the steep grassy slope which in turn leads onto a wooded plain. The access to this is guarded by a stone watchtower as is each end of the closed side of the quadrangle. The main entrance is through an arch under a portcullis and most of the windows are mere slits in the stone. All in all, a real medieval fortress with dungeons below and all the works! I have no idea when it was built nor any concept of the history, but I should imagine it was constructed several hundred years ago. Someone must have been living here fairly recently since the walls are papered. There are electric light fixtures and some attempts at modern plumbing. Obviously, none of these are functioning now and the whole place has the appearance of having gone slowly to seed for a number of years, even before war arrived to speed the process. Whether anyone will attempt to rebuild the whole estate at any time is questionable but I personally would have no desire to do so. It might just as well go on and die gracefully, since, without carriages rolling under the portcullis, powdered wigs and brocade gowns in a ballroom, feudal tenants and liveried servants it would be only a feeble attempt to revive a dead era.

I am enclosing with this letter a poppy which I picked for you and pressed this afternoon as a symbol of forgetfulness . . ."not poppy, nor mandragora" — so it's very appropriate. You could hardly call this area Flander's Fields but these poppies have their own historical significance. Do you remember reading Rommel's oft quoted remark when he visited and inspected Germany's West Wall defenses, "Who would think that beneath those waving poppies are buried the thousands of mines which will block any Allied landing attempt?" Somewhat of a paraphrase but that's the general idea. The poppies are still here but Rommel is well onto the first lap of his one-way trip backwards. However, the mine stories were no exaggeration. I doubt if any area through which the Germans retreat will be safe for an indiscriminate wandering for years to come. With the combination of the work of the sappers and engineers, a little care, proper training and knowledge, they don't present any tremendous problem for the Army, but there are occasionally tragic aftermaths among civilians returning to their homes after the lines have passed. We brought to a Field Hospital in our rear, a little French girl who had come back with her family to their farm and who was badly wounded by a booby trap set under the lid of the stove. An individual instance, but the same general type of thing which occurred on such a large scale in the post office explosion in Naples some months ago.

As you know so well by now, griping is an intrinsic part of Army life. In actual fact, I am not sure that, given the opportunity, I would change places with anyone at the moment. Much as I miss surgery, I don't think I would want to spend the whole war in a general hospital but there is very little actual hospital work as yet in France. Most of the severely wounded can be rapidly evacuated back to England. At least in this life you don't have any feeling of guilt or at least not very much. On occasion, one does feel a little guilty about even having a jeep or a truck in which to ride around when one sees a long column of dog-faces swinging along on their own feet to the front. They're the ones who do the actual fighting and will win the war, and they don't even ride on their way to do it. A tough racket with no glamour, little thanks and very few medals! There is nothing like the Air Medal—given automatically for five flying missions in the Infantry—all the dog-face gets after his first five experiences of exchanging shots or crossing bayonets is the knowledge that he'll repeat the same procedure scores of times before the campaign is over and without 50% additional pay for flying time.

This is a red letter day literally since a big packet of letters arrived and even some packages. Many thanks for the t-shirts which fill a very pressing need. You see, I've had to develop the habit of wearing an undershirt in summer because of the fact that it's an impossibility to wash one of these woolen OD shirts every day or even every week and having a clean t-shirt every day makes life much pleasanter. At times in transit, all you actually carry with you on your back is a field bag which is so packed that even one extra heavy OD shirt won't fit in but t-shirts can be squeezed in almost anywhere. They certainly extend the lifetime of the OD's.

This section of France seems to be Nirvana for the insect kingdom and a particular fertile breeding place for the damn fleas with which the ground in this area seems to be covered. I'm already a mass of huge bites from the damn things. We also have innumerable varieties of flying insects plus thousands of bats at night. Fascinating place for a naturalist interested in the insect world.

And so we came to the 4th of July with sound effects but no pinwheels—in fact, except for various units displaying the colors, it was much like any other day, and any other day at the moment was seldom much like the day before. For the first time since we hit France, I felt some of the restlessness that used to be so prominent in England creeping on again.

I bounced around in a jeep most of the day—and the word "bounce" is an understatement. The French roads were hardly sensational to start with, and when we turned loose a mechanized army on them, all except the main highway soon became very hard on the duff. When it comes to crossing fields or driving along the connecting lanes, the jeep takes on all the characteristics of a bronco, and the net result is similar, inasmuch as you feel very much the same as after a day on a horse. Another interesting result comes from a combination of factors—the dust clouds on the main roads, the mudholes and ruts of side roads, and the fact that in all combat zones, windshields are always kept down and covered with canvas to avoid any reflection from the sun that might be seen by attacking planes. All this ends up producing a beautiful cake on the skin everywhere except where tight-fitting driving goggles cover your eyes.

We constructed a magnificent field shower out of an old iron double bed which we lifted from a German barracks (stood on end, it made a fine framework), an old gas drum perforated at the base, and ready-made fire to heat the water. Very effective, and for the first time since hitting France, I felt fairly clean.

One day, in addition to my other strenuous duties, I played the roles of veterinarian and pediatrician. At one gun section the boys brought me a horse that had been hit by shrapnel. As a matter of fact, he turned out to be a much more cooperative patient than many others I could think of, and considerably more grateful at the end than the average run of human beings. From there, the path of medical science led to a French farmhouse, where a little gamin had a large abscess which I incised.

Although somewhat damaged, as it had been hit several times by shells, the farmhouse was beautiful, with a large courtyard surrounded by the house, stables, and barns in a solid square, all constructed of heavy stone. The house itself was lovely, and absolutely spotless—gleaming white curtains and linen, floor scrubbed, copper and brass pots and pans glistening. The family insisted that I have some cider and then several glasses of Bordeaux, all of which I accepted with no undue reluctance. My French had improved to the point where conversation was feasible, and we had a very pleasant hour or so. The father had been in the French army, had been taken to Germany, and released more than a year before to come home and be put to forced labor by the Germans on the coastal fortifications four days a week; the remaining time he spent with his family and farm, improving the food supply of the area. His young son, in his early teens, had been impressed for the same type of work seven days a week. The daughter, who had been at the Sorbonne when the war broke out, was engaged to a boy who was killed. All in all, they hated "les Boches" with some violence and the Italians almost equally for the "stab in the back" of 1940. The mother said brightly that it would be worth having the whole farm flattened to get the Boches out. The happiest day they had in four years was the day they watched the first files of German prisoners march through a nearby village. The daughter went every morning with flowers to the American cemetery out of gratitude for La France Libérée, and the family prayed daily for the Americans. When I finally had to leave they pressed three eggs on me, which I also accepted with more eagerness than polite hesitation, I'm afraid. Since I had to return to check the little moppet's postoperative convalescence, I collected more eggs in France than in the whole time since I'd left the States.

Our major contact with the outside world was an occasional issue of *Stars and Stripes* and *Yank,* and those only intermittently. And when they did arrive, it was in a ratio of about 1 to every 30 men.

I could understand much better now Oliver Wendell Holmes's comment, "War is an organized bore!" If I had been sitting in England at that point, I think I would have been close to the gibbering stage. At least after we landed in France, there was some raison d'être and sense of accomplishment. At its worst, it was nowhere nearly as bad as the best of the stretch in England.

After scrubbing down under our one great luxury, our home-made, air-conditioned (very much so) shower, I felt at peace with the world. It took some backing and filling and screwing up of courage to get started, but it certainly was worth it. For a couple of days, I had just put off showering, thinking, "Well, tomorrow the sun will come out and it will warm up." But it never did, so to enjoy the luxury of being relatively clean again, I underwent a certain amount of shivering and shaking during the procedure of undressing in the field, drying, and re-dressing. The water was hot, however, and by means of a certain amount of mental elasticity, one could have imagined that it was not a field shower but a hot tub somewhere in the United States. Baths in any form were relaxing and very conducive to daydreaming, I found, but unfortunately, the hot water didn't last long.

On July 11, a strong German counterattack led by the Panzer-Lehr Division was finally thrown back by the 30th and 9th divisions. Our battalion was not directly involved in that scrap but an evacuation hospital to the rear that had just arrived in Normandy was briefly overwhelmed with casualties, and a few corpsmen and I went back to help out.

One of the major problems confronting the American Infantry and Armored divisions was the *bocage*. Narrow, sunken roads traversed the countryside and at that point, the main road from Lessay through Perier to St. Lô and Toriguy was still held by the Germans. It seemed impossible to mount a sustained, mobile offensive based on armored divisions until the invention—attributed to a Sergeant Culin of the 102nd Cavalry Reconnaissance Unit—of "sawteeth" mounted on the front of some of the tanks. These "Rhinos," as they became known, sheared through the hedgerows and established pathways for subsequent vehicles and infantry. They were responsible, at least in part, for the success of the breakthrough that began on July 26.

It was interesting climbing up and down and around the area of the beachhead, through towns and places that one had read of in the past, participating in history instead of being entirely on the outside with one's nose pressed against the windowpane. I had been getting sick of that feeling sitting out the war on the Sceptered Isle. Some of the French towns were one huge rubble heap; hundreds and thousands of man-hours of work demolished in a few seconds. I hated to think how long it would be before a full-fledged Phoenix rose from the ashes. The only hope was that either Germany would collapse or the speed of modern mobile warfare would bypass and spare Europe's cities, towns, churches, palaces, fortresses, museums, and monuments—her tangible history. Even in such a comparatively small area as this peninsula, I reflected, where so much violent fighting had taken place, a surprising amount had been partly or entirely spared.

Following collapse of the German counterattack, life settled down somewhat. During the subsequent lull, a lengthy political (international and domestic) argument and discussion sprang up among some of the officers in the headquarters unit and others who dropped in and out occasionally to put in their two bits' worth. It was very heated as usual, and also as usual, more or less of a review rather than any fundamental disagreement, covering rather haphazardly some of the diplomacy, ideals, and intrigues up to and after the onset of the war—Russia, Spain, Finland, etc. Everything looked much brighter to all of us, with the Invasion beachhead well established, the Allies rolling north in Italy, Russia driving towards the German border in what now looked like a shattering and unstoppable offensive, and Japan being routed in the Pacific.

Obviously, we were in a holding pattern, and life became a little more civilized. Several of the units in our general area collaborated to construct an officers' club on the first floor of our "Shattered Chateau"—complete with a French steward (and of course an enlisted men's club nearby in another area). Very fancy! The interior-decorating phase (building a bar, salvaging and scrounging things like lampshades to put over nonexistent electric lights, murals, usable furniture, etc.) was a problem, but finally we were ready for a grand opening. Liquor wasn't a problem, as one of the units seemed to have a source, perhaps from captured Wehrmacht stocks. And of course we did have a certain amount of pure ethyl alcohol in Battalion Medical Unit supplies. When we moved on, as we inevitably would, at least someone would be able to move into a well-established and relatively furnished bivouac. The club was lit with candles or flashlights, under only rigid blackout conditions. Our "club" didn't exactly resemble the Somerset or the Chilton.

Bastille Day marked the first time since July 1939 that this area had been free of Nazi domination. It was too bad the Allies could not have entered Paris on or before the 14th, but that would have been asking a little too much.

We were then faced with one of the major problems of wartime

medicine—treating colonels, and not just one but *two*. What a
headache! Treating a colonel in the army is somewhat analogous
to treating a trustee of a hospital, and now we had a pair! We had
just about become resigned to treating one for bursitis (a dull ail-
ment at best, and certainly at its best in a chicken colonel) when
another one appeared from an entirely different unit with a chronic
otitis media (another remarkably uninteresting affliction unless
one has it oneself). He seemed to have found some fatal fascina-
tion for our battalion unit and developed the habit of taking a fairly
long daily jaunt just to see us. Why, I can't imagine, since I certainly was no ear specialist. Our newfound friend among the high-
priced help had his own medical sources easily available, but he
didn't respond to our subtle hints on that score. At least, it was
less depressing than seeing anyone of any rank blown into bits
and pieces.

The first post-Invasion magazines and papers from home began to roll in. It was amusing to compare our own experiences
and observations and tales from other units with what we read
about the period in articles and descriptions about other units.
Time was disappointing in its first post-Invasion issue but later
gave a very accurate account of a people whom I had grown to like
very much—friendly without being embarrassingly effusive or
emotional, intelligent, proud, religious, and moral. Even in the
rear areas to which civilians had returned, none of the various sex
problems appeared that were wildly rampant in England and reflected in the venereal disease rate. The few girls we saw were
clean and attractive looking. Home, family, and church were very
important in this part of France and girls did not wander around
at night unescorted or even unchaperoned.

I read in *Life* the story of the song "Lili Marlene," which I remembered hearing for the first time early that spring on a German
propaganda broadcast and humming all the following day. It

spread through the battalion rapidly—the simple little tune seemed to have some remarkable attraction for soldiers overseas. Apparently, it was first broadcast from the Nazi station in Belgrade to the Afrika Korps, picked up and popularized in the 8th Army, which appropriated it as part of the spoils of the victory over Rommel. None of us in England had heard anything about it until the Germans started a regular propaganda program from the Calais radio directed towards the Invasion forces—an excellent program as far as musical selections went, which rapidly became extremely popular. The main attractions were Midge (a girl singer with a fine boudoir voice), the daily repetition of a little ditty called "Invasion" (a catchy tune with comically pompous and boastful words designed to terrify us at the prospect of facing the Herrenvolk), and "Lili Marlene." The song was then taken over by the Allied Invasion armies. It was hard to figure out exactly what gave it the peculiar nostalgic quality that it seemed to have for everyone, but it was certainly there.

By mid-July, the weather changed and reading outdoors in the first hot sun we had in days seemed to relieve a little of my gnawing irritability at not having enough to do. Most medical officers felt the same way. That may sound somewhat surprising coming from an active war front, where you might picture all the doctors as working night and day, but that's a misconception. When we first arrived in Normandy, admittedly, I had no complaint about lack of activity, but about six weeks after D-Day, military action grew sporadic and doctors and more organized medical units began to pour in. The army became so damn well stocked with doctors and medical units of all descriptions that was impossible to find enough to keep them all busy, particularly since the degree of military engagement was so variable. God knows, I'd rather have done absolutely nothing for the rest of the war than take care of youngsters shattered to varying degrees, but the systematic wasteful distribution of technically trained men did annoy me at times. I should guess that 90 percent had less to keep them busy than I did. My own specific and naïve solution would have involved fewer specifically assigned doctors in large hospital units and more highly mobile surgical teams staffing small, well-equipped mobile hospital units. One could then have some stable large units in the rear and small hospitals or dispensaries for minor problems in quiet areas. However, everyone in the army had his own personal solutions for any and every problem.

When we first landed, the whole beachhead was full of wild rumors. There were still scattered German snipers wandering around, which gave rise to stories that the French were sniping at us. All such rumors were quickly disproved and died a natural death, but initially such tales, plus the inability of most of the boys to speak French, led to a certain amount of skepticism and mistrust. Soon, however, the boys came to admire and like the few French who were around. The hot news had been, of course, the stories of internal disturbances in Germany and of the shakeup of the Japanese cabinet following their crushing defeats in the Pacific. Both of these situations were strong indications of tottering regimes and were the first definite signposts pointing to the end of the road. It was peculiar, however, that the winter before, with nothing but open speculation, I had been supremely optimistic, whereas now, with so much behind us and all indications pointing towards a fairly rapid crushing defeat of both Germany and Japan, I found myself almost afraid to believe it.

As long as we never wrote specifically of time or place and did not discuss any immediate, pertinent, or impending events we were allowed to mention some of the various activities of war in letters. Except for the impressiveness and magnitude of the whole operation, however, which was obvious during the preparations, the crossing, and the landings, a campaign can be quite drab. The acquired instinct for avoiding mines or booby traps soon became unconscious and the continuous noise and rumble of guns, mines being detonated, and sporadic bursts of activity hardly entered conscious thought. If you happened to be up or awake during a night raid, however, war took on an entirely different aspect. A raid is a really extraordinary display of pyrotechnics, beautiful if disassociated from death and destruction. The whole sky and horizon are lit up by beams from searchlights and filled with a maze of bright-colored tracers streaming up and dotted here and there by flashes of exploding bombs and shells. The Luftwaffe was remarkably inept and ineffective during the daytime and even the night raids soon became infrequent and short-lived—a far cry from the day when Nazi planes ranged the skies in hundreds over Rotterdam, Coventry, and London and outnumbered and outgunned the available air and ground defenses.

George Koca, my medical sergeant, injected a light touch into the proceedings. He was a short, wiry, tough, and very conscientious and loyal man whose main hobby and worry in life at the moment was keeping the aid station free of goldbricks. In pursuit of this high ideal, he printed an impressive sign that became part of our permanent equipment at the entrance of the dugout aid station, which read: *If you have nothing to do, please do not do it here. Thank you so very much.*

The "Officers' Club" was still functioning, with *cidre* as the only liquid attraction. Fortunately for the livers of all concerned, the stock of Calvados had never been replenished after that first night. The "thunderbolt" straight Calvados, with enough crème de menthe to color it and take off some of the rawness so that it wouldn't cauterize the throat on the way down, was a delightful concoction (now a memory), but I don't think it would have met the minimum standards of the 4-H Club. The club still made a pleasant locale for a civilized and relatively comfortable poker game, which was a great step forward.

It was always surprising how little consecutive leisure periods there were during a day, even during the quiet periods. It seems to be a universal failing of the human race that the mere sight of a doctor sitting alone reading or trying to write a letter starts some sort of vague mechanism clicking so the individual feels an over-powering urge for a consultation. At home, you might call it the cocktail or dinner-party consultation, but I can't think of any particular appropriate name for it in the army. You could make the men come in during regular sick call (except for emergencies), but officers were incorrigible. Every one of them who passed in the general vicinity of an aid stations invariably dropped in for a social call, and that was always fatal to any short stretch of free time. You could almost see the gleam in the eye as yet another fellow officer eased up with an opening remark to attract your attention from a letter, book, or medical journal and then casually remarked, "You know, I thought you might be interested in my back," or "My shoulder always seems to *click* when I move my arm in a certain direction." What one learned to do was to evince an active interest, use a few unintelligible words from medical jargon, and extend a great deal of reassurance. Much like the Out-patient Department at the MGH!

On July 24, we received march orders to leave Isigny and follow directives to one of the smaller roads leading to St. Lô. This was no great surprise, as rumors were already circulating of an impending major offensive. Again, as in East Anglia, the "long wait" was over, and we hoped that the upcoming drive would begin a new, perhaps final, phase of the war.

7

The Breakthrough

ST. LÔ TO AVRANCHES

July 25–August 15, 1944

After the fall of Cherbourg, the German line extended from Lessay on the northwest coast across the Cotentin Peninsula southeast of Caen. In late July, when we left Isigny and joined innumerable other mobile units on the various roads leading to St. Lô, it was obvious that another drive was in the making. The same preparations were taking place all along the line at the point of the projected breakthrough from Lessay to St. Lô. At dawn on July 25, we could hear the roar of the 8th Air Force passing over and the stupendous, earth-shattering sounds of bombs being released along the German lines. Wave after wave passed over us as we cheered from below, until one flight dropped its bombs prematurely and devastated one of the roads packed with American troops. General McNair, one of the senior officers in the First Army, was among the hundreds killed.

The German lines were shattered, and the lead units of General Collins' VII Corps broke through and headed for the base of the Cotentin Peninsula. Our battalion powered through the shat-

Quadruple-mount machine gun in position on hill near
Avranches, looking toward Mt. St.-Michel. Early August, 1944

tered town of St. Lô and headed for Coutances and Avranches.
One of the key factors in the success of the operation was the uti-
lization of the Rhinos, which chewed out gaps in the hedgerows
and permitted the following tanks and infantry to pour through.

Rumors were running through the units of Count Von
Stauffenberg's assassination attempt on Hitler on July 20; the details were still garbled but we did know that it was unsuccessful.
It has been said that, subsequent to the explosion, Hitler began to
direct the battle in a fashion that severed all contact with reason
or reality. This may account for the ill-fated offensive against
Mortain and Avranches on August 12, which was contrary to the
wishes of the general staff and prevented an orderly withdrawal
from the pocket being contrived for closure of the Falaise Gap.

Like the Invasion itself, which secured the foothold necessary
for a power drive like this, the first few days of Operation Cobra
provided a succession of impressive, almost awe-inspiring pictures
of the tremendous strength built up by America in the preceding

two and a half years and welded into an unbelievably powerful military machine. Roads packed with tanks, guns, armored vehicles, half-tracks, and mobile artillery, all rolling inexorably eastward, with planes roaring ceaselessly overhead, made an unforgettable impression of sheer rolling power. When you thought for a minute that, in addition to the stupendous problem of transporting and supplying such a force across the ocean, the United States was mounting huge amphibious offensives in the Pacific, plus an overseas operation in Italy, you could not help feeling a thrill of pride in your own country and people, no matter how much you might hate war itself. I hated it—I hated the boredom, the tragedy, the destruction, the suffering, the maiming and death of young men, the ache of separation—but at such times I caught a glimpse of the principles for which we were fighting and found nourishment for the hope that something had been and was being accomplished; that some good would come out of all the suffering and pain. Such moments came rarely, but when they did, they made up for a great deal.

One such moment occurred as we roared through a town that the Germans had left so precipitously and in such disorder that there had been practically no fighting and very little evidence of destruction. The windows and doorways were hung with red, white, and blue bunting and even a few American flags that had been found somewhere. The people had just come out of hiding, and the streets were lined with cheering, shouting, weeping crowds, throwing flowers and blowing kisses and picking up the cigarettes and candy that the boys threw back. Unfortunately, we couldn't halt even long enough to reap some of the fruits of war in the form of wine and cognac that was being waved at us.

The last thing I remember as we rolled into the countryside again was the picture of a grizzled oldster in some sort of ancient uniform with a red, white, and blue bunting on his lapel standing by himself on a corner, saluting and shouting, *"Vive la France et l'Amérique!"* Those people weren't cheering a parade or gawking at fancy uniforms or brass bands. There is nothing very beautiful about a lot of dirty guns and dusty, grimy boys in field uniforms. They were crying and cheering because it was the end of four years of a ghostlife under cold, calculating aggression that had let them live but bled them white—and even more important, because they could again hold their heads up in pride as free people of a free country, and women could foresee the return of their husbands, brothers, and sons from military prisons or forced labor in Germany. Never having had it been taken from us, I don't think Americans can appreciate how much it meant to those people just to be able to hang out the flag of their country again. One home, which had been less fortunate than most, was little more than a mass of rubble; nonetheless, the *tricouleur* had been raised over a corner of the ruins.

As we rounded a turn in a countryside road, a beautiful little golden-haired girl was standing on the corner watching the troops passing by, her right hand raised in the V sign and her left hand stretched out, palm up. Apparently she had already recognized the Americans as a fine source of candy from preceding units. Her technique was certainly good, for she was being showered by all sorts of candy bars and food. Because of the scarcity of younger men, it was rare to see children below her age (four or five). By keeping so many Frenchman in Germany as prisoners of war from 1940 and by drafting so many others into forced labor, the Nazis hoped to keep down the birth rate in France to the point where her manpower would never be a threat to Germany.

By the end of the first week of the Breakthrough, the new drive was well under way. Surprisingly, but fortunately, the great majority of the wounded were not from our own troops but from the Wehrmacht. This push was really rolling over them. The myth of the Supermen, the Herrenvolk, was really a thing of the past! I saw only two Germans who were still fanatical Nazis, and they were really morons, pulling out plasma needles, Wangensteen suction, etc., because they thought we were trying to poison them. The others, however, were delighted to be prisoners and out of the war. They certainly were a seedy-looking crew—haggard, whining, and dirty. In the temporary shock tent, which we were repeatedly setting up and then moving, the contrast with the Americans was remarkable. Despite all their Nazi training and stoicism and heroics, almost every wounded German was whining and sniveling while the American boys beside them lay quietly smoking and talking and waiting patiently for us to get to them. There were certainly exceptions and without doubt I was prejudiced to some extent, but these are all generally held observations. Many of the German troops were ordinary "folk," not Herrenvolk, and had never had much taste for Naziism.

Obviously, at this stage, the German army was not what it had been in the early stages of the war. Some of the SS troops were still fanatical, and were certainly superb troops in the strictly military sense, but the ranks of the Wehrmacht itself had been watered down by taking both older and younger cadres into service with limited preliminary training.

It was sad to realize the agonizing labor the rebirth of France would take and maddening to think that even in defeat, the Germans were ruining not only their own country but France, Italy, Russia, and Poland. St. Lô, for instance, which had had to play the role of a French Cassino, was a complete shambles. No one can ever imagine real devastation who hasn't actually seen it. We rode through one street after another where thousands of people once lived and could not see one habitable room. The large church in the square, though still standing, was hardly recognizable as such, and here and there you might see an intact doorway or wall, but otherwise there was absolutely nothing but acres and acres of

St. Lô, July, 1944. A terrible shambles!

rubble and water-filled bomb and shell craters. Despite the rumble and roar of the army passing through, there was a ghostly silence everywhere. Not actual silence, certainly, because there are few things besides the Boston subway that can equal the noise of an army in motion, but an impression of silence arising from the rows of empty side streets lined with piles of shattered stone and wood and the absence of any living soul except the troops and the tanks, trucks, and half-tracks rolling through. MPs stood at each intersection. How a city like that could ever be rebuilt, I could not imagine. It would take years just to clear the mines, before even starting to build.

Where the people had gone from these towns, no one seemed to really know. I suppose they fled out into the country away from the cities, roads, and railways. Wherever they went, they all seemed to flock back on the heels of the first American patrols—that is, back to those cities and towns of which there was anything remaining. I saw no one in St. Lô.

Except at strategic points like road junctions and intersections, the countryside and rural areas bore fewer scars of war, but didn't escape completely unscathed. As we rolled along through a gloriously beautiful, lightly wooded green countryside, we saw an occasional shattered stone farm that the Germans had attempted to use as strong-point. Dead cattle lay stiff and swollen everywhere, typical litter of an advancing war. The smell of war and death was everywhere. The roads were strewn with the debris of a defeated Army—burned-out, shattered, or abandoned German tanks, vehicles, and equipment—and of course, German bodies, which no one had yet had time to remove. The cynics called them "reeducated Nazis." Despite an intense hatred for everything for which Naziism stands, and despite all the stories from Belgium, France, Russia, Yugoslavia, and Poland of the cold-blooded cruelty and brutality of the Nazis, I felt no personal hatred for the individual German, and was somewhat shocked to see a Frenchman spit on a pile of German corpses. But I can't criticize his action—I don't know what he had lived through and suffered. There is a considerable difference between war as seen from the point of view of a victorious army and as seen over years of defeat and oppression. Neither is pleasant or pretty; war is always a sordid business. But there was certainly no comparison between my lot and that of millions of people in occupied Europe and in prison and concentration camps.

The offensive slowed down intermittently to mop up pockets of resistance. Eventually I could relax, stretching out in a neat green orchard near a pretty little farmhouse beyond Coutances and wearily unrolling a sleeping bag. There was a very handy sunken road behind the hedgerow, just wide enough for a bedroll and pup tent.

In the early morning of the eighth day of the offensive, we received orders to move again, towards Granville and the west coast

Pup tent in a relaxed moment near Avranches

of the Cotentin Peninsula. We had been moving so fast in the past few days of this offensive that my letter writing had been very limited, but I recall this minor odyssey vividly. One thing that has stuck in my mind is a letter written by a wounded German captive bemoaning the fact that this was "no longer a decent war," that it was now "just a wholesale slaughter and bloodshed and a disgrace to the twentieth century." To me, this was typical of the thinking that characterized Germany. From their point of view, I suppose it was a "decent war" when the Wehrmacht and the SS units were rolling over Czechoslovakia, Poland, Greece, and, during the early phases of the offensive, into Russia. The worms had now become snakes and the glamour was gone.

Before the Invasion I had thought that anywhere in a combat area must always be interesting in some way, but the sights of such a scene soon become so familiar that the lines of tanks and convoys, the planes overhead, the shattered villages, the craters, and the noises and smells become a part of your life and cease to mean much in and of themselves. The tragedy inherent in gaping walls and crumbling roofs soon loses, meaning, even to the people involved. So you drive on, intent more on the code signs that direct you than on the rubble left in the wake of an army that would appall anyone brought directly from civilization.

There was no time for more than the elemental phases of personal hygiene and by August 7 I was caked from head (including hair) to foot with a four-day collection of dust, dirt, and sweat, and altogether presented a repulsive picture. Just how repulsive fortunately was not obvious, because the metal mirrors we carried didn't give us a very clear reflection. I did make some strong, rather ineffectual attempts to remove some of the layers with a helmet full of soap and water, and managed to shave. Added to the accumulation of grime was the fact that we had had practically no sleep, as a result of which two bright red orbs gleamed out from the depth of two black sockets "like two burnt holes in a blanket," to use the familiar phrase.

There were rumors of a complete German rout, but one learns to discount rumors until they present as facts. The trail of destroyed or abandoned German vehicles along some stretches of the road was astounding. If we could have collected all the equipment we could have assembled almost any type of mobile items, from a tank to a field kitchen.

There was no way of predicting even the immediate future. We had hoped to settle for an immediate objective and some rest, but not only did we pass another sleepless night but we were on the road at the crack of dawn reconnoitering. The projected shower never took place either, so rather than being a shining example of cleanliness and field sanitation, I now had another complete layer of caked dust except for two beautiful white circles around the eyes where my goggles were. I felt as though I personally carried half the soil of France.

August 8, 1944

My outstanding ability, merit and value to the Army of the United States has at last been recognized and I will begin to draw down the salary of a Captain. Apparently, this promotion was recommended and the papers submitted before the invasion but the bureaucracy involved with the procedure did not seem to be able to find out where I was. At any rate, tomorrow I'll change your allotment from $200 to $275 a month since this means that I'll have an extra $52 in my pay and the amount I win fairly regularly in poker keeps me well supplied with the necessities of life. I'm sure that you're happy to have married into such great wealth.

We finally arrived in Avranches on August 7, following the offensive that had begun near St. Lô nearly two weeks earlier. After the tremendous aerial bombardment that preceded the offensive on July 25, 1944, Patton assumed command of the offensive and the newly constituted Third Army, which was comprised of units like ourselves who had previously been in the administrative structure of the First Army. Avranches, which is just across the water from Mont St. Michel, was a key point in Patton's strategy, since the whole Third Army had to go through this town and then break out into the open plains of Brittany and into the major areas of the Ile-de-France as well as to provide units for closing the Falaise Gap. There was a narrow corridor between Avranches and Mortain where the 30th Division was holding against a counteroffensive by the Germans designed to cut Patton's corridor at Avranches. We distributed our 40-mm guns in a semicircle around a bridge over which the entire Third Army had to pass and which was therefore vital to the overall strategy, the culmination of which was, in theory, to roll up the Germans into the Falaise pocket. This

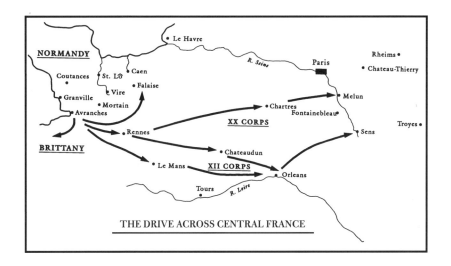

THE DRIVE ACROSS CENTRAL FRANCE

bridge over a rather small river led to a winding road up a hill to the town of Avranches, from which one could obtain a spectacular view of the valley in which our machine guns and Bofors were distributed. The Germans immediately recognized the importance of this particular bridge and every night as darkness set in at about 2300 hours, waves of JU-88s swept in, using Mont St. Michel as a guide point, to destroy it. Our battalion's role was to protect the bridge as well as possible so that the engineer company stationed with us could begin reconstruction as soon as the German raid was over.

In this key position, we saw most of the units of the newly constituted Third Army, including the Fourth Armored Division, the Deuxième Blindée (a French armored division that I believe had been originally formed in Africa and that was quite badly damaged just beyond Avranches by a separate German air raid), and various combat and supply units as they wove their way down the narrow road over the repeatedly reconstituted bridge and up the hill to and through the town of Avranches (where a statue of General Patton now stands in the main square). We dug in the aid station under some huge trees and used a hedgerow as a part of a protecting bunker. Fortunately, even though there were several direct hits on gun positions, there were only a few occasions when I had to go out in the peak of a raid and bring back casualties from the gun crews.

It was a weird feeling to be in the open road with the JU-88s dropping magnesium flares. As I could hear them roaring low overhead, I felt as if I were on a stage with a large spotlight directed solely in my direction. On one particularly intensive night of bombing, a frantic field telephone call came from a dug-in Bofors gun position near the bridge, which had received a direct hit from a bomb during a particularly heavy attack. As I headed down the road in pitch-black, except for the faint blue gleam from our headlights, a roar from a low-flying plane was immediately followed by the brilliant light from a magnesium flare. My driver and I dove for a ditch but the plane disappeared after a brief burst of machine-gun fire. We resumed our drive, this time at breakneck speed, in the daylight environment temporarily provided by the flare.

We turned off the road into a field and approached the gun position that had sustained a direct hit. The whole scene appeared to be one of complete disaster, with the bomb crater forming a concentric ring with the circular mound protecting the men servicing the gun, the 40-mm Bofors overturned, and several bodies strewn across the area. I rapidly examined each body and discovered that none had sustained a life-threatening or serious injury. The bomb had detonated so nearby that all the potentially lethal fragments had sailed over the men's heads, and the earth revetment had mitigated the force of the blast so that nonfatal concussions were the result. We managed to get the men all back to the shelter of the aid station and after the raid was over, arranged transportation back to an evacuation hospital, from which they were returned to duty in a few days.

We were extraordinarily lucky during our days protecting the bridge at Avranches; we sustained only a few disabling shrapnel wounds and no fatal injuries. But what a baptism of fire! It was fruitless to be frightened, but it was a little difficult not to be.

A few days after our arrival, when we were finally "dug in," we put up a primitive shower near the aid station and enjoyed that long-awaited bath, although by the time we had it up, the weather had cooled off considerably, and with a strong breeze blowing, the open-air shower arrangement was damn chilly. We now had extra transportation. We had "liberated" a Nazi staff car in remarkably good condition and painted it according to regulations (OD paint, white stars, red crosses, etc.), cannibalized other ruined cars along the road to supply various needed parts, and cut out the back to accommodate stretchers. We then took out one of the front seats and put in two tiers of braces for litters, giving us a small but fast and handy little ambulance. The self-sufficiency of a unit like a battalion is remarkable. You could always find mechanics, plumbers, carpenters, painters, and other artisans of all sorts within the outfit and there were plenty of tools, so that you could complete almost any project in a surprisingly short period of time. The transition from a battered piece of junk with innumerable missing parts to a fairly smart-looking little ambulance took only a day—a task that in civilian life would have taken a couple of weeks and cost a couple of hundred dollars—*wartime* dollars.

After settling in, I spent a whole day on the road going back to the rear echelon for some data and equipment. Much of the country was as ravaged as St. Lô but I did see one magnificent Gothic cathedral standing completely untouched on a hill in the center of a badly shattered town (Villedieu-Les-Poêles). It

looked very proud and beautiful with a huge *tricouleur* fluttering
from one of the spires. It reminded me of Italy in a way, since it
was built mainly on a series of terraces overlooking the surrounding country.

Our fancy new refurbished limousine took to the road for the
first time resplendent in its new coat of paint, adorned with white
stars and red crosses. It looked impressive—very much like a General Staff car, judging by the salutes we received. (The visibility
into the car wasn't very good and whenever any of us saw any
kind of closed car roll by, we snapped into a salute on the assump-
tion that it bore the tender duff of at least a brigadier general.)
When Joe put out his hand for a left turn a convoy on the opposite
side of the road came to a grinding halt and a lieutenant jumped
out of the leading jeep, came over, and said, "Did you want me,
Sir?" He looked a little amazed to find nothing but a couple of
captains. We all laughed. "Damn, I thought there must have been
at least one general in there!" he exclaimed. After bouncing in a
jeep so many times, it was quite a luxury to rest my bruised and
battered duff on some real cushioned seats.

Our fifth day at Avranches brought my first complete tour of a
genuine bordello—unoccupied, admittedly, but a bordello nonetheless. I went along as a volunteer with several others and men
who were hunting for a Nazi sniper who had been shooting at
some of our men in gun positions in the valley. The bordello
seemed a likely hiding place because of the general direction and
its location (high on a hill) and because of the fact that when the
Americans entered Avranches, two of "les poules" had tried to
hide a dozen Germans in the otherwise deserted establishment.
The search of the area was fruitless but our glimpse of the demi-
monde was interesting, if a little revolting. It had been run by the
Boche and was typically German in its combination of gross eroti-
cism and cold, distinctly asensual efficiency. As a result of de-

scribing this diversion in a letter to Blanche, I was told by return mail that "under no circumstances" should I have entered such a place.

After our fruitless search for the sniper, I went from the bordello to the other extreme of life. Franz Siegel, our intelligence officer, had to talk with a family who lived well outside the town in a beautiful park. The house, a picturesque, impressive chateau, was normally their summer home, but because of conditions in Paris they had been living there for some time. The huge square building had a Mansard roof, stone lion heads at every angle and embrasure, and much bric-a-brac everywhere. The family were lovely people with a charming combination of Gallic warmth and self-assured pride. We saw the grandmother, her daughter-in-law, and two beautiful children with huge dark-brown eyes and amusing poise and self-assurance. An ancient retainer hovered around, chattering every so often about Lafayette, "the hearts of the French beat with the Americans," etc. The grandmother, a charming white-haired lady, cordially invited us over to ride, to spend the evening, and anything we'd like, but unfortunately we couldn't accept any invitations.

I certainly enjoyed the family very much, but we couldn't stay long. When Franz had obtained the information he needed, I went out to one of the gun sections where there was a natural pool and small country stream. A swim felt wonderful after the broiling heat of the dusty road. We then dried off on a grassy slope leading down to the pool and headed back to headquarters and the aid station.

8

The Battle for Central France

AVRANCHES TO VITRY LE FRANÇOIS

August 15–September 18, 1944

After over a week of protecting the vital bridge at Avranches and facing the nightly raids of the Luftwaffe, our battalion was ordered from its positions around the bridge and directed to rejoin the XII Corps (now under the command of Major General Manton Eddy). Presumably, the reassignment was due to the failure of the German counteroffensive on August 8 from the direction of Mortain, which had reached within a few miles of Avranches before collapsing. As the Germans began to withdraw towards the Falaise Gap, the threat to the narrow corridor at Avranches was dissipated and the left flank crumbled. The Luftwaffe diverted their attentions elsewhere and intensive protection of the bridge was no longer needed.

The XII and XX Corps of the Third Army had driven almost without opposition across central France from Normandy. Our battalion with the XII Corps had gone from Avranches to Rennes, in Brittany, to Chateaudun and to Orleans. Within a few weeks, we had moved from Orleans on the Loire to Fontainebleau, where

we crossed the Seine, then on to Montereau, Romilly, Vitry le
François, St. Dizier, Bar-le-Deuc (crossing the Meuse en route),
and finally to the Moselle, where the whole Third Army was stalled,
as were all the other armies along the western front. The whole
three months of the campaign in Lorraine and Alsace and later in
Luxembourg would be bloody and frustrating. Never enough supplies! Never enough ammunition! Never enough fuel! Morale
was surprisingly good, which reflected Patton's policies and personality in tactical warfare. Even then, we recognized his bizarre
reactions, his personal inadequacies, his peculiar prejudices, and
his habit of venting emotions irrationally and often to his own dis-
service; but it is fair to say that we all felt comfortable (an odd
word to use under the circumstances) serving under him.

During this portion of the campaign with the Third Army, I
never personally encountered or saw General Patton until much
later in Luxembourg. Dave Dunn, however, a young surgeon
whom I first met with the Clearing Station of the 5th Infantry Division and who later was transferred, as I was, to the 30th Field
Hospital, tells a typical story of the flamboyant general under whom
we both served until the conclusion of the war. On a hot day during the offensive across France, the 5th Infantry Division had incurred some casualties whom the clearing station was treating until
they could be transferred to the rear echelon medical units. Dave
was working on some of the casualties with his sleeves rolled up,
probably looking as disheveled as many medical officers did when
temporarily flooded with wounded, when General Patton drove
up in his jeep with his ivory-handled revolvers and a machine gun
mounted on the rear. He swept into the receiving tent. Dave,
trying to be military, snapped to attention. Patton glared at him
disparagingly and snapped, "Roll down those goddamn sleeves,
Captain! What do you think this is—a goddamn Gypsy camp?"

In late August, Patton's units had crossed the Seine at Melun and Fontainebleau. While Hodges drove north to Belgium, Patton headed eastward towards Verdun, on the Meuse, and finally towards Metz, across the Moselle. Until then, the entire operation had been the dream of any general with the enthusiasm and the vigor of a Patton or a Rommel. At this point, however, we all became aware of problems in our romantic dream of a glamorous, unstoppable offensive rolling endlessly across the Meuse and the Moselle rivers, through the Siegfried Line, across the Rhine, and on to Germany and Berlin. Little did we realize the drab, mundane logistical problems that beset a mobile army. It became obvious to all of us that we were running out of gasoline, out of food, even out of cigarettes. As everything ground to a halt, we heard more and more about the "Red Ball Express"—quarter-ton trucks that were constantly making runs of several hundred miles back to the coast to find gasoline for our tanks, half-tracks, trucks, and jeeps. Without it, we were dead in the water. Rumors circulated that all the fuel was being diverted to Montgomery's drive up the coast to Brussels and Antwerp and eventually to the lower reaches of the Rhine, and that the pipelines to Montgomery had to be tapped surreptitiously to obtain what little gasoline we were allotted. Like all rumors, these probably contained a modicum of truth. Supplies and gasoline had to reach the forward units, and the farther forward a unit was, the more difficult it was to maintain the supply lines

At any rate, the vaunted Patton offensive ground to a halt at the Meuse. Advance reconnaissance units had moved forward as far as Metz and into some of the undefended forts. Sections of the Siegfried Line were alleged to be undefended. The Wehrmacht was in a state of unaccustomed shambles, without an organized defensive line and with units scattered in disjointed retreat with no recognizable plan of defense. When logistics forced Patton to halt on the Meuse, the Germans regrouped, and by the time the

Third Army had fought its way across the Meuse at Verdun and Chalons, the Germans had reoccupied the forts at Metz, re-established the Siegfried Line, and formed an organized defensive line on the Moselle.

So there we were—and would be for some weeks to come!

Although everything was in very short supply, the army finally began to move again. Bridgeheads were established in late August across the Seine at Melun and Troyes, and armored units drove forward to the Meuse and ultimately to the Moselle. Reconnaissance units had crossed the Moselle and entered several of the forts around Metz. Since the major units did not have the fuel or supplies to continue the offensive, the advance units were forced to retreat and the bridgeheads across the Moselle were withdrawn as the Germans rapidly regrouped and initiated a number of counteroffensives. A strong defensive line was established before the Saar and Metz and along the Moselle. The drama and the glamour were over, the "shouting and the tumult died," and the war descended again on the shoulders of the PBI—"poor bloody infantry!"

Operation Market Garden in Holland, which began on September 17, finally ended when the British withdrew from Arnhem, the third and northernmost of the three bridgeheads established in the most organized airborne assault since D-Day. Thus ended the hopes for a quick and decisive end to the war. It was obvious that we were in for a long, hard fall, which would come to be known as the "autumn stalemate."

Following the breakthrough from Normandy into central France, Patton's army was distributed among three main thrusts— one section to move into Brittany and isolate the strongholds of Brest and St. Lorient (which actually did not fall until the end of the war), another to join the units designated to close the Falaise Gap, and a third to maintain the spectacular offensive towards the

Seine and the Loire and into Ile-de-France. We were ordered to follow the advance armored units of the XII Corps that had rolled through Rennes and Le Mans towards Orleans, which was captured on August 17.

There has been endless postwar speculation as to whether Patton's XV Corps, under Haislip, could have closed the Falaise Gap earlier. Bradley made what was probably a prudent decision to halt those units near Argentan, where Montgomery had drawn a boundary line to keep the American and Canadian units from firing on each other in an area of general confusion. About half of the Germans in Normandy escaped the trap; the remainder were casualties or captives, and most of the mechanized equipment, tanks, and artillery was lost. Shortly before the final closing of the pocket, on August 21, French and American troops had landed on the Riviera and were driving north through southern France towards an ultimate junction, in September, with the southern flank of Patton's army near Nancy.

In mid-August Eisenhower had released the information that General Patton was in command of the Third Army, and apparently all the press and radio commentators avidly followed the progress of his advance units through France. There was relatively little active combat—most of the German combat units were scattered and dispersed, and the rear echelon units, stunned by the speed of the advance, often did not realize that there were American units within a hundred miles until the first tanks and mechanized units roared into town. Patton himself (with characteristic modesty) allowed that the advance was "probably the fastest and biggest pursuit in history." Certainly, it was a striking reversal of the fall of France in 1940. One of our German prisoners commented on a letter that it was "no longer a decent war." It all depends on whose ox is being gored, I suppose!

At one point in the dramatic drive, we thought that we might be involved in the liberation of Paris. Just the thought of rolling down the Champs Elysées was enough to generate a massive adrenal response and an emotional explosion. It was not to be, however. We came as close as Fontainebleau but continued east across the Seine, so our brief dreams of glory faded. Paris was liberated on August 25, 1944 by the French Deuxième Blindée Division (which had suffered some heavy casualties outside of Avranches) and the American 4th Infantry.

At some point after we had crossed the Seine, we received a dispatch from Patton's headquarters announcing the award to the 550th Battalion of a Distinguished Unit Citation, relating specifically to actions during the breakthrough in Normandy and the corridor at Avranches.

September 12, 1944, Romilly, France

The other notable event of the day was the arrival this morning of a citation from Army Headquarters commending the battalion among some other units for action in this particular campaign, referable particularly to Normandy but I suppose more inclusive than that alone. Unfortunately, I cannot send you a copy since the citation mentions specific times, places, planes shot down, etc. It was very nice and the men have taken a lot of pride in it. Quite long and included most of the usual stuff—"As a result of superior training, skill and coolness"—etc. and—"loyalty, enthusiasm and extreme devotion to duty"—etc., etc.—"exemplifies the highest traditions of the Armed Forces of the United States." So with the mail, the sun, the appearance of the first Red Cross Clubmobile and a Citation, everyone is quite happy.

The only tangible effect of the citation was the distinction of wearing a patch with a wreath woven into it on the lower left sleeve of a dress uniform.

It is surprising how much you can come to enjoy or at least be content with a life in the open. Despite the bugs and the various inconveniences, it was quite agreeable. The trouble was that so much depended on the weather. The conditions of our existence in the drive across France would have been miserable in winter, and even on cold rainy days it was damn unpleasant, but when the sun was blazing in a blue sky and the grass was green, soft, and dry, it wasn't bad at all. Ordinarily, I rigged up the pup tent so that it was off the ground and hung from a branch, which gave me more room, protected me from the rain and heavy dew, and still gave me a couple of feet between the tent and the ground so that I could stretch out in a bedding in the shade with a warm breeze blowing across my feet. Sleeping in ditches, foxholes, or sunken roads was occasionally necessary, but usually a nearby hole was sufficient.

Inevitably, the war entangled civilians in its passage. Once, I was called to a local French hospital where I found the nuns who ran the establishment trying to treat two little boys who had been hit by shell fragments. It was pitiful, not only because of the boys' youth but also because the nuns had absolutely nothing to work with; no supplies, no dressings, no medicines, nothing! I had anticipated something like that and brought plasma, splints, dressings, morphine, and so forth with me. One of the boys was terribly wounded, almost dead. After a sucking wound to the chest had been closed, other wounds dressed, and bottles of plasma poured into him, he was much better, and the other youngster took relatively little time to fix up. When they were in condition to be moved, we stopped an ambulance and got them transported to an evacuation hospital somewhere in the rear area. I drove back to see them the next day. They were much better, although one was still very precarious since in addition to his chest wound, he had some abdominal injuries, which required laparotomy and closure of multiple intestinal perforations.

I rounded up some abandoned German medical supplies,

added some of our own, and brought them all down to the nuns. By that time, they had another civilian case for me. After we sent her back to another, larger French hospital, the Mother Superior called me aside and said she had something *"pour votre femme."* She and her sister, also a nun, were sweet old women—very tiny, with bright, sparkling black eyes. They showed me all over the buildings (built by St. Louis, king of France in the thirteenth century), with a beautiful little chapel, and chattered on and on, telling me about France and asking me about America and my wife. They said they would pray for us every day of their lives, and gave me their address. The little gift they sent Blanche was a small shrine, intricately carved and constructed, which was duly dispatched home and received with great pleasure.

The emotional drama of seeing a nation in the frenzied throes of national liberation is hard to express. Within a few years, I was sure, the French would settle back into their frugal, light-hearted, agreeable way of life and again assume the attitude towards the world best expressed by the shrug of the shoulders and *"on ne sait jamais"*; but at the time they were in the midst of a national emotional catharsis so universal and contagious that it made you want to laugh and cry with them. In the sudden joy of liberation, freedom, and revival of national pride and honor, every man, woman, and child was freed from inhibitions and self-consciousness and all were putting on an unrestrained public exhibition of their happiness such as is permitted to humans very rarely. It was thrilling to witness, making us forget for a time the misery and unhappiness of war—to say nothing of the petty annoyances that form the basis of the great traditional army custom of bitching.

Obviously, there was tragedy everywhere in a country in which a war was being fought, but as the drive and sweep of the army gained momentum, there was less of the massive concentrated destruction that was characteristic of an established line and more

areas where the Nazis had been swept aside or encircled or had
fled precipitously before the weight of the onrushing columns,
leaving the country and towns fairly intact. It was, of course, in
those areas where the joy was most unrestrained, since it was not
tinged with the sadness of loss, of home, or of family. The advance moved through a succession of cities, towns, and villages
where the streets, doors, and windows were packed with cheering, shouting inhabitants. Everyone was smiling and laughing,
and tears of joy rolled down many cheeks. Veterans of this and
other wars were out to salute proudly the columns that were rolling through their towns. After years of courageous resistance the
French underground were free to carry their guns publicly and
wear arm bands denoting that they were soldiers of a free France
(FFI). Mothers held up babies clutching crude homemade American flags in their fists and the standard greeting everywhere was
the upraised hand with fingers forming a V. The *tricouleur* and
the stars and stripes waved everywhere, usually faded or homemade but certainly more than adequate to express their feelings.
There was no material for fancy or ornate displays but every town
strung homemade banners over the narrow streets with captions
in French or English: *"Honneur à nos liberateurs,"* "Thanks to
our allies," *"Vive l'Amérique,"* etc. Along country roads, people
ran across fields from their work just to stand beside the column
and wave. Everywhere people held out bottles of wine to the tanks,
tracks, trucks, and jeeps, blew kisses to the troops, and threw flowers, fruit, and vegetables of every description to the boys, who
tossed back cigarettes and chocolate.

None of this, however, held a candle to the reception given to
the first French units as they headed into the line. The French
had been trained and equipped by the Americans but they fought
under their own flag, and the thrill of seeing their own sons, brothers, and fathers coming back into free France with a victorious

army must have been tremendous. In town after town, they literally had to fight their way through the crowds. Never again will I witness such joyful mass hysteria. It was unbelievable.

Our track from Normandy to the Moselle during the victorious rush of Patton's Third Army across central France was erratic, and I never knew the names of all the villages and towns we traversed. But fifteen years afterward, en route by train to Paris from Lyons, I suddenly spotted a familiar church spire, the top section of which had been rebuilt of new material. The sight triggered an instantaneous complete flashback. Everything was utterly familiar—the church, the village, the landscape. I saw again a German machine gunner, firing from an opening in the steeple. Our reconnaissance jeep pulled back and a Bofors 40-mm mobile-gun unit demolished the upper part of the steeple, along with the gunner. The resistance collapsed and our units moved through. The railroad conductor could not tell me the name of the village, nor could anyone else; but the entire episode was crystal clear.

Unless it had already been devastated in the war, like the chateau where we lived in the early days in Normandy, we never used a French home as a billet. In the words of a headquarters order, "We have come to liberate France, not to occupy it." The patches of forest that dot the plains of France are very handy for bivouac areas, and during the summer of 1944 we intermittently lived a life in the woods. Practically every such *bois* was privately owned and had some sort of empty chateau at its edge or in a clearing. (One chateau we ran into had been in use as a center for refugee children, but most had been deserted since 1940, when the owners fled before the Nazis' advance.) It was quite comfortable in the woods, and fairly secure, since it would be hard to spot even a battalion from the air when it was spread out through dense forest. One night, beyond Sens, we were bivouacked on the grounds of Henri Rothschild, adjacent to the hunting lodge, which had been used as a German headquarters but when we came was deserted except for a housekeeper and an ancient gamekeeper. The lodge was large, but a little dismal when we arrived, as it had poured rain all day. Lanes just wide enough for a truck cut through the trees in all directions, massive branches interlacing overhead to form wide natural arches.

According to the gamekeeper, an old walrus-mustached veteran of World War I, this small patch had been home to hundreds of game birds, but the Boches had shot most of them. The gamekeeper wandered about the grounds in a uniform with gold buttons stamped "HR" and a mammoth gold badge denoting his official status as watcher of the birds. When he discovered that I understood and spoke a little French, he started in with a dissertation on how much he hated the Boches *("les vaches")* and what they had done while they were there, branching off into a battle-by-battle description of World War I including how wonderful the Americans had been at St. Mihiel and what he had done in liaison work between the infantry and artillery. Proudly he brought out the Croix de Guerre and a flock of other medals. Quite a nice old gentleman, despite his alleged ferocity, but he would have gone on all night if I hadn't managed to move away politely.

Once the rain stopped, about an hour after we arrived, it was quite lovely. The trees were dense and heavily overgrown with ivy so that the interior of the forest was dark and cool. My tent was set up on a tiny clearing near the edge, so that I could peer out through the leaves glistening from the reflection of the setting sun on the remaining raindrops to where the thick woods ended abruptly a few yards away, revealing miles of rolling plains crossed by long, straight, bare dirt roads. The wheat had been harvested and the plains stretched out flat and unbroken. In the distance, I could see long convoys rolling continuously as a series of tiny dots moving across the countryside.

After a delicious dinner of C-rations heated on the radiator of the jeep, three of us spent a couple of interesting hours with a man who had really seen a lot of the phases of the war against fascism. He rode out from a nearby village on a bicycle with his little girl sitting on the handlebars and spent most of the early evening talking with us while his daughter munched happily on chocolate. His father had been in command of an army corps in Spain and he was a lieutenant in a tank battalion that fought for thirty-two months against Franco until the fall of Madrid, at which point he and his wife fled to France. His wife had been injured and his three young children killed during the bombing of Barcelona by the Stukas. When France went to war against Germany, he enlisted in the French army and fought through the initial campaign until France collapsed, at which time he managed to rejoin his wife. By posing as a Spaniard who had come to France to work for the Germans, he procured papers and evaded the Gestapo, although his brother-in-law was caught and shipped off to Germany for forced labor. His unit received supplies and military leaders from the Free French by parachute, but eventually, he and his wife were arrested and were thrown into a local concentration camp. In the confusion attendant upon the rapid American advance, they managed to escape, and were living in a tiny two-room house in the village, near which he had set up a little bicycle shop. He invited us to eat with them the following evening and we had a magnificent dinner, most obtained from local fields and streams—Byrrh as an aperitif, rabbit, fish, grouse, lemon meringue, sweets, etc.

Every house in every town seemed to have at least one French flag, to say nothing of the dozens that draped the war memorials, the *mairies* and the *hôtels de ville*. The rows of cheering, shouting French lining our route was an old story now; what at first had been a real pageant had become part of the routine of a convoy. After a few hours on the road, you almost wished you could stop

Two German prisoners (directly behind sign) being
brought in, near Rheims, France, September, 1944

waving for a time, but seeing the joyful faces of the people on the
sidewalks and the windows, you couldn't help smiling with them
and waving back. Their attempts at homemade American flags
brought some unusual results; it was obvious the average Frenchman hadn't the foggiest idea of the correct number of stars or
stripes. The thought was there, however, and we saluted some
monstrosities of flags as smartly as if the colors were passing in
formal review.

After some days of spasmodic actions in the countryside and in
small towns, we were back in civilization in Vitry le François. The
headquarters battery was camped in a small park in back of the
hôtel de ville. The city itself had been badly battered by bombing
and shelling from both sides, and was almost a ghost town. Where
the people lived, I couldn't imagine, but there were always a number in the streets and in the main square during the daytime to
watch and cheer as the Americans rolled through. The church

was almost intact, although every pane of glass had been shattered by blasts. It was a massive building, very ornate and of a peculiar type of architecture unlike anything else I'd seen in France. Quite ugly in some ways.

Mass on the morning we arrived was an ordeal. The monsignor, a handsome man in his sixties, waxed so enthusiastic and effusive in his sermon about the gratitude of himself and his people towards the Americans that it became acutely embarrassing for those of us who were scattered throughout the congregation. Everyone turned to stare and smile and what the hell could we do but stare straight ahead, feeling very self-conscious indeed—particularly since the heroes, if there were any, had already preceded most of us during the main fighting for the actual liberation of the town. After Mass the monsignor collected us together and explained that he had acted as a chaplain in the last war for a battalion of Americans who were temporarily attached to the French.

The Germans had been particularly brutal in this town, shooting hostages, sending girls off to army brothels, and on and on. So the people had a particularly violent hatred of les Boches, as was evidenced that afternoon in the square in front of the church. The process of rounding up isolated detachments of Jerries was practically continuous. We happened to be passing by after lunch when a small group of FFI (Free French of the Interior) brought in two Boches from the woods, beating hell out of them as they came amidst general vociferous approbation of the population. These two happened to be renowned SS men and hated for their brutality. The whole picture wasn't very pretty, and hardly cricket; but there is nothing pretty about any aspect of war.

Fortunately for the Germans, most of them fell directly in the hands of the Americans, who treated them damn well and shipped them back to prisoner-of-war camps. Most of us, however, expressed an opinion at some time or another that it was too bad

SS Men under guard by FFI near Rheims

that the French didn't handle all the prisoners, which might give them a clearer picture of the "master race" theory of life. I obviously could not hate them violently, since I had never suffered directly from them, but I couldn't work up much sympathy for any of those bastards, especially the SS, after having seen and heard some of the results of their four years of brutality.

We had some magnificent wines and champagne at Vitry le François. The French in this section buried most of their stocks four years earlier, to hide them from the Germans, and were in the process of digging them up again. Wonderful stuff, although there wasn't too much when it was spread around. An outfit a short distance away captured a whole truckload of cognac that the Boches were trying to cart away, so we also got enough of that for a short nip all around after dinner. It was a little ironic to gnaw through a couple of hard biscuits, stuff down some canned Spam, and gulp down powdered coffee, all accompanied by superb wine and cognac.

Women with shaven heads for collaboration with the
Germans near Verdun, December, 1944.

By September, the war was following a pattern. First, the American columns rolled through a town with more or less fighting, depending upon the area. Then the FFI joined in the rounding up of all pockets of isolated resistance and finally, women who had slept with the Boches were rounded up and their heads shaved smooth. They were beaten intermittently by the women. After this ritual, a town seemed to be able to settle down into a comparatively tranquil existence. Although this rough-and-ready punishment was usually well behind us in our mobile warfare, I saw it carried out at Vitry. A French woman who voluntarily slept with a German invader degraded the national honor as much as an ordinary run-of-the-mill collaborator (who were also given short shrift), I suppose, but the spectacle of a group of females, hardly prepossessing to begin with, humiliated publicly in this fashion is not elevating.

When you could sit in a barracks room eating lobster paté on

crackers and drinking Veuve Clicquot, it was a great war. The
wooden barracks was originally built for the French army, near
Verdun. The lobster paté was from a can sent to one of the officers from the United States and the champagne was the product of
an incredible deal I had wangled. While wandering over the country on routine communications, I came across a huge cache of
liquor that the Germans had left behind in their hasty retreat. By
means of some fast doubletalk to the officer in charge of the guard,
I absconded with a whole case of champagne (thirty bottles) and
two cases of cognac (twenty-four bottles). I distributed my catch
among the battalion (with a little held back in reserve for cold
weather—good for rheumatism)! If I could have spent all my days
in such fashion, the war might not have been too bad!

Our status in early September was monotonous—no mail, constant motion, relatively little activity, even less news. Medically
speaking, it was also dull—certainly nothing to complain of, but
without the stimulus of new cases, diagnostic problems, and civilian hospital work, medical reading loses some of its point. War
surgery and the problems of military medicine are not conducive
to mental stimulation. Surgery in the field follows one definite
pattern, with only one type of case, a young man with single or
multiple traumatic injuries—a situation as far removed from most
civilian surgery or medicine as if we were in another profession
entirely. The idea, so prevalent among the laity, of the medical
experience gained in war is poppycock. General advances are
made through the tremendous amount of data accumulated on
shock, burns, and the treatment of wound infection and trauma in
general, but the individual doctor's problem was not to *lose* knowledge. One medico summed it up well by saying that from the
point of view of medical experience, the only advantage to a war
was that it gave a few timid surgeons the courage to operate. (My
attitude certainly changed after I was transferred, much later, to

an auxiliary surgical unit, where complex surgical problems were the rule rather than the exception.)

I made a new friend at Vitry le François—a little French boy, age ten. Pierrot was a fascinating little boy, very handsome and very brave; one of the most attractive kids of his age I had ever seen. He had a severe case of hero worship for Americans, hated *"les salles Boches"* intensely, and was inordinately proud of the fact that his father, a member of the local Maquis, had personally killed three Germans. He followed me around all day, trotting along in his bare feet, politely inquiring whether he was bothering me. After I assured him that he was not, he embarked on a very serious discussion of the war, Naziism, democracy, and so forth, speaking slowly and carefully so that I would be sure to understand him. He wanted to know all about England, America, me, my wife. I had to go into great detail on the whole campaign from the landing at Omaha Beach on, with maps and diagrams, and tell him all about where we had been and what we had done. Within a short time, he virtually assumed the job of orderly, taking my laundry away to have it done and my trousers out to be pressed and bringing in eggs every day from the country for breakfast. Being with a youngster like that, intelligent, amusing, pleasant, and cheerful, somehow made me terribly nostalgic. If it hadn't been for the war, I might already have had a good start on a similar little boy.

France, Friday, September 8, 1944

In some ways, this is a particularly depressing part of the war because one knows that, while more battles will have to be fought, more people killed, more cities captured and more destruction spread about Germany in particular, this is all particularly fruitless. What can you do with a nation of people who will fight and die hopelessly for a principle based entirely on cold blooded brutality, aggression, intolerance and most of all a complete lack of intelligence, humanitarianism or philosophy? Seeds that are sown that

deeply cannot be eradicated easily. I am sure that breaking
Germany into small states will never solve the problem. But the
job of maintaining the status of Germany as a nation while
re-educating the people into a democratic, cooperative and
humanitarian philosophy of life seems colossal. As far as I can see,
the only other choice is a war of extermination which is what, from
this point on, the Germans are driving us to fight. We are no
longer in the somewhat idyllic position of fighting in defense of an
ideal, but are forced, after having crushed what at one time seemed
to be the overwhelming power of aggression, into the position of
insect eradicators wiping out individually and collectively all
remnants of the past decade which are still fighting with the
instinct of cornered rats rather than with any hope, reason or
idealism. Carthage was leveled and sown over with salt, but it is
hard to conceive of a similar end to a state of 80 million people in
these days. I suppose that in theory, it is just as possible now as
then, except for the difference in scope but unless some force for
good arises within Germany itself, what other end is possible?

9

Autumn Stalemate

SAAR OFFENSIVE AND BATTLE OF THE BULGE

September 18, 1944–January 13, 1945

It was obvious in early September that some of the steam had gone out of the dramatic offensive across France. It had become impossible to provide adequate fuel, food, and supplies to Patton's Third Army units and still maintain the combined British and American offensive to the north through Belgium into the Netherlands. Antwerp and the Channel ports hung on stubbornly; it was not until November 28 that the first convoy could enter Antwerp. Patton's plan to initiate an offensive into the Saar after completing the drive to the Moselle was deferred in favor of Montgomery's plan, Market Garden—the airborne assault on Eindhoven, Nijmwegen, and Arnheim.

Within three weeks of the fall of Paris and the overwhelming defeat of the German armies in the battle of central France, the Wehrmacht had recovered its balance and was no longer "on the run." In fact, it was again holding a coherent front at the Siegfried Line at the border of the Saar, at Metz, and along the Moselle River.

At the end of September, Patton was attacking but also repelling counterattacks on the Moselle. We entered the "Autumn Stalemate."

After a German counteroffensive across the Moselle River had been repulsed, our battalion headquarters was eventually established at Pont à Mousson with the batteries deployed along the river with the potential dual objective of protecting against another counteroffensive, or conversely, to support a river crossing by units of the Third Army. For the moment, however, we were halted at Vitry le François.

Life had been quiet enough to permit an occasional social interlude. One evening, the local doctors—in fact, the only doctor, since Vitry had been almost completely destroyed by the war—invited me to dinner at his home. After an evening of good food and wonderful liquor, I returned to quarters. Like most French dinners, the meal lasted for over three hours; and it was marvelous. Despite the tremendous obstacles of shortages in everything, it was always amazing to see what the French could do to turn out an outstanding dinner. All the courses were very simple, but each was done superbly. We had tomato soup (touched up with wine), then a course of tiny beans with an excellent sauce, followed by chicken with a particularly delicious sauce. Dessert was sliced baked apple covered with a wine sauce, accompanied by grapes, a fresh peach, Camembert, and coffee. Finally came liqueurs of considerable variety.

The next afternoon, when I was out on a call to one of the outlying batteries, I stopped in a fairly good-sized town that had been practically undamaged by the war, as its location gave it no strategical or tactical value. I spent most of the afternoon wandering in and out of stores and shops, looking for something to send to Blanche. I did buy a couple of small items, but on the whole, it was discouraging. Jewelry and trinkets of any sort were incredibly expensive; and even junk jewelry was beyond belief. There was nothing in leather, nothing in clothes; there was not even a

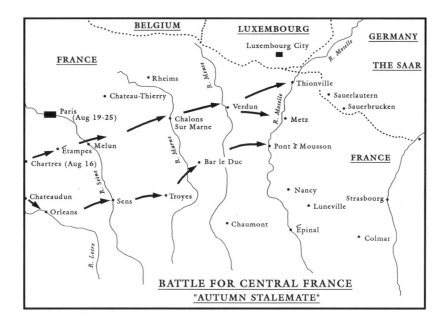

BELGIUM

LUXEMBOURG

GERMANY

Luxembourg City

FRANCE

THE SAAR

• Rheims

Thionville

• Chateau-Thierry

• Sauerlautern

Paris
(Aug 19-25)

Verdun

• Sauerbrucken

Chalons
Sur Marne

• Metz

• Étampes Melun

Chartres (Aug 16)

Pont à Mousson

FRANCE

• Bar le Duc

Chateaudun

Sens

• Troyes

• Nancy

Strasbourg •

• Orleans

• Luneville

• Chaumont

Épinal

• Colmar

R. Meuse · R. Moselle · R. Marne · R. Seine · R. Loire · R. Moselle

BATTLE FOR CENTRAL FRANCE
"AUTUMN STALEMATE"

drop of perfume in the town. In the little shop where I did buy a few odd items, I had a long chat with the owner—a very smart-looking woman of about forty, beautifully groomed, neatly and attractively dressed and charming—a type you might expect to find running a smart shop in Paris. She did have a shop in Paris, but had been marooned out here unable to get back because from the beginning of the Invasion there had been no established transportation facilities for civilians. The Germans had seized all forms of transport for military purposes. Even in Paris, she told me, the shops had little or nothing of any real value, and everything was exorbitantly expensive. The Germans could, and did, print all the German occupation francs they wanted. They forced the French to accept this worthless currency, and were delighted to see prices rise well above any level that a Frenchman could afford, thereby cornering the market entirely for themselves. From what she had to say, my illusions of finding any exotic creations for

Blanche in Paris or elsewhere were somewhat crushed. Not that I could get to Paris anyway—it was off limits to troops of both armies and only SOS (Service of Supply) troops whose work was there were permitted.

That evening I read an article from the South Pacific that referred to the Jap nightly air raiders as "washing machine Charlie." The Japanese planes must have had the same engines as the asynchronized motors of the German planes, which were dubbed the "Maytag Express." These little differences were useful to us, making it fairly easy to tell whether friendly or enemy planes were approaching during the night.

Hitler had promised that he would drag Europe down into chaos with him. He certainly was doing his best, with the flying bombs in action and the threat of the V-2s, a major problem for England until their bases on the Continent were captured by Allied forces.

Again we were pulled back out of the line at the Moselle, to the area of Vitry le François. I went out for dinner with a young architect and his wife and two youngsters. It may have been his last dinner at home for a time, since he was an officer in the French Army and, having been liberated by the Americans, was leaving for active duty in the near future. Our dinner and evening were enlivened by a German raid in the valley below where the wife's family chateau was seated, making fireworks worthy of the Fourth of July. The dinner was excellent with innumerable courses, two red wines, good champagne, etc. We ate and drank leisurely, talked, and smoked. After the air raid died out we finally called it a night and I returned to the battalion well after midnight.

Letters from home dated September 7 (after the beginning of the "Stalemate") were waiting for me. I knew damn well that there would be a letdown at home with the slow-moving war, which was very much an anticlimax after the sweeping victories and rapid progress of August, but I hoped that perhaps things would change tremendously soon. The closer to the end, the harder and bitterer the fighting was. It would have been wonderful to see the Allies roaring across Germany the way we roared across France, but war doesn't always work that way. Thought of where we were only three months before, however, when we had a bare toehold on the Continent, raised my spirits somewhat.

Rheims, which we had gone through with one of the Third Army's Infantry divisions, was still nearby. Franz Siegel, our S-2 officer, went back to a newly established army headquarters on the outskirts with the dual purpose of getting supplies, orders, and matériel and incidentally paying a visit to the local director of the G. H. Mumm Company, who was an old family friend of his father, a wine merchant in Germany before he escaped the Nazis and came to the United States in 1930s. I went along with him, hoping to scout up some medical supplies at a depot en route. By the time we arrived it was almost noon, so we had lunch in town and looked around at the famous cathedral and then went out to Mumm and Co. and looked up Monsieur Mazzucci, who was delighted to see Franz again for the first time in some years. He was a charming man in his late sixties, very good-looking and an amusing and interesting raconteur. His work involved an enormous amount of travelling and he had been practically everywhere in the world (including twenty-six trips to America) and spoke six languages fluently. We went on a tour of the plant, ending up in a small, bare tasting room that contained nothing but a well, wall tables extending the length of both sides, two closets containing various types of glasses, and a spittoon. Each table was divided in three parts, with bottles of wine to be tasted lined up against the wall. The taster pours a little wine into a glass, sniffs it, fills his mouth, meditates for a short time, and then lets go into the spittoon and moves on to another bottle. After doing a little sampling ourselves, we went into the cellar (there are twelve miles of tunnels under the plant) and traced the trip of the grape from vine to glass. We then returned back to M. Mazzucci's offices, talked wines, war, France, and America, and drank more champagne. He pressed on each of us a case of vintage Cordon Rouge that had been stamped "Pour le Wehrmacht." With the Germans evicted, he felt it should be reclassified as "Pour les Americains."

By September 26 we were on the move again, back to Pont à Mousson on the Moselle. It was a miserable day, with rain pouring down my neck and into my boots and forming a puddle under my tail in the jeep. As we drove, mud splashing on the side formed a thick, soft crust all over me. To dream of being warm and dry was almost like Paradise regained. After a long day of shivering and dripping on the roads, we moved into a battered and beaten ex-German building, boarded up the windows and holes in the wall and roof, repaired an old stove, and started a blazing fire. I was finally stretched out on a cot in dry clothes and socks and revelled in the waves of heat. Wonderful! We attached the radio to a portable power plant that we had thought to carry with us, and I set up a flashlight on the table stand next to my cot to shine on the pages when I was reading or writing. All these amenities lent a sense of relative luxury and the blessing of being dry and warm; Solomon in all his glory never had anything that tasted better than the hot bouillon we brewed up. Living seemed very elementary and we wondered why it becomes so complicated between wars.

By the end of September we were in a small house on the outskirts of town near headquarters. It left much to be desired as a house but at least had a semblance of a roof and walls, which was an improvement over a pup tent. A stretch of tent living gave me a serious case of acute claustrophobia from crawling in and out of the damn things, trying to turn around sit up, get dressed or undressed, etc. It was like living in a small closet. This house had a fairly intact cellar, which saved us some digging, and I set up an aid station in another section. Because we were spread out considerably we split the aid station into two sections. I had plenty to keep me occupied, but fundamentally war is damn dull business. Even the occasional excitement loses its novelty and you become sick and tired of the whole scene. One advantage about a unit like ours, however, was that we had so many different types of mission that in a course of a few months we saw about every branch of the army and air force in action.

September 29, 1944—Pont à Mousson

This particular town isn't too interesting and is quite badly battered. The few people who have remained are frightened and live mainly in cellars. The Germans in their present slow withdrawal have apparently not been too gentle. It is difficult to gauge the accuracy of stories but from the few people who have managed to slip through the lines, you hear talks of the Germans evacuating whole towns and villages to Germany (I suppose for forced labor) and burning towns and homes. In some ways they are a peculiar race. Individually, they may be quite "correct" (except for SS troops and Gestapo) in their relationships but in groups of any sort, they become brutal bastards. That may be one interesting facet of German psychology. Apparently, it takes the presence of companions to give the individual courage to exercise the cruelty which has been characteristic of this war. That may also explain why the jovial beer drinking German of the Rathauskellar can transform himself without much apparent effort into the Jew-baiting Brown Shirt or the Hun who drove into Russia murdering babies and raping women or the Boche in France who could calmly shoot hostages and burn villages in cold blood. They are a very simple barbaric race at heart with a thin veneer of civilization developed during the past 100 years but easily rubbed off. This simplicity of mind, characteristic of the Visigoths, Huns, Vandals and all primitive barbaric tribes, may be what makes them so difficult to understand. Knowing them and recognizing them as a "civilized" nation, we can't bring ourselves to believe they are actually as simple, direct and emotionally primitive as they actually are. That's why Hitler could publicly announce to the world in print what his actual program and theories were in the early edition of *Mein Kampf*. In the pre-war years, no one could believe that the leader of a modern state actually believed in, much less intended to carry out, all those wild and brutal fantasies. It is still incredible to run into Germans, either adolescents or adults, who believe wholeheartedly in this fantastic line of tripe. If they as a race, have clinically adopted Naziism as a means to an end, you could at least explain it to yourself even while hating and fighting it, but, that any people could be so simple as to accept all of this hysterically is really incomprehensible. Unfortunately, these very times make them more dangerous and difficult to defeat than if they were just ordinary gangsters. A gangster with a fanatical, barbaric view of life and a self-imposed mission makes a difficult opponent. As I said so many times before, just what in hell we can do with them after the war, I'm damned if I know. Perhaps something worth-while may be born in a post-war Germany but it will be a long and painful labor. If we could only adopt their own policies, it would be very simple—kill the dissenting sections and sow under their cities with salt—another Carthage! The world being what it is, however, you can't very well do that without negating everything for which we've been fighting. I honestly think, however, some-thing could be made of southwestern and southern Germany plus Austria which are, as you know, the predominantly religious regions which have never accepted Naziism to the extent that other areas of Germany have. Northern and eastern Germany, however, would take a lot of re-education, I'm afraid. Just how much will be accomplished, I haven't the vaguest idea, but it's a nice thought.

I had to take a boy back to the Divisional Collecting Company, which has been transporting injured and wounded and sick to the Clearing Company and then to local field hospitals serviced by auxiliary surgical teams. He had a nasty laceration of the femoral artery just below the groin and his injury would not stop bleeding without continuous pressure from the heel of my hand on gauze. We were not equipped to go in and repair the artery in the Battalion Aid Station. After we got him back to the 30th Field Hospital (to which I was later transferred), I sat around for a while with three of the doctors. One, who was starting his fourth year overseas, was a little discouraged with the war as a mode of living. He was amusing about his depression, and admitted that bad as this was, it was infinitely superior to Iceland. They were going in shifts to a movie that was being shown at one of the evac hospitals, but I didn't feel that I could go because there was too much activity back on the Moselle. Before I returned we had a few drinks, and talked about the war, medicine, schools, hospitals, and mutual friends. It had been a long time since I had any such professional contact and it was incredibly stimulating.

Shortly before we moved forward again, Major Steve Ondash, executive officer of the 2nd Platoon of the 30th Field Hospital, took me aside and asked how I would like to work in a field hospital. The question startled me, but it seemed so unlikely that I thought no more about it until Steve came over to see me the next day at the battalion with a remarkable proposition. Apparently, it was possible with the consent of both commanding officers to effect a direct exchange of medical officers between units, and that was exactly what he and Lieutenant Colonel Mulligan, in command of the 30th Field Hospital, wanted to do. It was not quite as simple as it sounded, however. Lieutenant Colonel Kim was somewhat recalcitrant about letting me go but finally agreed halfheartedly provided he could interview my proposed replacement. That wasn't possible initially, since the platoons of the hospital were widely split. In addition, forms had to be initiated by the field hospital, sent through channels to army headquarters, and finally back down the line for approval by both commanding officers. ("Through channels" is a remarkable system for bringing everything to a grinding halt.) I did not spend much more time thinking about it, although after a year and a half as a battalion surgeon

I had just about exhausted the possibilities for interest and learning and would have enjoyed immensely the high-pressure surgical problems with which the field hospital units are concerned during periods of military action. I was surprised when the whole transfer became effective some weeks later.

In the meantime, we returned to the lines in preparation for an offensive through the Saar planned for November 13, designed to break through the Siegfried Line and head for the Rhine and a direct crossing near Frankfurt.

Shortly after the return to Pont à Mousson, we were pulled out of the forward line again and re-established in the rear echelons near Verdun—our first billet near a large city. Presumably, this was a part of Patton's general philosophy of rotating units out of combat at regular intervals for brief respites. As far as I could see, moving us anywhere would be unlikely for a time at least, and I was certain we were in for a moderately long stop at our location on the Moselle. But move us they did, and it looked as if I would get a few evenings of peace and quiet where I could sit down at leisure to read and write. We had rather luxurious quarters—again, an ex-German barracks. For the first time since hitting France, I was in a room with intact windows. We had a stove set up and the room was warm and pleasant. Verdun even had a movie theater! It was practically garrison soldiering, but I can't say that I objected to it. An uninterrupted night's sleep and a warm, dry room looked good at that point!

We also had the time and the facilities to visit Verdun and the St. Mihiel salient—the site of the most vicious and prolonged fighting of World War I. Even twenty-six years hadn't healed the scarred fields, although the deep, zigzagging trenches that stretched out endlessly over the countryside were overgrown with grass and had become smoother and shallower. The shell craters existed as numberless grassy hollows rather than the ugly bare scar of a fresh burst. Even if it were not for this mute evidence, you would realize there was something peculiar about the whole countryside—the natural surroundings showed absolutely no evidence of age. All the trees were fairly young scrub pine or saplings. Without the small but heavy growth of wood that dots the French countryside elsewhere and the symmetrical rows of tall poplars that ordinarily border the rural roads, the whole terrain had a bleak, desolate, unnatural appearance. Here and there one would encounter memorials, of which the Tranchée des Baionnettes was the most searing and tragic. This was the site where a unit of French *poilus* were awaiting, with fixed bayonets, the order to go "over the top." Suddenly a massive German barrage came down on and around them, and buried the entire unit. Only the bayonets and tips of rifles protrude above ground. An open, roofed memorial had been built over the tragic scene.

We passed the site of a village that had completely disappeared into history, leaving nothing but a few stones already heavily overgrown with vegetation to match the foundations of homes, farms, and churches. In a beautifully kept cemetery rows and rows of white crosses surrounded a monument on a flagpole flying the stars and stripes, a mute reproach from our fathers' generation for allowing the world to slip back into the same chaos that they fought to abolish forever. They have companions now in France—the youths who died twenty-six years later with the same hope.

After leaving Normandy, we moved with the mobile and armored units of the XX Corps through Rennes to central France, as described in the preceding chapter.

The last time I had seen the inside of an operating room was back in Normandy, during that period of stagnation preceding the breakthrough at St. Lô, when I worked intermittently in an evacuation hospital. One notable day, I had my hands in surgery after a long exile. I took one of our officers into the hospital in order to talk with some of the medical officers about his case. After he was admitted, I ran into Bemie Soutter on his way to the operating room. I trailed along and worked with him until well into the afternoon. You really miss surgery when you have been away from it so long. It was very pleasant, not only to scrub again but to talk with someone from MGH, reminisce, exchange notes on where everyone was, and so forth. It was too bad the hospital was so far from our headquarters, because otherwise I could have spent a lot of time with Bemie and the other surgeons.

During the siege of Bastogne in the Battle of the Bulge, Bemie had volunteered to go into the town by glider to provide much-needed surgical care to the men of the 101st Airborne Division. Before the glider took off, he arranged to have a sign displayed near the door where the volunteers entered. Echoing a commonly seen sign posted in railroad stations throughout the United States, it read—"Is this trip really necessary?"

The next day we made a range for small arms (rifle, carbine, pistol, and tommy gun) in a nearby old fort and brought the men back in small groups for target practice. It was hardly the fancy range of the United States training camp and the targets were bottles and cans, but everyone had a good time. This type of unit does comparatively little small-arms firing, so familiarization in shooting is in order at intervals. The badly battered fort contained a monument in the center commemorating the fact that in the last war, one company of French infantry and one battery of artillery had held off a whole German division for three days until they were finally crushed by weight of numbers. The American troops must have been there at some time also, because I found an old-style United States helmet pierced by a bullet hole and rusted almost to the thinness of tinfoil by the years. There was a magnificent view from the top rampart, no one shot anyone else, and it didn't rain, so all in all, it was a successful day with no complaints.

After a short respite back in the Verdun area, the battalion was returned to the Moselle line at Pont à Mousson for another stretch. Finally, after days of only spasmodic activity, we were again pulled out in support of the Saar Offensive, which Bradley had given Patton permission to begin on November 8 with ten divisions. The weather could not have been worse. Torrential rains flooded the whole area and turned the roads into quagmires. Patton persisted and by November 15 was preparing a "final" attack through the Siegfried Line to the Rhine at Frankfurt. Obviously, the German offensive through the Ardennes, which began on December 16, caused dramatic alterations in those plans. Interestingly enough, in reading about Patton after the war, there are indications that he had some premonitions about a possible German offensive against the weak and thinned-out line in the Ardennes area held by Middleton's VIII Corps.

The battalion remained at Pont à Mousson for a time but was eventually pulled out and travelled in convoy through St. Mihiel to Trier and ultimately to the Thionville area by November 20 to provide support in the Saar Offensive.

On the day after our return to the front line on the Moselle, I had to leave at the crack of dawn to preside at a general court-martial miles away. What a ride! There was a heavy fog along the whole valley and it was so damn cold that it settled on everything like a thick blanket, almost resembling a light snow. The open-air, top-down driving required by Patton's regulations may well have saved some lives, but personally I had no great desire to prolong my own life in such a manner. The combination of cold, fog, and frost added to the usual vicissitudes of travel by jeep, leaving Asmo (another officer assigned to the court-martial) and myself a couple of sad sacks at the end of two or three hours. The army should conduct genetic studies that would breed a race with a tremendous amount of padding over the coccyx and butt to adapt to the type of transport available. Bouncing along on these oversized cocktail shakers innocuously called "jeeps," I always looked enviously at somewhat porky gentlemen who carry their own cushions. After the court-martial the ride back duplicated the ride down—except that it was colder. Invigorating? As the Venetian gondolier said when he fell into the canal, "It shouldn't happen to a Doge!"

I had practically a private suite on our return to Pont à Mousson. Lieutenant Mark Thomson, who shared the quarters with me, went out almost every evening, sometimes on duty in the line and sometimes conducting a courtship with a local belle. I had a drink with them one evening and surmised that Mark's courtship was permanently molded in the languishing phase. The young damsel eyed him very warmly but her father and stepmother were definitely of the French school of thought that assumes that a courtship should be carried out in the presence of the immediate family. Mark could not carry on any lengthy conversation with her without them gently inserting themselves and to my knowledge nary a peck came out the whole affair.

Pont à Mousson, Monday, November 6, 1944

Just finished reading Yank for this week in which the News from Home Section was headed by a statement by Professor Hooton of Harvard that he favors a woman president for the United States. Says Hooton, "A woman's reproductive system is so complicated that the rest of her must, of necessity be simple and what is required in statesmanship today is simplicity." ...

I imagine that most of us overseas will vote for Roosevelt who stands as a symbol of people of the world of hope for the future. I honestly think that his defeat would be a blow to the people of the allied and liberated nations and would not smooth any future relations with Russia and England and might afford Goebbels a bit of propaganda material with which he could bait the German people along for a few months more than they might under present conditions. So much for the election tomorrow, but I trust we do not have to face an election for a fifth term overseas.

Tuesday, November 7, 1944, Pont à Mousson

In addition to spasmodic injuries in our battalion and adjacent units, my local practice has reached the consultation stage with the local population so today I went to see a French boy at a local doctor's request. I'm not sure I could shed much light on the reason for this youngster's swinging fever to 104 and, as you might imagine, the French hospitals near here have very limited diagnostic and laboratory facilities. If he were truly an acute emergency, I could admit him to an American Evac hospital for study but these local illnesses do present these kind of logistic problems.

Wednesday, November 8, 1944, Pont à Mousson

Among the items of news from home is the note that women have been admitted to the Harvard Medical School which I must say doesn't seem cataclysmic to me although others seem to view it as nothing short of a revolution. As you know, shortly after I left medical school, the Army and Navy subsidized about 75% of the medical education by taking students into the Forces as privates and seamen. The remaining 25% were women and 4-F's. The course was cut to under 3 years and nine months hospital training was allowed after graduation. Now, however, both the Army and Navy have cut this program tremendously and since Selective Service does not defer young men because they are planning on a medical education, the medical schools are having a helluva problem filling up their classes. The old days when Harvard was able to select a class of 125 from over 1000 applicants are gone. I doubt if, under the present circumstances, even the best schools would be able to fill their quotas. This would entail not only a tremendous decline in the quality of men (and women) graduates but also a marked fall in the total number. If the war continues for much longer, the problem of supply of doctors could be cataclysmic since there will be the natural attrition from death, a decreasing inflow to the medical education programs and the inevitable battle casualties among combat surgeons. I doubt that Selective Service

will, at this time, defer healthy young males through the 7 years
which, even under the present accelerated educational program, it
would take to get through the minimum of premedical, medical
and hospital training. With almost a half million total casualties
already, there is a much more pressing need for younger men and it
would hardly be fair to all the men fighting now who have given up
years towards all types of careers which are equally important to
them. Secondly, it would be hard to expect the Army and Navy to
continue the subsidization plan up to the previous 75% level.
They have all the doctors they need right now and barring any
tremendous increase in physician casualties, the greatly slashed
programs should provide all the replacements they will need in the
future. Basically, they wouldn't know what to do with an increasing mass of new junior medical officers and feel they can use these

Photo taken from a bridge over the Moselle looking towards
the cathedral in Metz, France, winter, 1945

men earlier to a much better advantage in other capacities.
Thirdly, continuing the shortened medical program as it exists
wouldn't help any future need for doctors in the United States. All
it would accomplish would be to provide a huge mass of partly
trained young men who would pull back after the war, not to
relieve the critical shortage of practicing physicians and surgeons
but to clamor at the doors of hospitals for further training. To
continue the "Royal Succession" in medicine, it would be necessary to have a gradual influx into the profession of young men from
extended residency programs. Continuing to train men through a
greatly shortened and accelerated training would only flood the
country after the war with a number of poorly trained younger men
who, because of their number, would not be able to obtain further
training. That's worse, if anything, than a true shortage of doctors
since it would obviously bring medical standards to a dangerously
low level. Easy solutions do not seem easy to come by and the
problem exists and will become more acute and more apparent as
the war goes on. If the war goes on interminably, a gradual release
of combat veterans to be replaced by newly trained young medical
officers would provide a rational but hardly a psychologically
acceptable solution to the problem.

In mid-November we received orders to proceed to St. Mihiel
and thence to Trier. This sudden move coincided with the opening of the Saar Offensive. Patton hoped to break through the
Siegfried Line and ultimately into central Germany; but it was not
to be. The offensive ground forward very slowly, as the weather
was frightful and we were constantly mired in mud. After a slow
gain of thirty to forty miles, the whole battle plan was changed by
the onslaught of German Panzer divisions breaking through the
thinly held line of Middleton's VIII Corps in the Ardennes on
December 16, 1944.

We rolled out, glad of a change of scene and resigned to a frigid
ride under the usual wintry sky. Convoys were not what they used
to be. The French were pretty well recovered from the mass hyste-

ria that came with the Invasion, the breakthrough, and the drive across France. A slow, grinding push never leaves the delirium in its wake that a steamrolling series of spearheads will, but there was still the open friendliness and waving en route, albeit a little dampened by the weather. I huddled in an overcoat, following the map automatically, smoking and fortifying my already strongly held theory that wars should be fought between April and October with a truce for the rest of the year.

After arriving at our assignment, we found a children's school for use as a command post, which was somewhat of an improvement over a section of a furniture factory. Except for being chilly, a status to which we had become quite accustomed, it was not a bad setup. The building was quite modern, with central heating, but unfortunately there was no coal available so that was a total loss. The modern latrine would have been very nice except it was designed for the age group two to six by whom it was to be utilized. Everything was in miniature—a row of minute footpaths along one wall and another row of tiny little johns along another. A fascinating problem in mechanics! Mark Thomson and I were again pretty well off. Since we were the only two present who spoke French, we jabbered away with the directress of the school and she invited us to use a room in her house, which was actually a part of the school building. It was quite nice, clean, with a desk that I used regularly, a fairly respectable bed that it was my turn to occupy (Mark was exiled to a cot on this trip), and a small wood stove, which with continuous and assiduous attention might warm one corner of the room. It was hardly the Ritz, but I considered myself damn lucky.

Under different circumstances, Trier might have been a fairly pretty town. It was nestled among several hills and from various points you could look for miles over the countryside—that is, when you could see more than a few hundred yards. The usual leaden

W.M. McD. and Lt. Bob Fehr in front of litter-bearing jeep at one of A Battery gun positions.Pete Lisowski, the driver in back. Near Metz, December, 1944.

sky had been tossing off a peculiar combination of hail, snow, and rain and the natives with whom we exchanged a few words assured us cheerfully there was no improvement in the climate until April at least—"nor anywhere in Germany, either," they usually added to complete the picture. The people leaned over backwards to be hospitable to us, although civilians in a war zone lived under continuous tension and they were invariably nervous and jittery.

As we moved into the Saar the population included an increasing percentage of Germans. Since I could by that time get on pretty well with the French language, I had intermittent contact with them—particularly in the town, in which there was no civil affairs officer, so I was functioning out of the organizational pattern in that temporary capacity. Outwardly, at least, they were no problems. The German segment of the population seemed a bit surly but also obsequious and cringing. They would follow any flatly given order to the letter, but none of us had any intention of wandering around alone in the pitch-black nights. I was sure that a

German underground movement would never present any immense problem. My impression was that the average Jerry became so accustomed to dictatorial authority and was so impressed by military power that the independent thought and emotional drive necessary to support a nationwide resistance movement was nonexistent. Verified stories abounded of the peculiar attitude of even fanatical Nazis when they were taken prisoner. A good example was the tale of an infantryman who captured a German and while taking him back was jumped by a Nazi patrol. While beating them off, he had his prisoner dutifully loading one gun while he was firing the other—and that was a man who had been fighting hard and well for months without any attempt at desertion. Their basic psychology was so different from ours that, to the American soldier, the German was almost incomprehensible. There is no question that the German was a tough, dogged, fanatical fighter, which didn't jibe at all with his persona as a prisoner, when he was placid and docile—even though he might remain stupidly fanatical in philosophy and completely lacking in any conception of what we consider the basic tenets of humanity, Christianity, and civilization. Just after the breakthrough in Normandy, I visited the temporary stockades within a very short distance of the rapidly advancing front, filled with thousands of prisoners and guarded by a few scattered Americans and a few strands of barbed wire. Only a short time before, they had been fighting viciously and violently; once captured, they gave the impression that even the small guard and the wire were unnecessary. Americans or British in a similar situation would have been off over the countryside in droves in no time.

The Maytag Express didn't seem to be what it used to be, but the German Air Force still had an interesting habit of strafing prisoner stockades. I remember how amazed we were when we first saw German prisoners strafed by their own planes. Reading about horrors, atrocities, and psychological abnormalities, never brings home their reality—coming face to face with them is always a shock. I suppose the theory was that no true German should ever surrender, but when you consider that more than six hundred thousand prisoners had been taken on the Western Front alone, it seemed a little impractical for even the most fanatical Nazi to think that much could be accomplished by strafing an isolated stockade. The practice seemed even more vicious than Himmler's orders to shoot any soldier who retreated or even evidenced a defeatist attitude. The American guards were much more amazed than the prisoners themselves, who seemed to accept it as part of the routine. A prison stockade out in the country was the last place where the guards ever thought they would have to dig foxholes.

10

The 30th Field Hospital

END OF "THE BULGE"

January 13–February 5, 1945

The courage and determination of the Wehrmacht was manifested throughout all of our contacts. By the end of 1944 it must have been obvious to most of them that they were fighting in a losing cause, but the majority fought stubbornly and bravely in defense of something—homeland tradition, discipline, family—it was difficult often to understand. I would obviously exclude the SS from these comments since they were comprised of a highly selected fanatical, brutal, cruel, and disciplined subset that reflected the bizarre tenets of Naziism as expounded by the disordered mind of Der Führer.

The American soldier appeared in a different light. Taken directly from home and civilian life into a completely foreign environment, trained (often briefly) in the aura of military discipline and sent out in a dangerous and frightening war against some of the best, most experienced troops of history, the citizen-soldier of the U.S. Army conducted himself bravely and effectively. Obviously, it was the pilots of the air force, the sailors on the combat

Red Diamond Express, Junglister, Luxembourg, January, 1945. "The Bulge."

ships, and the men of the infantry and armored divisions who bore the brunt of the fighting and who were exposed to the major risks of a modern war.

It was during the latter phase of the Bulge that I suddenly received orders on January 13, 1945 transferring me to the 1st Platoon of the 30th Field Hospital, which was working closely with the 5th Infantry ("Red Diamond") and the 4th Armored divisions of the Third Army in Luxembourg at the southern shoulder of the Bulge. I embarked on a completely different type of medical and military experience, from my previous life as a battalion surgeon.

When word of my transfer came through, a large farewell party was organized. I spent the afternoon signing over equipment, telling my replacement as much as I could about the odds and ends of the battalion, and packing for the trip to my new assignment. The job I was headed for was very different from the one I had had throughout the campaign. Instead of being the big frog (in fact the only medical frog), I would be one of a number of small frogs as well as senior frogs. As Ogden Nash wrote, "Every flea has little fleas upon his back to bite him—and little fleas have smaller fleas—and so ad infinitum." I couldn't plan on having enough space in which to pack all the junk I had accumulated, so I repacked and reorganized everything to a more or less stream-lined motif. Then it was time for dinner, after which we broke out practically all the available liquor for the farewell party. It turned out to be a wild affair—good fun, though very alcoholic. Various officers from the batteries came in to say goodbye and have a drink or two or more and Mark came in to spend the night.

He and I sat up with two other friends, drinking and talking until well after 2:00 A.M. Much as I liked the idea of getting back to some real surgery again, it is hard to leave good friends with whom you have lived, fought, drunk, travelled, and worked for so long—but turning down the transfer would have been damn fool-

Junglister, Luxembourg, January, 1945

ish. Medically and surgically, I was rotting.

The next day, we left on a long, cold ride north to my new station. John Miles, captain of A Battery, got permission from the colonel to ride up with me and we had an enjoyable trip despite the open jeep and the subzero temperature. As we entered Luxembourg, the terrain was a peculiar combination of stretches of flat farmland alternating with rugged areas of deep ravines and sharp, steep hills where the road wound through heavy pine forests that had a peculiar dark beauty, their somberness unrelieved by the heavy snow on the ground and on the branches. We went through the relatively undamaged city of Luxembourg to the Headquarters Unit, 1st Platoon of the 30th Field Hospital in Junglinster, where I faced the pangs of saying goodbye to Pete, my driver, and to John Miles.

The field hospital was designed in the Spanish-American War as a relatively mobile unit providing acute and emergency surgical care. The commanding officer held the rank of lieutenant colonel and the hospital itself was divided into three platoons (or HUs), each under the command of a major in the Medical Corps. At different points in history, there were varying numbers of junior officers and warrant officers, both administrative and medical, and corpsmen of various grades and at different levels of training. In the intervals between wars, most of the field hospitals became National Guard units, and it immediately became apparent to civilian consulting surgeons such as Drs. Churchill, Berry, Cutler, and others in the days prior to and after Pearl Harbor that these units had become anachronisms in the era of sophisticated surgery of trauma. They had great potential as basic mobile units but the tremendous variation in the training and experience of the doctors in the National Guard who constituted the professional hierarchy made it impossible for them to function adequately under prospective wartime conditions. Thus, a new and imagina-

tive structure was devised under which a skeleton professional
headquarters unit, usually consisting of little except the lieutenant colonel, the adjutant, and a few enlisted men and functioning
mainly in an administrative capacity, was maintained. Small, flexible, highly skilled teams, known as auxiliary surgical groups, were
often temporarily grafted on in order to provide excellent surgical
care. These new units were composed of smaller teams, each
consisting of a senior surgeon, an assistant, and an anesthetist.
Any one or more of these auxiliary surgical groups could function
as needed with a platoon of a field hospital. (Sometimes the headquarters crew stayed with one of the platoons; more often, they
set up alone somewhere in the rear area more or less in contact
with the three independent platoons.) Each of the three platoons
usually functioned independently as a highly mobile group of two
or three surgical teams, located close to the lines near the clearing
station and collecting companies of a division, designed to operate on "nontransportable casualties." (These were mainly chest
and abdominal wounds, but included serious and critical multiple extremity injuries). A wounded soldier was first seen by a
corpsman with a Red Cross on his arm and helmet, then brought
to a battalion aid station (such as I had just left), where the surgeon could give immediate first aid—dressings, splints, plasma,
antibiotics, and narcotics as indicated. The casualty was then
brought to the clearing station where an ambulance of the collecting companies took him immediately either to a nearby field hospital platoon or farther back to the evacuation hospital. These
latter units also received postoperative cases from field hospitals
as soon as they were transportable. The end of the line was the
general hospital, located either in a theater of operations overseas
or within the continental United States, where convalescent facilities, physiotherapy, rehabilitation equipment, and reconstructive and plastic surgery were all available. Many casualties could

1st H-U (hospital unit) 30th Field Hospital near Jaulnay, France.

be returned to action after convalescence; others were discharged from military service to home or to veterans' hospitals.

Often the commanding officer of a platoon was an administrator, but in our unit the original commanding officer was replaced by a highly skilled surgeon, Mike Mulligan, from one of the auxiliary groups. Mike not only served as CO but also ran his own team (often assisted by Dave Dunn or myself), in addition to two other teams from the Fourth Auxiliary. When I joined the unit, we were located in Junglinster, north of Luxembourg City. The admitting surgical operating tables and postoperative wards were under a series of tents just outside of town, well marked (we hoped) with Red Crosses, and we slept in whatever billets were available in and near the village. I was assigned to the vaults of a small bank, which turned out to be a haven for most of the rats in Luxembourg. The problem of keeping them from crawling all over our litters was solved by placing helmets in basins of water under the legs of whatever props we were using to hold up the litters. Charming!

The people of Luxembourg were not only extremely friendly and pleasant, I was told, but also very well educated. Thanks to an excellent school system a large number spoke English surprisingly well. Like so many other places in Europe—more than any other I'd seen, in fact—Luxembourg would have been a delightful place to live if it had not been for the Nazis, who left their trademark there as elsewhere. At the time of my arrival, the 1st Platoon of the 30th Field Hospital was set up in the village of Junglinster, where we were fairly comfortable in spite of the expected sound effects of war day and night.

The function of the hospital, and my new role, looked very exciting. It was a damn good job—a wonderful opportunity to see and do surgery again. In my old job, I always had a gnawing feeling I was slowly forgetting everything I had ever known about medicine and surgery. I was glad, however, that I had spent those many months as a battalion surgeon. The job had an independence that my new post lacked and the knowledge that I was a big frog in a little pond, that the men relied on me, trusted me, knew me, and were grateful to me, was satisfying—but it still wasn't surgery. I knew that I would enjoy tremendously the feeling of being busy again in a hospital routine, albeit a very humble one in a wartime environment.

It felt strange to be decked out again in a cap and mask, etc. The surroundings were hardly like the MGH, but the operating rooms themselves were wonderfully familiar—if I concentrated on the table, the instruments, the drapes, and the operating gowns and didn't look beyond to the walls and the floors or the high combat boots of the surgeons showing beneath their gowns. In peacetime, it would have been hard to imagine setting up pre- and post-op wards, blood bank, operating rooms, autoclaves, X-ray, laboratory, etc., under such circumstances, to say nothing of pulling everything down on a moment's notice, piling it all onto trucks, and moving on. Not only was all that done regularly and routinely, but it was done damn well. A man might be wounded, operated on, and sleeping peacefully in bed or on his way farther to the rear within an incredibly short period of time.

The blood bank was of particular interest. Seeing how the boys pulled a foot out of the grave when the blood started pouring into them made me realize even more fully how important was the work that the volunteers at its blood donor centers were doing. There would have been no dearth of volunteer donors if everyone could have seen how much blood we routinely infused into one boy's veins in a few hours. It's no exaggeration to say that it was a matter of life or death to most of them. Without it, we wouldn't have been able to get them in shape to stand an operation.

Within a day or so of my arrival, various officers and men from the hospital and the Fifth Division went back to Luxembourg City to attend a solemn high mass in the cathedral in gratitude for the liberation. Patton's advance units had come through the city a few hours before the Nazis, who were coming down from the north, so this service was a fairly dramatic occasion. Even though I was not involved in that operation, I shared vicariously in the praise and admiration lavished on us by the bishop and the people.

As the Third Army continued its offensive against the southern shoulder of the Bulge, we followed closely with the Fifth Infantry Division.

The process of moving to Echternach on the Sur River took up most of the day and evening. Having left our holding company behind with postoperative patients, we were practically ready to open for admissions by nightfall. Complicated as it may sound to pick up a hundred-bed (all three units) surgical hospital or any of its three platoons by the roots and set it down somewhere else, the whole move ran very smoothly and quickly, for in all the units the men knew the procedure and their own individual jobs perfectly. We, in the First HU, were now set up in a large rambling chateau previously occupied by the Germans. The hospital itself occupied the whole first floor, plus one space as an overflow ward on the second floor. The officers and enlisted men had living quarters on the second and third floors. It was a damn nice setup. The estate was beautiful, although I was too busy to look around very much. We were a little crowded for space but a field hospital unit doesn't need anywhere near the room of a civilian hospital doing that much surgery, because we functioned mainly as an operating center and evacuated cases postoperatively as soon as they were transportable. We could do a tremendous amount of surgery with a comparatively small amount of ward space.

We had various arrangements for division of the work, depending on the volume or expected volume of cases coming in. For a time, I was with the team working the twelve-hour graveyard shift, from 20:00 to 08:00, so all my sleeping was done in the afternoon or early evening. Of course, if there was any sudden tremendous rush of cases during the day, the night teams stayed on to help out the day teams in the OR or, more likely, work in the preop ward during the supposedly off hours. It was an imposing schedule at times but there were lulls when the fighting quieted down so, over a time, it probably balanced quite well. All the officers were young, as seemed to be the policy in assignments to the newly organized field hospitals, but I remained the "infant" of the group. The two majors, obviously the oldest, were, I should guess, pushing forty pretty hard if not across the barrier. The other officers were all captains (except one second lieutenant) and ranged from their early to mid-thirties. Geographically, distribution was very varied, with practically every section of the country represented. There was no one else from New England and New York in this particular unit but Dave Dunn came from Pennsylvania so that brought the eastern representation up to two.

By January 18, we were established on the Sur River and life had taken on more than a vague resemblance to that of a mole. After a few days on a very busy schedule, I almost forgot what daylight looked like. I usually finished up in the OR and postop wards somewhere between 8:00 and 9:00 in the morning, had a tremendous breakfast, and turned in for a long day's snooze. Since the night crews all slept together and our rooms were completely dark all the time, there was very little to disturb us except the occasional bombings at night and intermittent artillery fire during the day. It was a little hard at first, to get adjusted to a program of sleeping during the day and working at night. I woke up several times during the day, but on the whole pounded out a pretty good seven hours until I finally stayed awake around 4:00 P.M. Since there was no immediate rush to get up, and the other two medical officers in the room were still asleep, I often laid back drowsily, read a little, and thought about life at home. I eventually dragged myself out, washed and shaved in a basin of ice-cold water, and had dinner at the peculiar hour of 5:00. Then there were a few reports to straighten out and finally I went back to the room to scratch off a few quick lines of a letter before going down to relieve the day shift, who had been handling a lot of cases during the previous twelve hours and who seemed pretty damn tired.

The news looked pretty good, what with the steady mopping up of the von Rundstedt's salient plus the first reports of the Russian winter offensive in Poland.

As the Fifth Infantry Division was steadily flattening the southern shoulder of the Bulge, life suddenly became extraordinarily hectic. I learned what it was like to turn in so tired that it was hard not to fall asleep while getting my boots off. From the point of view of the steady rush, the pace reminded me of the Cocoanut Grove fire on a small scale, but it was damn good to be working really hard again. This was certainly a different life from that of a battalion surgeon, and I enjoyed it tremendously, although I was afraid that there would be times when letters to Blanche would suffer. "Enjoy" isn't quite the right word. No one felt much like frolicking around and whistling with a lot of terribly wounded kids lying around and when we were operating on some of the grim cases, but as long as there was a war, I preferred to do the work that I liked and have the satisfaction of seeing the difference between the preop and postop wards. It was astounding how much could be done. Every case that came in was a major operation, comparable to having a ward full of major abdominal and chest cases at the MGH—and we used to think we were overwhelmed if we ran three or four serious operations, to say nothing of doing them on tables set up in a dining room with a continual racket going on outside and the building shaking from time to time.

When you get up, eat dinner, work five to six hours, have a quick bite at midnight, work another eight to nine hours, eat breakfast, and go to bed again, there is not a lot to say, particularly when it takes place in the confines of one large building. All this may sound dull but actually it was far from that. I felt very much in the rut of surgery, transfusions, Wangensteen suction, dressings, medical talk, eating, and sleeping without much contact with the outside world. A quick scanning of *Stars and Stripes* was about all I had to make me aware that anything else was going on in the world except the war as it existed in that particular sector.

A large number of German casualties came through, all very much in the same pattern. It seemed to me impossible to do anything about rehabilitating or re-educating these characters. In the hospital we saw very little of their vaunted arrogance, but what we saw made the future look hopeless. They could be really stupid in a way that it's hard to believe any human could be, which I suppose in a way represented the product of some dozen years of unthinking regimentation. Peculiarly enough, they did not seem to have any real pride in themselves or in anything in particular. Far from evidencing the supposed Teutonic stoicism, even the officers whined, complained, snivelled, and begged for coffee, for butter, for cigarettes, etc. Not that they were easily beaten. They were trained for war; they had thought, loved, and breathed war for years—there was no other life for them. They fought hard and well until the going got too rough for their instincts, but once beaten and captured, the majority seemed to react exactly like decorticate animals. All of this, of course, is not true of the SS or the military caste, in whom there had been bred an arrogance that was itself an instinct like eating or sleeping, but we didn't see too much of that particular ilk for various reasons. I might have thought that there was some hope for them if they had evidenced some reactions of either guilt or of deep, thought-out hatred. They did not, although most of them had killed soldiers and civilians, men and women, in cold blood.

January 23, 1945

Last night was horrendous! Because of the amount of work, I climbed out of bed and started in about late afternoon and worked steadily through with the exception of about 15 minutes in the evening, until 9 A.M. Since this stretch included a five-hour and a four-hour operation, I was practically comatose by mid-morning. Then the crowning blow fell when we had to move again crossing the Sur River. I packed up, but fortunately managed to wrap up in a blanket and sneak a few hours sleep before it was actually time to roll on. . . . Somehow, even with the columns of tanks and guns on the road, the noise of war and the inevitable destruction, [the country] maintains an aura of serenity and peace, even among the people who have been remarkably tranquil about the presence or the passage of war. Sleepy as I was, I enjoyed the ride particularly since it was the first time in some days that I had even seen the

outside world in daylight. We arrived here on the Prum River and
started work immediately so the only unpacking I had done was to
dump my things in a corner of a damn cold room in the building
we occupied—an ex civilian hospital of some sort. By then it was 6
A.M. and it began to look as if I would be able to turn in around 8
A.M. for a snooze—a wonderful prospect. Our operating schedule
bogged down for about an hour while the generator was being
repaired after having been hit by an 88 shell.

The 30th Field Hospital was supporting the clearing stations
of the Fifth Infantry and the Fourth Armored Division as they
moved into Luxembourg to crush the southern shoulder of the
Bulge. As is obvious from the historical review of the period, a
number of the Germans were able to withdraw from the salient
that had been made in the Allied lines by the Ardennes offensive,
and the pressure from the Ninth and First armies to the north and
the Third Army from the south was not sufficient to cut off totally
the pocket of Germans, but a huge number were taken prisoner
and we took care of a number of their casualties before returning
them to evacuation hospitals and ultimately to prisoner-of-war
camps. There was heavy fighting, and we were operating around
the clock and taking care of an extraordinary number of casualties
on both sides. Eventually, the salient was crushed and an American line re-established from which provided the base for the ultimate final offensive to the Rhine and into Germany and Austria.

January 25, 1945

After an initial flurry in our new location, I thought this might be a
slightly more relaxing night since we seemed to be caught up with
our operating schedule but with a new influx of admissions from
the Clearing Station and Collecting Companies, it didn't work out
that way. In fact, I never sat down at all since I got up this afternoon at 4 P.M. until almost 6 A.M. There was a short lull in the
operating schedule because we called for repeat x-rays and another

transfusion on the next case who was coming up for surgery. I
tried to think of what it would be like at the MGH if we ran into a
continuous 24-hour operating schedule, all major cases. Of course,
we only ran two tables, but even at that, with the comparatively
small staff we had, I think that there was more major surgery done
here in a month than in a year at any civilian hospital.

That may not have been an entirely accurate statement, because
we were not always in a routine like that, thank God. I might have
nothing to do at all for several days, whereas a civilian hospital
will run a pretty constant number of daily cases, year in and year
out. I'm sure of one thing, however, and that is that I saw and did
more traumatic surgery, primarily of the chest and abdomen, in a
few months than I would for the rest of my professional life. There
was no other place in the medical setup of the army where you
could get such a wealth of surgical experience, but obviously I
would not have been sorry to see it end suddenly. A lot of the
results were damn good, and it was satisfying to be able to do so
much, but it was no fun to see these kids rolled back from the
front a few minutes away, terribly mauled and beaten. In addition
to everything else, this was a helluva time of the year for the
doughfoot to be fighting a war, what with the snow and the bitter cold.

We were getting more and more wounded Krauts brought in.
Two of the operations turned out to be extremely long but also
highly interesting, involving both the chest and the abdomen. We
took care of the German casualities with the same standards as
anyone else, but they were surprisingly unpleasant, and individually as demanding as a whole ward full of Americans. We just
treated them and ignored them which was, I guess, the only policy
we could follow.

We did have access in one way or another to surgical journals,
and I came across an issue of *Annals of Surgery* that contained an

article by Colonel Churchill, chief of the West Surgical Service at the MGH and now senior consultant to the Mediterranean Theater of Operations. This was of interest since it contained descriptions and photographs relating to field hospitals and auxiliary surgical groups and a schematic diagram that gave an excellent projection of the operational system. The pictures were not of the winterized version of a field hospital, since during this time of year we preferred to take over a building or buildings somewhere and use the cellars for operating rooms if the military action was particularly heavy. I was told that later on, when weather permitted, we would use tent space, as it was, perhaps surprisingly, easier and more efficient than the type of building usually available, albeit somewhat more dangerous in terms of aberrant shelling. Of course, danger at any time in life is relative, and compared to life with a combat infantry battalion, this was almost relaxing.

On arrival at the field hospital patients were brought into the receiving ward where data were recorded and clothes cut away. They were then taken to the preop ward, where they were kept until a final diagnosis was made and they had been stabilized for operation with blood and plasma. Traction, splinting, chest taps, redressing, packings, emergency ligation of arteries, penicillin, sulphadiazine, morphine, stimulants, gastric intubation, and other various therapeutic maneuvers were employed as indicated and X-rays were taken of chest, abdomen, skull, and extremities according to the type of wound. When a patient was out of shock and could tolerate an operation, and the diagnosis was established as to the type and location of the internal injuries, he was taken to the operating room, which had complete equipment necessary for anything except neurosurgery or reconstructive orthopedic surgery (done farther back in the chain). He was then returned to a combination recovery room and surgical ward without, of course, all the luxuries of a civilian hospital. As mentioned earlier, we evacuated cases as quickly as possible and practically never kept a postop case longer than seven days. Our individual work was both specific and flexible. I was responsible for all postop cases, which entailed regular rounds several times a day seeing that the wards were set up and functioning properly, writing postop orders, carrying out any necessary postop procedures, and in general watching the patients very carefully. In addition, I was more or less responsible for the preop section during the night shift. We had shock teams attached for preoperative work, but they were usually medical men on detached service from some inactive evacuation or general hospital and not too familiar with the handling of emergency surgical cases. Therefore, one of us from this unit was available at all times to check the preop wards at intervals. Like an emergency ward at home, it is the busiest and most confusing place in the hospital, and I spent a lot of time there. Even on a quiet night something usually turned up; one night, for instance, I interrupted a letter to do a chest tap on a Kraut who was brought in with a tension hemopneumothorax.

The rest of my time on duty I spent in the operating room—usually assisting one of the surgeons from the auxiliary groups and occasionally operating myself, since both the majors (Mulligan and Bohrer) were, in addition to being excellent surgeons, damn nice guys and let me do as much as possible, and were always willing in appropriate situations to help me operate rather than the reverse. Eating and sleeping made up the rest of my routine.

January 27, Luxembourg (on the Prum River)

Your Christmas letter was wonderful but I felt badly because you had been imagining such a miserable Christmas for me whereas actually, as you know by now, I did have a reasonably pleasant time despite the German offensive to the north which was reaching its

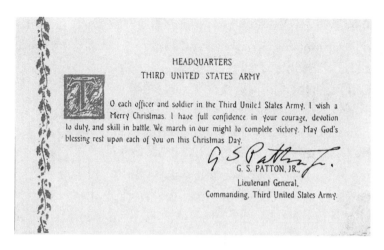

HEADQUARTERS
THIRD UNITED STATES ARMY

O each officer and soldier in the Third United States Army, I wish a
Merry Christmas. I have full confidence in your courage, devotion
to duty, and skill in battle. We march in our might to complete victory. May God's
blessing rest upon each of you on this Christmas Day.

G S Patton Jr.
G. S. PATTON, JR.,
Lieutenant General,
Commanding, Third United States Army.

Pattons' prayer handed out to the troops (front)

peak at just about that point. There was a burst of German air and
artillery activity along the whole front coinciding with von
Rundstedt's drive but it didn't do much locally in the Saar except
add a little color and drama to Christmas Eve about which I'll give
you more details some day. I am delighted, a least, that the orchid
arrived on schedule and sounded better than I had expected.
There is a lot of fuss made about December 25th with the men
overseas and everyone goes to no end of trouble to make it as
pleasant as possible but you never see a mention of the Christ-
mases of the women at home which are a thousand times more
miserable because of the constant gnawing doubts and anxiety
brought on by the ignorance of where their men are, how they are
and what kind of a Christmas they are having. I have tried to
imagine at times just how miserable I would be if I didn't know
where you were and how you were and have ended up thanking
God that I know you're safe and warm and comfortable at least. I
was glad to hear that you had some Lanson 1928 at Marie and
Eddie's over Christmas, because some of the champagne we used
at the farewell party (a restrained noun to use for that little occasion) was Lanson although of a later period and not a vintage wine.
. . . I am sending one of the little cards which General Patton sent
to all the troops on Christmas, praying for decent weather so that
planes could fly in support of the ground troops again.

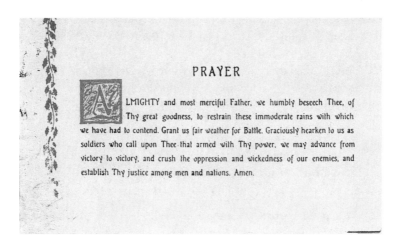

PRAYER

LMIGHTY and most merciful Father, we humbly beseech Thee, of Thy great goodness, to restrain these immoderate rains with which we have had to contend. Grant us fair weather for Battle. Graciously hearken to us as soldiers who call upon Thee that armed with Thy power, we may advance from victory to victory, and crush the oppression and wickedness of our enemies, and establish Thy justice among men and nations. Amen.

Pattons' prayer handed out to the troops (back)

January 30, 1945

Activity continued to slack off in terms of the workload and a shower unit was able to get to us today. It must be over two weeks since I've had anything except a helmet bath and it was a great luxury and well worth the loss of sleep since obviously, I had to give up part of my day's sleep after the night shift in order to catch up with them. Then I went to Mass in the nearby village so what with the cleanliness and godliness cutting into my sleeping hours for two successive days, I'm drooping slightly tonight.

The walk to the showers and to Mass was about the first time in many days that I have been outside in daylight but it was snowing slightly so there was no bright sun to put an unaccustomed strain on my retinae. It had been snowing almost constantly but never heavily in the form of a blizzard. The flakes seemed to be widely separated and drift down slowly, lightly but steadily, so that it looked like a print of a Winter scene from Dickens and not the raging blizzards to which we were accustomed in New England. It was very cold; the snow never melts and it crunches underfoot with that sound which is all associated with very cold dry wintery weather but it was not at all unpleasant. I had no particular desire, however, to sleep out in the snowdrift as we have had to do on occasions in the past. . . . A letter from home with a clipping on

> Bemie Soutter amused everyone here highly since most of the
> surgeons in the unit have worked with him in the ETO. They
> particularly enjoyed the fact that the continuation of the article on
> the inside page was headed "Soutter"—nothing else. He was
> extremely liked everywhere by everyone who met him and all his
> friends were delighted by the decoration for his flight into
> Bastogne and that he received his majority a couple of months ago.

We were very little affected in my old unit by the early phases of the Bulge except for increased air and artillery activity on the part of the Germans, presumably to try to hold us in our positions. General Patton responded impressively to his responsibilities and initiated drives for the relief of Bastogne by, I believe, the Fourth Armored Division, and then other units were to swing north also to try to crush the southern shoulder of the Bulge and cut off the Germans in a large pocket within Belgium. It was a difficult strategic and tactical maneuver to mobilize large units of infantry and tanks and to cross behind one's own lines when the supply routes were well established at right angles to the projected offensive. As far as I was concerned, this was handled extremely well and I had the opportunity to see the MPs organizing and directing the crossing routes when I was transferred to the 30th Field Hospital attached to the Fifth Infantry Division, the main unit that was smashing the German troops at the southern shoulder of the Bulge. Along with the Fifth Infantry and the Fourth Armored Division, we drove steadily north through Luxembourg and were posted as the offensive proceeded at various points in Luxembourg itself, including Junglinster, Eich, Berglandster, and Echternach. By late January 1945 a huge number of Germans had been captured in the Bulge, the lines had been straightened out, and again, it was obvious that a major offensive was about to be resumed into the Rhineland through the Siegfried Line to the Rhine. January 28, 1945 was officially designated as the end of the Battle of the Bulge.

When we were in Junglinster, the Germans were still heavily entrenched across the river and at regular intervals would shell the town. General Patton came roaring into town one day in typical fashion, with his helmet liner shining (*we* were not allowed to go without helmets because the liners would shine in the sun), his ivory-handled revolvers at his side, and machine guns mounted on his own jeep and his own command car and on accompanying jeeps. This small parade made quite a show, which would have enchanted us except we knew that the Germans across the river had the area under observation and would, without question, send over a barrage as soon as they saw anything as dramatic as this going through. Patton roared on, saluting and waving, and we immediately dashed for the vaults of the bank before the barrage arrived. So much for exalted missions of leadership! They do carry with them some unfortunate sequelae. Nonetheless, I think it's fair to say that Patton was, with all his foibles, respected by the rank and file of the Third Army. There was a certain confidence engendered among the troops in his ability as a tactician. While everyone recognized his idiosyncracies and oddities stemming back to the slapping incident and peculiarities which he evinced in dress, behavior, and public statements, he handled troops well and we were happy to have him as a leader in a tactical situation, although I would certainly never have wanted him making political decisions on an international scale. Moving northward, we drove in the southern shoulder of the Bulge. In order to reach the ultimate objectives, the rivers Our, Sur, Prum and Kyll had to be crossed. With the stabilization of the line, we moved forward across them along with the Fifth Infantry and the Fourth Armored Divisions in what we all hoped would be the final assault on Nazi Germany.

At the Rhine, we turned southward until we were across the broad river from Frankfurt and then established a forced crossing with an engineered bridge at Oppenheim. Dave Dunn and I became fast friends during that period, and have remained so ever since. It was about that time when, as he sat facing me in the truck while we moved to a new location in the daylight, I noticed that his sclerae were icteric, and urged him to go back for medical care in an evac hospital. He might well have been sent home, but he decided against leaving the unit. He did follow instructions about rest and diet and fortunately what was obviously an attack of hepatitis passed off without serious sequelae.

When the war quieted down, making night rounds on the postop ward, or sitting at the desk in the dim light writing orders, checking the records of intake, output, temperature, pulse, etc., it was so damn much like the days at the MGH, despite the differences of circumstances and situation, that memories came back in surging ways—memories of lengthy telephone calls to Blanche late at night, rushing through admissions to get the Reservoir-Beacon Limited, meeting her at the church on the way to the North Station, getting a little drunk with Charlie, Addison, and Doug on Redheart Rum (Charlie's favorite fluid), and our mutual unseen friend, Jenny, a telephone operator at the MGH. It was a world unto itself until December of '42, when the boundaries stretched out to include 1688 Beacon Street, the Ritz, the Copley, the Harvard Club, the Lafayette, and that general area. It still wasn't a very large world but all those places suddenly seemed not just different but entirely new, as if I've never seen them before.

January 31, 1995—Echternach, Luxembourg

I was terribly sorry to hear of Angus' death in a B-17 over Germany. I never did see him in England and I'm not even sure that he was in the areas where we were prior to the invasion. Most of the air fields near us were B-26 units. Even with the number of friends and acquaintances who have been and will be killed, the number of impersonal tragedies I've seen, each new one is no less of a shock.

It's a brutal business and nothing else but there's no point in talking or writing about it any further.

Rafe Jones just got back from two days leave in Paris and was very disappointed. There was absolutely no heat or hot water anywhere in any of the hotels used for billeting officers (or any hotels for that matter), so much of the point of a trip to the big city (hot bath, warm room, etc.) was not there. On top of that, all the nightclubs and bars were closed, the weather was miserable, the ride by truck was like a cross-country jaunt in a refrigerator and shopping was next to impossible because of the prices. In short, he was glad to be back and sorry he went at all. I have no desire to go now whatsoever. I'd prefer to remember Paris as I knew it before the war and see it again with you in happier times when the fighting is over. Incidentally, this unit was the subject of a radio broadcast over the mutual network tonight at 6 P.M. which would make it about noon at home, I guess. The correspondent who gives the broadcast regularly was around all day talking to us and to the patients and watching the work in order to gather up material for this particular program. I wouldn't think that there was a chance in a million that you would be listening to the radio at that time, but if you were or if anyone happened to be, I would be interested to hear what he said. We obviously couldn't pick him up here since it was sent out for home consumption and not over any of the military, French or English stations.

By the first week in February, it was obvious that the Battle of the Bulge, or the Ardennes Campaign, as it was officially entitled, was over, the lines stabilized, and the new and "final" offensive was impending. We were all in good humor; even living conditions did not drive out the hedonistic and Apollonaustic side of us. By the end of 1944, it was apparent even to us moles that the initiative had passed from the Germans, never to return. The ordinary civilian-soldier "in the trenches" was cautious about optimism, particularly after the disappointments following the dramatic summer of 1944 and the apparent resurgence of the Germans during the early phase of the Bulge. By now, however, the

Russians had crushed the last real, desperate German offensive at Kharkov and had opened an apparently overwhelming offensive of their own. The campaign in Italy was moving ahead finally, long after the actual surrender of the Italian government. The submarine sinkings, which reached a high point of seven hundred thousand tons of allied shipping per month in early 1943, had dropped steadily ever since, even though events like the tragic sinking of the transport *Leopoldville* off the coast of Brittany on December 23, 1944 still occurred, with heavy loss of life in the 66th Infantry Division. The V1 and V2 bombings had been curtailed by the capture of most of the launching sites in Belgium and Holland and the Luftwaffe was increasingly ineffective. We all hoped and thought that this would be the "Final Offensive" in the European Theater and that we would then regroup and move on to the Pacific. Even though the war was going well in that area, we all expected to participate in landings on Japan. That was, perhaps, the only dampening effect on our overall ebullience about the future.

11

The Siegfried Line

INVASION OF GERMANY

February 5 – March 24, 1945

Patton's "final offensive" drove through the Siegfried Line into Germany and to the Rhine, near Coblenz and at the confluence with the Moselle. The 4th Armored and other mobile units cut through the southern slopes of the Eifel, covering fifty-six miles in the last three days of the drive, which had progressively gained momentum after crossing the Sur, the Prum, and the Kyll and cleaning out the pillboxes and fortifications that comprised the West Wall. On March 7 the advance units reached the Rhine. Concomitantly, the northern corps of the First Army reached the Rhine at Cologne and the 9th Armored Division captured the Ludendorff Bridge at Remagen intact and established the first bridgehead across the Rhine.

By March 14, the Third Army had crossed the Moselle southwest of Coblenz and drove south, enveloping the German units in the Saar.

February 2, 1945, Luxembourg

Certainly, the news is wonderful what with the crushing Russian

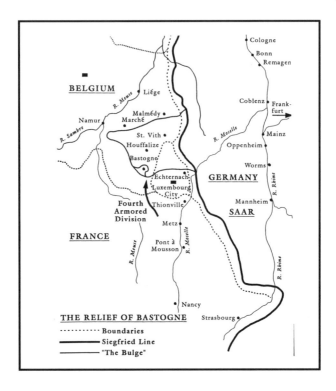

offensive still rolling. The offensive in this area and along the whole western front is picking up steam and the Pacific is looking better all the time. The cold weather has broken suddenly in the past two days and the snow melted away before I could get a really good picture of Luxembourg in the Winter—the thaw is far from an unmixed blessing, however, since we are all now wallowing ankle-deep in *mud*. For an armored division, this presents a major problem but the comparatively mild weather did make some of the functions of life such as evacuating and bathing less of a torture.

Despite spending all one night with intermittent fluoroscopic examinations in an attempt to get a Miller-Abbott tube through the pylorus of a youngster with multiple intestinal injuries, I found myself lapsing rapidly from my semblance of pessimism and couldn't help feeling that we were on the last lap. The contagion of optimism was running up and down the army again, as it did in

the halcyon days of the past summer. I was always very suscep-
tible to optimism, grasping too readily at any theory that offered
the prospect of ending the war. But I was not alone in this optimism; even trying to think objectively, it still looked as if the Krauts
were on their last legs. Just how far and just how long those legs
would carry them, no one knew, but I couldn't imagine it being
much farther or longer.

Another move! The trip, while not long, gave me a chance to
see a little more of the beautiful country (less attractive in the midst
of a sudden thaw than it had been under a heavy blanket of snow).
Armies and war make a helluva mess out of soft ground. Mud,
mud everywhere, thick gummy layers; but the scenery was magnificent. The landscape was, of course, inevitably blotched by
the scars of war and the villages battered in varying degrees. It
was always a helluva job tearing down the hospital, moving on,
and setting up again, but this time we were not immediately overwhelmed by patients. Our location, well beyond Echternach, was
pretty good—we were strung out in a series of buildings along the
main street of a village, with the hospital itself in a connecting hotel and tavern, and living quarters in a couple of adjacent buildings. The village was almost completely evacuated. Most of the
medical officers were living in a small bank. Four of us, all on the
night shift, lived together in a small room upstairs that seemed
very luxurious since the two windows were still intact (except for
one pane) and there was a small john next door. No running water but by carrying a couple of jerricans upstairs every day, we had
a practically ideal plumbing system. With no prospect of any immediate work, most of us trudged off through the rain to the clearing station a quarter of a mile down the road where they were
showing *Going My Way*. I enjoyed it so much that I hardly noticed that the tent was leaking like a sieve and that we were steadily
being soaked through. By the time we got back from the show, the

mess hall (if you could describe it as such) was serving Spam sandwiches and coffee, since we had had only one meal that day. So
what with the long convoy, sitting around talking and drinking
coffee, this, that, and one thing and another, it was quite late when
I turned in. Even when we were still on the night shift, we all tried
to do our snoozing at night whenever possible. Daylight sleeping
was unsatisfactory—there were always people coming in and out
of the house, if not the room, columns of tanks and trucks rum-
bling by the window, occasional shelling, and people shouting and
talking on the road. Somehow or other you became fairly well
accustomed to the noise of guns, but nearby extraneous noises
could be very disturbing to any stretch of uninterrupted sleeping.

The "final" offensive was well under way at this point in early
February. The 4th Armored Division moved through us in support of the 5th Infantry and it looked as if we were ready for the
major river crossings to move through the Siegfried Line and into
the Rhineland. The very fact that we had so few casualties was
testimony to the fact that the offensive was going well. We were
beginning to leapfrog the platoons so that one surgical team would
move up to a river crossing to be immediately available for any
casualties. This in itself indicated an optimistic outlook, because
placing a unit such as this in the front lines raises the possibility of
a counteroffensive that would overwhelm the outfit. But nobody
ever questioned the tactics and I think that having their doctors
and surgeons right with them gave the infantry responsible for
each river crossing a sense of security.

At the time of the Sur River crossing, there was a sudden influx
of patients in the advance platoon, catching us shorthanded with
two of our surgeons sick. After some twelve hours of steady work
I finally snatched a few minutes to rest, but had to go back and
scrub again shortly. I helped Mike do a really astounding case,
which took him four hours in all—right upper abdominal para-

median incision, resection of a lacerated first portion of the pylorus and duodenum, exploration of the common bile and pan-
creatic ducts, repair of lacerated pancreas, anticolic gastroenteros-
tomy, repair of bisected gall bladder and cholecystostomy (through
a stab incision in the flank) suture and packing with a concentrated plasma liver pack of a huge rent in the left lobe of the liver,
evacuation of a large retroperitoneal clot, repair of multiple small
bowel perforations, and finally closure. He did a magnificent job
on what looked like a hopeless situation. By the next day, the boy
was alive and doing well, with a good fighting chance. Even after
seven transfusions in the preop ward, he was still absolutely
pulseless when he hit the operating table and had to be resusci-
tated before we could open the abdomen.

February 10, 1945—at the Sur River

Thoughts of being a knight in shining armor seldom, if ever, occur
to the average soldier. The average American may have a certain
idealism, but he is not a fanatic; in the final analysis, the ordinary
infantry soldier is out in front fighting because he has to, and not
because he wants to. That doesn't in any way detract from any
glory or credit due to him, because the heroism he shows has
nothing to do with why he is where he is. I haven't thought much
about any of this angle of the war for the same reason, I guess, but
most of the stories of the war play it down. You always hate to be
an iconoclast and there is always the fear of discouraging or
disillusioning people until the war is actually over and it doesn't
matter anymore. Unfortunately for the human race, there is just
enough of that in the abstract that is appealing. The very thrill
accompanying anything that is dangerous, the color of flags and
marching men, the pride of race or nationality, primitive stirrings of
some animalistic instinct, the subconscious desire of the average
male to distinguish himself in what amounts to physical struggle,
histrionic urgings, patriotism, revenge, thousands of emotional,
irrational and instinctive reactions drive men into battle—so that it
has never disappeared as a national pastime. All of these factors

which drive nations to war and the individuals to enlist, disappear very quickly in the face of the reality of what war is and are replaced by a vague sense of comradeship which is primarily what keeps a man going—of course, added to these latter as a driving force, there is an instinctive hatred of whoever is in the opposing line trying to kill you. Nobody really knows the fundamental horror and brutality of war except the infantry man and he has no mock heroics about it. He fights because he has to and because of whatever personal pride or sense of duty drives him on; he lives a life which is so miserable because of the constant fear and unimaginable physical discomforts that it is hard to believe that human beings really go through it, and once out of it, he never wants to go back—at least I've never met one who does. However, you cannot very well play that up in the papers during a war so what you get is a story of a division advancing so many miles in so much time, rather than a picture of men shivering with cold, cramped with hunger, dirty, senseless, terrified by their own fear yet stumbling forward in what seems to them to be a hopelessly confused mangle of death and destruction.

The majority of men in uniform never experience any of this, or actually know the hopelessness of having life and death set against you continually as time drags on and on to some indefinite future. That is the lot of the infantry men and the rest of us would never have a very clear idea of what it is. Isolated instances of danger will never give it to you. That is nothing but high stakes gambling.

In addition to the routine work, which was nothing in itself, what took up much of my time was the fact that we were starting a small-scale research project on the problems of postoperative anurias in severe war wounds, which has been one of the main problems all over the ETO. We talked, argued, and discussed the problem for days, and finally, Mike managed to get a captain and several technicians from a medical laboratory (army) attached to us temporarily to carry out some of the laboratory determinations we wanted. I spent most of the day and night getting the whole thing organized. A plan of attack had to be made up and kept up on the postop wards for the cases to be studied, including a type-written routine for persons working in preop (what data to record, blood and urines to be sent to the lab, etc.), and certain determinations that must be recorded during the operations.

February 14, 1945—across the Sur River

I've been going since 10 A.M. this morning (yesterday morning) and it's now 4 A.M. tonight (or tomorrow) which actually makes it February 14th in time to wish you a Happy Valentine's Day—all very confusing, isn't it? We are still not through for the night and I have a short break now since, after finishing up one Kraut, we found there was no one immediately ready for the OR. The next case coming up can stand one more transfusion preoperatively. I am dead on my feet but I haven't had a chance until now to think about it. I should have written to you this afternoon when we had a half hour or so but Tag and Comerford from the 550th dropped by to see me on some jaunt they were on looking for supplies and before they left, we had started operating again—so the golden opportunity passed.

February 15, 1945

It was quite a shock to go outside after operating all night and see a blue sky, a bright sun and feel it was almost a warm breeze—almost too good to be true and certainly too good to last.

Perhaps I spoke a little too hastily of a quiet evening since a Kraut has just arrived with a bullet wound through his chest. For a time, at any rate, he was taken care of by oxygen, some plasma running but soon he was in shape, we had to open him up, clear out the clotted blood and leave in a water-sealed drainage tube. That didn't take too long so unless he was a premonition of things to come that evening, I was able to relax. Dave Dunn was still sick but Rafe was back on duty so that relieves some of the pressure in preop.

The offensive had been going extraordinarily well and we were spending almost more time moving than operating. On top of having two doctors sick and organizing the research project, our two shock teams were recalled to their units and only one sent in return—headed by a major who was pleasant enough but like all doctors on shock teams needed considerable orientation and indoctrination in the routine, the hustle, and the apparent confusion of the surgical hospital.

You can be damn sure that everyone over there made himself as comfortable as possible under his own particular set of circumstances and took full advantage of every available "luxury." Just because a few men were out on patrol on a bitter night and others were bundled up in foxholes, it didn't mean that every man in ETO went out and dug a comparable hole in which to sleep. If you had to be uncomfortable and miserable, it was just tough luck and you made damned sure you wouldn't be the next night. The man in the foxhole tonight may get indoors tomorrow night and he neither felt bitter tonight because other men were more comfortable nor guilty tomorrow if he managed to get inside and find a mattress while someone else was out in the cold. Everyone in the combat zones lived together and did their best for each other.

On February 27, the unit was off again. This all came up quite unexpectedly late in the morning so it was a furiously hectic day, closing the hospital, evacuating some of the patients and arranging for a holding company to take over the rest, packing up all the equipment, both hospital and individual, and doing the thousand and one things that moving such a unit entailed. I was glad to be off again, since our new setup might be very interesting from the last reports.

Unfortunately, we were scheduled to leave so late in the day that most of the trip was in darkness—which would have meant no pictures, little chance to see the route, and blackout driving, which was always somewhat unpleasant. But as it turned out, it was another example of the "Hurry up and wait" system with which one became familiar after a very short time in the army.

Eventually, we decided it might be practical to open up our bed-rolls and it was, since we didn't pull out until daylight. We were glad—it would have been a terrible anticlimax to have crossed the Kyll into Germany in complete blackout after waiting all these months. As we pulled out, the Luxembourgers gave the boys a bottle of champagne on the condition that it be drunk as they crossed the German frontier. It was quite an occasion, just as it is for every unit that moves into Germany for the first time.

The best way to describe the country itself is in the words of some correspondent who said, "What's happening here shouldn't happen to anyplace but Germany." Town after town was battered to a pulp, with roofless buildings, charred walls, masses of rubble cleaned off the main roads, dead cattle and horses in the fields—I didn't see one intact building. Even the roads and fields were scarred with the chaos and devastation of war. The fences were stripped, shredded, and still smoking slightly, heavy roadblocks smashed open with demolitions, pillboxes opened and gaping after they had been taken and blown up, farmlands turned up by the tracks of tanks and other vehicles and pitted with hundreds of shell craters. German litter was strewn everywhere—tanks, 88s, tracks, wheeled and horse-drawn vehicles, helmets, clothing, gas masks, and dead Krauts. It would be hard to say much about the Siegfried Line itself since from the roads you didn't get too clear a picture of the whole defensive setup. There were, of course, the inevitable pillboxes cleverly camouflaged and in some cases, actual houses built around them, wide anti-tank ditches and tank traps, thousands of individual covered foxholes and gun positions, lines of trenches, and the usual Kraut souvenirs—mines and booby traps everywhere. There was no question but it was a tough nut to crack.

For the first time in the history of the modern German state, the people were seeing war on their own soil, reaping the harvest of their glorification of war. The full realization of the ruin that their armies have wrought in every other country of Europe was being brought home to them tenfold. I doubted if they'd be quite as anxious again to extol the virtues of the "heroic" military life.

Obviously, all this destruction was necessary to break through the defenses, but it would have been nice to have found one building intact somewhere we could have used as a hospital. Since we didn't, we were completely set up in tents; which represented a lot of work for the men, because even a comparatively small mobile surgical unit needed a miniature tent city in which to operate. We set up on the slope of a bare knoll of a larger mountain that overlooked the countryside for miles around. It was spectacular at night when the artillery that ringed us let go in unison. As we sat watching the constant flashes extending as far as we could see up and down the line Mike shook his head and said, "It doesn't look as if there will be any buildings left intact ahead of us either." It was quite a spot from which to watch our own local war going on, and if you were tired enough, the noise didn't keep you awake. Looking out over the villages dotting the valleys was quite pretty since distance obliterated the pervasive ruin and destruction. When there was a lull in activity, the picture was one of tranquility and peace rather than a bloody shambles—very deceptive.

We saw few German people. Amost the entire civilian population had left the war zone, and those who stayed merely stared at us with blank, apathetic faces that exhibited no particular emotion except the awareness of defeat. If there was a house with any remaining civilians, there was invariably a white sheet hung from a flagpole or window, and that became a standard picture of the German towns. One young girl smiled a little and waved hesitantly, but no one responded. It didn't surprise me that there were so few people, but rather that there were any at all. I couldn't imagine where they could have been during the attack, but they had obviously been hiding out somewhere, in disobedience of the German government's blanket order for evacuation of all civilians ahead of the advancing Allied armies. Most of the towns and villages, however, were ghost towns and the only signs of life were stray dogs and hens wandering around the streets. Even the army installations avoided most of the towns because of the ruins and because of the ever-present possibilities of mines and booby traps. As we crossed the river Kyll a sign read, "You are entering Germany through the courtesy of the Fifth Infantry Division." From a pole at the end of the bridge was a miniature gallows, with a bust of Hitler hanging abjectly by the neck.

We opened up for admissions quickly, because we had moved forward into the area near the battalion aid stations and almost immediately after the first tents went up, casualties were coming in.

The Siegfried Line looked almost impregnable, but it wasn't. This phase of the war had absolutely maddening aspects. Those bastards had a habit of sitting safely behind the thick concrete walls of the pillboxes, firing until things looked a little discouraging, then coming out with their arms raised and trotting off to a prison camp. Giving a clear picture of life in those days would be impossible. It was chaotic. I hardly knew what day it was or even what *time* of day it was. Mike and I were on the same shift and we both faced the problem of traversing the distance from the OR to our sleeping quarters without falling asleep on the way.

Ernie Pyle probably reflected the thoughts of the average GI better than any or all of the other correspondents in the war. In one of his articles he asked what he could say to a man who came up to him and demanded, "Tell me, Mr. Pyle, just what is it that you don't like about war?" I heard him criticized because so much of his material supposedly detracted from the ideological picture of this war as a noble crusade. That may very well be—certainly, it was inevitable, unavoidable, and brutal.

Bridge over Rhine through windshield of jeep. Oppenheim, Germany, March 1945. *(left)*

Echternacht, Luxembourg (actually a little north of Bollendorf, Germany.) Bridge across the Sur River, February, 1945. *(below)*

Bridge across the Kyll
River, Echternacht,
Luxembourg, February,
1945 *(right)*

Dave Dunn, a colleague
in the 1stAuxilliary
Surgical unit, "celebrat-
ing" entry into Germany.
Note bottles (mouth and
pocket) and flowers
around left ear. *(below)*

February 22, 1945

If I made any over exuberant remarks recently (as I think I did) on the advantages of living in tents, allow me to retract them all. They were made under the hypnosis of a day of sunshine, blue skies, a warm breeze and pleasantly cool starlit night. Tonight, the situation in the Rhineland changed remarkably and having come off duty about an hour before, five of us were huddled shivering around a little tent stove with a howling wind threatening to bring a number of square feet of canvas down around our ears and a driving rain causing a small river to pour through one end of the tent and out the other. We thought we had been very foresighted in selecting this spot which is near the crest of a small mountain but there wasn't any astounding amount of drainage downhill as far as I was able to observe. The whole area seemed just as muddy after a few hours of rain as in the depths of the lowest valley we had been in to date. The ambulances and trucks, tanks and half tracks were churning up a sea of sticky mud.

March 3, 1945—Rhineland, Germany

It came over the radio that the 9th Army had reached the Rhine. In reading the latest *Time*, I came across an article which may not paint a brilliant, rosy picture of post-VE day prospects for troops in Europe but which, on the other hand, was eminently practical and sane. In the final analysis, it was not really discouraging or disheartening. This article was helpful because it was realistic enough so I could accept it but was not a bitterly discouraging summary such as that recent book, *U.S. Troops in Europe May Expect to Go Home Via the Suez and Tokyo.* I've always felt it would be a terrible blow to the boys in the Pacific if the majority of the troops in the ETO demobilized while the war in the Pacific was still unfinished. If, on the other hand, Britain and the United States (and possibly Russia—since it begins to look more and more as if she might join in against Japan) send whatever they have available as fast as possible against the Japs with the help of China and other nations, the final cleanup of Japan may come fairly soon after VE Day. I would much rather face a certain prospect of being part of a really total war against Japan for a short period from the probable prospect of being in the comparatively small groups struggling on interminably. The general outline as set forth in this article was by far the best I've seen prophetically and it offered the possibility of getting home fairly quickly after VE Day, having a short furlough or leave and remaining in the United States during a period of regrouping before starting off into the last final push and before coming home permanently. I don't know how all this will sound when it reaches you but it is meant to be encouraging.

This will be only a very quick note since I can do nothing else tonight. As described, we moved and opened up for admissions last night. I worked until after midnight, went to sleep, started in again early this morning and I've been going ever since until now—now being 4 A.M. so it's now into another day (March 4th) but it's too confusing to talk about beginning this work yesterday morning rather than this. I'm confused and sleepy enough as it is now and must hit the sack because I'll have to be up in a few hours to help clean up the cases still waiting for operation. Sorry about this letter but I'll try to do much better tomorrow.

The usual tactic in a fast-moving offensive is to leapfrog the surgical units so that one is always near the front line and is eventually joined by another. The third team may then leapfrog the other two and set up ahead, to be rejoined later by the rest of the unit. This type of operation can go on endlessly, with varying combinations depending on how fast and how successful the offensive is. I wasn't sure what would happen in a successful counteroffensive when obviously we would have to go on operating and taking care of the wounded, and so would end up behind German lines. Fortunately, except for the units in the line at the time of the Bulge, this did not happen very often. Anyway, we did reach the Rhine and the crossing.

After crossing the Kyll into Germany and through the Siegfried Line, we moved rapidly through Wolsfeld and Kaisersech and on to Wald Bockelheim. Before each river crossing, one of our auxiliary surgical units moved up as close as possible to the river, sometimes in a cellar or in a building, and set up quietly for action.

Road out of Wolsfeld, Germany (in Rhineland), March 1945.

After the units had jumped off to the river crossing, we were in a good position to pick up the first nontransportable casualties within a few minutes of their being wounded. This tactic led to the process of leapfrogging described above. We were in constant flux with sometimes one, sometimes two, and rarely three surgical teams static at one point but all of them functioning along the line of the division's advances. Collecting and holding companies took care of postop patients and transported them back as soon as possible.

Eventually we crossed the Moselle near its junction with the Rhine at Coblenz and drove south in to the Palatinate, and encircled the German troops in the Saar.

March 4, 1945—the Rhineland, Germany

This offensive into the Rhineland has really been a workout and it has cut into my free time and brought it down to next to nothing. Outside of that, I haven't a kick in the world. It's a wonderful job;

time races by so we hardly notice it passing. Therefore, I seem to be getting home sooner! Very logical reasoning, isn't it? I might take up where I left off two days ago when I scribbled off a rapid fire letter as the tents were being pulled down about my ears. About four minutes after I sealed the envelope, I piled into a truck and we took off in late afternoon which rapidly became a real twilight as we rolled away over the turned up, littered roads of this godforsaken countryside. All I could think of was how much material Albrecht Durer missed by living and painting in another age. If I ever saw a background which would have fitted any one of his paintings to perfection, it was a panorama of that night. The twilight itself enhanced the effect and in that atmosphere, it was an eerie spectacle presented by the ruined deserted villages, the road winding through small wooden patches where gnarled trees were stripped of anything but the trunk and heavier branches and by the constant flashes lighting up the darkening sky. Oddly enough, even the noise of war and the roar of the motors of the convoy didn't seem to dispel the ghostly silence of the charred and empty towns, a real setting for Gotterdammerung!

There was no silence noticeable, however, when we moved in and opened for admissions in complete darkness. This time we found one moderately intact (everything but the windows) building which was big enough for the hospital itself—preop, surgery, postop and lab. Living quarters were incidental at first since there was too much to do. By the time I did get to bed, I could have gone to sleep on a board of nails but someone had put up a squad tent so I just hauled my bedroll off the truck, found a little corner and fell asleep. As a matter of fact, I didn't unpack anything except a bedroll, washing and shaving equipment until tonight when the pressure of work eased somewhat. Yesterday, I was up around 8 A.M. and worked steadily for some 20 hours until 2 A.M. when I scribbled a note to you; then to sleep for about four hours. Started in again early this morning but as things are quieted down considerably, we were able to knock off around 10 o'clock tonight and let the night crew finish up alone. I was really tired at that point but Mike, Bill Higgins and I had a couple of drams together before turning in so I feel considerably improved—wonderful thing, liquor!

As I mentioned earlier, tonight was the first chance I had to

unpack anything. We even have a home of our own now with
Mike, Bill, Rafe, George and myself living in a squad tent which
was set up today. Electric lights have been strung from one of our
generators and a small stove set up in one corner, so compared
with the past two nights, this was real luxury—almost! A fair
number of civilians have already begun to trickle back to what is
left of their homes. Obviously, we had no contact with them but by
appearance, I wouldn't think that there was much thought about a
Fifth Column organized underground. They look like a thoroughly cowed and apathetic group—very little swagger or bluster
left now in either the prisoners or civilians. The former are
flocking back in ever increasing droves, all of them violently
anxious now to deny any interest or affiliation with the Nazi party.
And as for the SS—well, you would think that they had never
heard of that little group. Most of the SS, of course, discard the
insignia as fast as possible. I should guess that there were just
about as many Krauts who are now trying to get off the sinking
ship as there are Turks, Egyptians, Syrians, etc. who are trying to
climb on the bandwagon now that victory would seem imminent.

    I don't think you should worry about trying to make every letter
an epistolary miracle particularly when you are bogged down with
a bad cold. To me all your letters are wonderful. I don't imagine
that for every hour of our life together, the conversation would
sound to a hidden auditor either like a cocktail meeting of Dorothy
Parker and Ogden Nash or like a tryst between Heloise and
Abelard. Why should either of us expect every letter out of almost
500 to date to read like a sparkling literary gem to the public?

    In your last letter, I don't think you have too clear an idea yet of
a Field Auxiliary Unit when you expressed surprise that we had no
plumbing. We practically never have any sort of a setup with
running water and therefore have had to devise all sorts of make-
shift gadgets for preoperative scrubbing, etc. All water is brought
from an established engineer water point by truck in five gallon
cans. Therefore, you can see that we're not often exposed to the
luxury of civilized plumbing which is why I can sympathize with
the back to nature movement.

    Electricity for the operating room is provided by a portable
generator, which was hit at one point, by an 88 shell, putting us out
of action for a time . . . .

What with security censorship now imposed along practically the entire front, what is there to say about the news and the events of the war except you can feel, almost physically, the lift and drive everywhere. You might have little inkling of what was happening, but I think you would sense it in the faces of the men, in the way a jeep is driven, in the shower units with men freshly out of the line— I'm sure this must be pure fantasy and imagination but it really seems that way. Even a tank turning a sharp corner has a peculiar exuberance. War is particularly like a manic-depressive psychosis with periods of wild exhilaration of victory, liberation and enthusiasm alternating at times with a brutal, grinding, slogging, soul chilling, almost hopeless struggle when the infantry are building up positions, slowly grinding down defenses and paying bloodily for advances of a few yards which ultimately will result in the wild breakthroughs and screaming headlines of a later date. There is no question but what every combat soldier sweats out his chance of returning home on rotation and lives only for the day when he can climb on a westward bound ship. He hates the whole goddamn mess but, on the other hand, he would feel cheated and be thoroughly miserable I know to step off a transport in New York and pick up a paper announcing in huge black type that his division or army had broken through and was off on a wild dash with a mobile combat team. You can never completely understand war and the men involved are so full of such strange paradoxes that they can't understand it themselves.

The infectious spirit of a breakthrough must spread quickly to the enemy as well. It is hard to understand how Germans could commit themselves to a bitter last-ditch fight one day and then the next day be walking towards the American rear areas in groups, alone and unguarded in the initial stages of their trip because the advancing spearheads don't want to be bothered with them. They are really an extraordinarily degraded looking group and insofar as it is possible to generalize, they seem to be neither the brutal, human fanatic nor the weak-livered animal-like specimen who has neither a true will to fight and continue the war nor the moral or physical courage to do away with the small groups of ruthless leaders who have calmly dragged the German people into complete ruin as a nation and as individuals. As far as I'm concerned, the Germans have put on a revolting, degrading performance in both

victory and defeat. You would not think that the whining, snivel-
ling wretches who trudge back into the POW enclosures or who
are carried into the Clearing Stations at Field Hospitals are the
same bastards (at least some of them are) who swept along mouth-
ing the Nazi battlecry enthusiastically during von Rundstedt's
short lived triumph of the Bulge only a few weeks ago, and who, if
they did not actually participate in the incredible atrocities at
Malmédy and elsewhere, at least condoned them—which is every
bit as bad. I always feel that I am being carried away in any
conclusions by a temporary emotional reaction or am swept along
by a tide of racism but it's impossible to escape condemning the
whole people of Germany for one thing or another. How can you
feel any sympathy for the hundreds of thousands of men who now
protest they had never wanted to have anything to do with Hitler
or the Nazis? If they didn't . . . the inevitable question arises,
"Why the hell didn't they have the guts to get rid of the Nazis
themselves?" There may be very few who are sincere in this but
they are a group of spineless fools who will kill other men and
perhaps die themselves because someone orders them to do so but
who don't have the courage to face death by rebelling against their
leaders with these alleged convictions of theirs. I may be blinded
by being too close to the war but I can see no excuse or apology for
any one of them.

March 5, 1945, Rhineland, Germany

We cleaned up all the surgery by noon today and took off in two
shifts this afternoon to a shower unit several miles back from the
front—and it really felt good. I hate to think of how long I go
sometimes between any form of bathing but it doesn't seem to
make that much difference in this environment.

This unit is quite a center because of its location and officers
from division headquarters and from the regiments come and go
from the front lines and drop in at intervals, scattered and irregular,
depending on the situation, to pass the time and chat with whom-
ever happens to be free or off duty. It makes it very interesting
because you always pick up bits of information, stories and keep in
touch with the local and general situation better than any other
way. I started in this track because I was going to tell you an

episode which amused me and I want to preface it with a little information! Lt. Colonel Codman, one of the more regular visitors from the staff, dropped in this afternoon for the first time since we were at this location, looked around at our remarkably intact hospital building standing out in the midst of the surrounding ruins and rubble, and said, "My God, some artillery officer must have gotten hell for leaving this standing!" That's just about the situation too; as I've told you, we've been contemplating trying to bribe artillery spotters to leave at least one building intact whenever we're planning on moving into an area. Otherwise, it looks very much as if our hospital would be in tents all the way across Germany.

March 7, 1945, Rhineland, Germany

We are back in tents and are in the midst of celebrating this historic date (my birthday) with a bottle of Martel's cognac which I have been carrying around for a number of months in anticipation of some such emergency as this arising. As a matter of fact, I've been so busy since I got up this morning, I never thought of my birthday at all until we decided to call it a day around ten this evening and had the few remaining cases finished up by the night crew. At that point, it seemed like an excellent excuse for a little morale toping— unfortunately a bottle of brandy doesn't stretch very far in a group but it was pleasant while it lasted.

Last night, after I finished your letter, I turned in for a comfortable night's snooze and was buzzing away peacefully when I suddenly began to have odd nightmares about the Chinese water torture and awoke suddenly to find water dripping steadily down my face as well as all over bedroll and causing little rivulets to trickle down my back and into various cracks and crevices between the blankets. Fortunately, I was too damn sleepy and tired to do any more than reach out with one arm and stumble around for a raincoat which I pulled over my head and then fell promptly asleep again in this slightly soggy collection of wrappings. Last night's outburst was apparently the last straw for this aging tent since the same thing happened in various other places around the canvas so I was not the sole sufferer. There is certainly no way of drying out the bedroll so I guess we'll have to take it as is.

Even though I may gripe at times about the long droughts between mail from home, it still is amazing how the APO functions and gets mail to us even in the midst of a wild and rapid offensive movement. The only thing to do is make hay while the postal sun is shining. I know that the mail we write does not always get out under these circumstances for days on end so there may well be periods of drought on your end also.

This is the end of the birthday and please remember that today begins my annual five week period of superiority when I technically am a year older than you are, so I trust you will assume during that time a suitable attitude of docility and respect due to my advanced years and resulting advantages of wisdom and experience!

It is beginning to take more will power or self control than I can muster to combat this ever increasing optimism. We all give ourselves these long talks—"Remember what happened last Summer"—but they don't do too much good. Surrendering troops of the Wehrmacht are pouring along the roads to the extent that it almost looks like a German offensive and innumerable trucks are kept busy shuffling them to the rear—but there is still a way to go and I'd better stop this tack or I'll begin to think that I am taking a westward bound boat tomorrow. There is still a lot of work to be done.

There was an excellent article in *Life* on the "Odyssey of a Wounded American Soldier" which gave a good picture of a chain of medical evacuation in this war. . . . Unfortunately, it does not give a very good picture of the role of the mobile auxiliary surgical units in the field hospitals since . . . we were not actually in the direct line of evacuation but are sort of a siding where severe surgical emergencies can be operated on close to the line. The boy who was followed in pictures from the battalion aid station all the way to the states was wounded in both arms, and practically all extremity cases bypass us completely, unless they are in serious danger or have a chest, throat, or abdominal wound in addition to the extremity injuries. On an active period like this, we will do anywhere from 10-30 chest and abdominal cases (both American and German) in a given 24 hour period although obviously there are slack periods . . . .

To console us in our oblivion, however, we received a very nice letter from one of our cases of a couple of weeks back, who is now in England. He wrote that in two separate hospitals through which he passed, after we evacuated him, medical officers looked at his chart and said, "Oh yes, Mulligan—an excellent surgeon"—which he is. Then he went on to say that "All I heard everywhere from both patients and doctors was that the 1st Auxiliary surgical unit for the 30th field hospital was the best medic unit in the Third Army" (which I already knew anyway). He was a nice boy and is apparently doing very well. The letter pleased everyone just as unit flattery always will in the Army. It's quite permissible to brag slightly about your own unit—in fact, it's supposed to be a good idea psychologically and I guess it is. Anyway, it certainly is standard practice in good units. Not that anyone would give a damn if no one ever heard of them individually, but they get very irritated if they think that Stars and Stripes is not giving their division due credit for its part in what has been done.

March 9, 1945, Rhineland, Germany (near Coblenz)

It begins to look as if someone who spoke Russian would be a big asset to any unit soon. The squeeze play is really on but I haven't gotten in touch with the Cunard Line about a westward bound reservation. I must do that soon. There may be quite a rush this spring. It sounds as if I have been indulging a little wine, doesn't it? I am not quite as badly off as this may sound but I can't quite see how the Nazis can defer final judgment much longer. I remember last Summer very well and I am making no attempt whatsoever at any prophecies involving time and distance but there is not much room left for another stand even if they had another complete line. The sands are running out but as long as they are still trickling, this isn't over. I wonder if any German ever stands in the ruins of today and says to himself, "It didn't seem very important when it was Rotterdam, Warsaw, Belgrade or Kiev." As far as I'm concerned, now that the great part of the war is being fought within the borders of Germany, the so-called postwar education is already underway. I can't think of any better way to dispel the myth of the Herrenvolk than to have the German people see the khaki columns rolling through their towns and cities in an endless stream while this grey column straggles in the opposite direction but this time without the goose step glitter and boastfulness of yore—and perhaps proclamations announcing the rules and regulations for civilians signed by officers with names such as Rosenberg or Abrahamson would help too. I doubt very much if postwar lectures extolling the virtues of the dove of peace would have accomplished quite as much as the present practical demonstration (nearing completion I hope). There is another side to war than the one glorified in the German armies of the movies, *Sieg Westen,* et al., which showed nothing except the Germans marching with beautiful precision down the Champs Elysées, the hordes of German tanks pouring into Yugoslavia with practically no opposition or the crowds of paratroopers dropping in for their bloody picnic in defenseless Holland. With all the very exciting, dramatic and glorious new stories, I doubt if there was any German sitting comfortably in the theater watching the pompous antics of the unbeatable armies of supermen [who] never thought of the civilians of France, Belgium, Holland, Greece, Norway or who ever speculated a little uneasily on the old proverb, "There are two feet on which a shoe can be worn." Well, they liked war, they wanted it, they've preached that death on the battlefield was the most glorious fate that could befall man. They enjoyed the spectacle of an army parading by, they lived on the principle that "might makes right!" So all this should make them very happy—if not happy, at least educated. They were all exposed to education some 20 odd years ago but unfortunately at that time, we didn't offer any laboratory facilities with the course and anyone would admit that a science course is valueless without experiments to show the validity of the principles under discussion. This time, however, the full curriculum is offered—with a slight change in the ordinary educational curriculum since the laboratory demonstrations precede the lectures.

I used to think in the earlier days of the war when we were all full of bitter frustration at our helplessness and inability to stop the scourge that the inevitable revenge would be sweet, but now that it is well underway, I don't feel any particular spirit of revenge, no sensation of satisfaction except that which armies of free men have been able to accomplish in the four years (almost) since the first Nazi military triumphs began in 1939, and no particular deep hatred. On the other hand, there is no horror at the devastation that is Germany or any sympathy with her people. All I see is a spectacle of a completely ruined country, an impoverished people,

wounded and dead Germans and columns of grey clad prisoners
and react with a deep and unemotional realization of the eventual
inevitability of divine justice. There probably isn't a man who has
crossed the German border who hasn't thought of the dictum, "He
who lives by the sword, shall perish by the sword."

We have just been reading and commenting on an eye-witness
description of Cologne which I guess is the first completely
devastated city of major proportion which American troops have
yet seen—a huge addition of St. Lô and Cassino. It must be a
terrible sight. Even the description makes you think back to school
days and Coleridge's, "In Köln, a town of monks and bones, and
pavements fanged with murderous stones, of rags and hags and
hideous wenches; I counted two and seventy stenches—."

We settled into something of a lull today with nothing to do
except postop work; how long it will last, I don't know, but those
who are off duty are taking the opportunity to hold a joint celebration of March birthdays of which there are a large number among
the officers—over half a dozen I think—which is a large percentage
of our small group. With a bottle and a half of spirits and food
contributions from various packages, it sounds like a very small scale
affair—a couple of hoots all around and a little food, then off for a long
snooze, I hope—it doesn't look as if anything will turn up.

*March 10, 1945, Rhineland, Germany (crossing the Moselle near
Coblenz)*

I thought I'd tell you the story which amused me which I picked
up today in talking with some boys of an armored division which
spearheaded the Third Army's drive to the Rhine. As is common
in a rapid thrust like that, one village was completely bypassed and
the first the people saw of the war was a column of trucks loaded
with German prisoners of war rolling back to the rear. One Kraut
who had been on furlough to visit his family saw the trucks, left his
house and when one of the trucks slowed down at an intersection,
he climbed aboard, waved goodbye very happily to his family and
headed west—no more war for him, and I guess he decided not to
take any chances by wandering around loose in a grey uniform.

We passed another motley crew by the wayside today—the most
variegated collection of uniforms I've ever seen. They were
French, Yugoslavian, Russian and innumerable others which I

didn't recognize. The swift advance had liberated a prison camp
loaded with soldiers of all nationalities captured at some time in
the past by the Germans. They were gaunt, haggard and their
uniforms were in tatters but you would have to go a long way to see
a happier group of men. The worms are all turning everywhere
now. The slave laborers from all over Europe who had been
dragged off to Germany to work long, backbreaking hours for the
Reich and who had been liberated by the advance had been lining
the roads to hoot and jeer at the members of the master race who
were heading towards the POW enclosures. Not very sporting,
perhaps, but then the past five years haven't been played exactly
according to the rules of the Marquess of Queensbury, so you can
hardly blame them. In fact, I'm sure that if it were not for the
American troops around, their reactions would have been a little
more than vocal.

March 12, 1945, Palatinate, Germany

I thought perhaps that some time today I would be able to sit down
at more leisure and write you. What an illusion! Except for a quick
breakfast and one meal late tonight, I haven't had a minute all day.
We were up shortly after six A.M. discharged the patients we could,
left the rest in charge of the Holding Company, pulled down the
hospital, piled everything on to trucks and rode off through the
mud over the worst damn roads I have ever seen which were, of
course, jammed with advancing convoys everywhere. After a long
cold wet ride in open trucks, we pulled into a setup which was
pretty adequate and which I'll describe to you tomorrow, unpacked
and received our first case almost immediately—before we had
electricity for lights, x-ray, etc. connected from our generators . . . .
It is one helluva job for everyone to pack up a complete surgical
hospital, put it on wheels, move it some distance, unpack, set up
and be ready for admission—all in a little over 12 hours. Each
individual and enlisted man, however, knows exactly what is his
job in packing, unpacking and setting up and they are justly proud
of what they can accomplish. Without actually knowing, I would
be willing to hazard a guess that there isn't another field hospital
platoon which could touch this one.

Even in combat, we are offered opportunities for leave but that really holds limited appeal except for a little free time with warmth and light to stretch out to read and write and a chance for a hot shower or bath. . . . For instance, last Sunday, Mike wanted either Dave or me to go all the way back to Brussels in an effort to get some special adrenal extract we wanted. I almost said, "Go ahead Dave, I don't particularly care about the trip." Then I kicked myself mentally and decided that getting in that much of a rut was entirely too much of a good thing, so we flipped a coin to see who would go. He won the toss and I am a little ashamed to admit to myself that it was more a relief than a disappointment that I wasn't going. I would have enjoyed spending a couple of days there once I got started but like every other similar thing which has arisen in the past 17 months, it hardly seems worth the effort. Everything is fairly quiet today, but we did encounter one of the real tragedies of war which turned up when a little German girl, age 3, was brought in. She had been shot (accidentally, I suppose) by a German sniper and the bullet shattered several ribs, passed through her lung, then through the spinal cord (giving her a complete paralysis from the chest down). I rigged up a little oxygen tent for her out of one of our individual gas protective coverings and we are now waiting for her to get into some kind of shape for operation. We can fix her chest wound and do a laminectomy to expose the spinal cord but I'm afraid that, from the course of the bullet, as well as we can estimate it from the various x-rays, the cord itself will be completely transected. In that case, it will be impossible to do anything but close up. Neural tissue of brain and spinal cord will not regenerate as peripheral nerves will do. That, of course, condemns her to a life of a bedridden paralytic. A terrible tragedy . . . .All we can do is to do everything we can for her and keep her in as good a quality of life for as long as possible.

Somewhere along the line in my letters, I think I have forgotten to mention "Liza," the Red Cross girl who stays with the unit when we are not on the line—a bubbly enthusiastic girl who also does a fine job; writing letters, sending home the Purple Hearts, getting candy, cigarettes, reading material, etc. for the patients.

After the war, she married Mike, who commanded the unit, which was a fitting romance to close out our particular group.

March 14, 1945, Palatinate, Germany

I'm not sure what kind of letter I can get off tonight although I'll try
to write intermittently during the coming hours. With Dave away
in Brussels until tonight, we are a little shorthanded and we have all
been going in high gear since 7 this morning and it is now 2 A.M. I
decided long ago that under the extremely uncertain time elements
by which my life was run, it would be fatal to ever let a letter go
until the next day—particularly tomorrow since I'm leaving to
spend a few days with one of the other platoons. Tell you more
about that later. One of the Army consultants in anesthesiology is
arriving to give one man from each platoon a chance to learn some
technique from him. That's something I know little about so I am
delighted at the chance.

I have already wished you a happy anniversary since yesterday's
letter stretched into the morning hours. I certainly would hate to
think what would happen if I had neglected to mention the day and
the occasion. I think I sent you one of Dorothy Parker's little
poems which in part reads, "—a precept coined in Eden, and
existing yet, women and elephants never forget." Quite true.
Various little presents are enroute but the main one is still in
Luxembourg where some lovely nuns are still working on the
needlework which they began weeks ago when I met them and
which was designed particularly for you. That's the last item and
should be ready any day. The problem now is how to get back
there to pick up the finished projects. Well, I'll get it off sooner or
later.

At this point, I am temporarily detached to another platoon of
the hospital in order to learn some sophisticated details about
anesthesiology particularly regional block which I think could be
invaluable, almost indispensable to certain types of surgical
procedures. Since our units are widely separated, I crawled out of
bed only a few hours after I wrote the somewhat sleepy letter to
you last night, rolled up my bedroll, threw my shaving equipment,
clean socks and underwear into a bag and took off. It's a long trip
running parallel to a section of the front. It was a beautifully clear
almost warm day so it was very pleasant. Of course, the dirt roads
of this general area are incredibly bad and the sunshine of the past
two days has been enough to turn the layers of thick mud into a
fine powdery dust. Every time other vehicles, particularly tanks,

singly or as part of a convoy pass, we were sprayed with the dried
silt which works its way through the pores of any cloth so that I
was a spectacular sight when I arrived in late afternoon. It looked
as if I had been crawling through a coal mine. Fortunately, however, this platoon, in distinction to our own, is in really luxurious
quarters (an ex-German civilian hospital out in the country) and
there is heat, electricity, hot water (tap, bath, shower) for the asking
and plenty of room. It looks like a delightful place to spend a few
days. At any rate, I dumped my luggage in an empty corner,
headed down immediately for a shower room and after a lengthy
and vigorous scrubbing managed to discard my numerous, newly
acquired, layers of German topsoil and emerged a cleaner if not a
better man.

I took a short ride into Coblenz which we had bypassed when
we crossed the Moselle southwest of its junction with the Rhine.
With a historical tradition and a lovely setting, it must have been
beautiful once; now it was just a rubble heap, with large areas completely flattened and the remaining section nothing but mere shells
of buildings. The streets were only paths cut through masses of
debris. I didn't see how it would ever be possible to rebuild some
of these German cities. Merely clearing the rubble away would be
a task of enormous proportion and by itself would take years of
steady work. No matter how many photographs one saw, no one
could really envision the enormity of destruction unless he drove
by acre after acre of complete devastation and saw the same scene
repeated time and again—block after block of buildings reduced
to a heap of dust and stone, railroad yards battered so as to be
unrecognizable except for twisted, distorted fingers of iron rails
pointing up to the sky, huge bridges hanging crazily into rivers,
craters of every size from small, shallow mortar holes to large gul-
lies from heavy bombs everywhere and filled with stagnant water.
The worst of it was, no sign of life except for the convoys rum-
bling through the streets and occasionally an emaciated dog nos-

ing through the ruins. The whole picture was incredible. I honestly couldn't imagine that some of these places would ever be rebuilt, but rather would remain uninhabited, terrible reminders to the German people of what they had loosed on the world that had finally come back to them with a vengeance as a permanent monument to the criminal madness of their chosen leaders.

One of the officers found a set of negatives in one of the battered buildings, showing step by step the execution by hanging of a scrawny civilian by a squad of German soldiers. A really macabre set! I thought of making a set of prints but decided against it—too damn gruesome.

March 20—Rhineland and Palatinate

I'm now back at the homestead with my little intellectual leave completed. It was generally quiet. Mike and I just finished a really rapid fire job on a German—removal of right kidney and ascending colon, an ileocolostomy in just about an hour flat. We had to be fast because he was so damn near death. Mike did a beautiful job. That was the last case so I suggested that I cover here, while every one else went over to eat, figuring I could get off a quick note to you and be ready to turn in when they came back. Dave is finally back on his feet after his bout of hepatitis which we noticed in Luxembourg when he turned a fairly brilliant shade of yellow but wished to stay with the unit rather than going back to the hospital.

We have just moved in to quite an elaborate setup which consists of a small but very modern German hospital which had been carefully spared by our bombers and artillery since the rest of the town is a shambles. We moved the German patients and civilian staff to one side of the building and took over the other for ourselves so it's very luxurious—wards, operating rooms, white clothes, autoclaves, offices. In these days of rapid movement, however, nothing lasts for very long—tile floors today, tents tomorrow! Rags to riches and vice versa. You never know from one day to the next and it's hard to imagine now that there are any Germans left with which an Army could be formed. Of course, at any given time, I can see only a localized area of the front but they are streaming back by the thousands—demoralized, confused, cut up into small segments, pockets and groups and most of them delighted that they are prisoners and that, as far as they are concerned, the war is over.

That's not true of all of them, of course. I saw one of their high priced help yesterday—a Colonel who was sitting morosely in a jeep at a local POW enclosure, waiting to be sent to the rear. He was a real character of impressionism—a man in his 50's with a magnificent uniform complete to the high peaked cap, shaven head, weatherbeaten leathery skin, closely clipped mustache, monocle. Compared to our own divisional officers (majors and colonels), who ride with their men and wear practically indistinguishable uniforms, he formed a striking contrast between the German and the American system of both life and war. This was even more impressive if we looked at the Kraut enlisted men in the same enclosure—a filthy, lousy, unshaven and unshorn lot in dirty, unkempt, ill fitting, shabby uniforms. After a few feeble attempts to enforce respect for his rank which were either ignored or laughed at by the guards, he lapsed into a sullen immobile silence and his only reaction was to shrink a little further down into his beautifully tailored overcoat every time a passing GI stopped and snapped a picture.

Following the crossing of the Moselle southwest of its junction with the Rhine, on March 14, the advance units moved rapidly down the west bank of the Rhine in the Palatinate towards Mainz and Mannheim, enveloping the remaining German units in the Saar and Palatinate. Following the repulse of a German counterattack on March 19, the offensive continued through the rolling plains of the Palatinate.

By March 25, the campaign in the Palatinate was almost over. The Third Army had cleared the west bank of the Rhine from Coblenz to Mainz and were ready for the major river crossing at Oppenheim.

Meanwhile, in the northern sectors, Montgomery was preparing a crossing of the lower Rhine near Dusseldorf and Bradley's units of the First and Ninth armies had secured the west bank of the Rhine from Dusseldorf to Coblenz. The Saar section of the Siegfried Line, which had been under attack in November and December of 1944, had withstood a number of assaults until it had been outflanked and attacked from the rear. It was during the Saar Offensive that I had been transferred from the 550th AASA-AW battalion in that area to the 30th Field Hospital in Luxembourg, functioning primarily with the 5th Infantry and the 4th Armored divisions. Thus, over the space of about two months, I had completed a semicircle through Luxembourg, into Germany, and down the west bank of the Rhine to an area that had been the objective of Patton's offensive in the Saar many weeks before.

12

Crossing the Rhine

THE BATTLE FOR GERMANY

March 24–May 4, 1945

During the night of March 22-23, six battalions of the 5th Infantry Division slipped across the Rhine at Oppenheim, south of Mainz, and established a bridgehead. (One of the classic stories of the crossing tells how General Patton expressed his satisfaction by urinating in the Rhine as he crossed over the bridge.) They were ferried across in assault boats directed by navy coxswains who had been brought from the coast and had recently been moving the "Red Diamond" Division. Engineers rapidly threw a treadway bridge across the Rhine and other units of the Third Army followed under an extensive smoke screen.

The 1st Hospital Unit of the 30th Field Hospital crossed shortly after the bridge was completed and set up at Waldorf, on the outskirts of Frankfurt, which was captured on March 31. In Waldorf, we set up facilities in a German barracks to handle any wounds incurred during the establishment of the bridgehead and the subsequent expansion after the offensive into central Germany.

We had very little activity in the operating room. Casualties

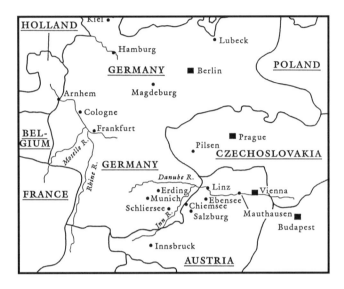

were minimal, amounting, I believe, to slightly more than twenty men killed and wounded.

From Waldorf, we proceeded through western Germany in a southeast direction towards Bavaria. We were then returned to Friedberg, where, consistent with Patton's policy, we were taken out of action for a rest period. There we remained from April 6 to 29, at which time we returned to active service, moved with combat units through Denkendorf, and crossed the Danube to Erding, near Munich. It was there that we received the final word of the German surrender on V-E Day.

March 23, 1945, Oppenheim to Waldorf (near Frankfurt) Germany

Life continues to be hectic. We had been on the road all day and pulled into a German city in the pitch black, bivouacked overnight in a school without unpacking anything and moved on in the morning. All I did was roll up in a couple of blankets and go to sleep in the corner. This morning we moved on a short distance and now have a magnificent spot at a German hospital in the country but unfortunately, I doubt if we will stay long. We have set

Frankfurt, Germany, March 1945

up one operating table with minimal equipment and have left
everything else on the trucks ready to roll.

Now for the Odyssey which makes a fantastic tale! As you know
from the news, divisions have been striking out in every direction,
cutting up the Germans who are facing the Third and Seventh
Armies into large and small pockets, slicing huge chunks out of
German held territory and smashing fast and hard through
scattered and disorganized resistance. This has really been a
picture of a nation built on the false framework of an artificial
philosophy coming apart at the seams. We are moving with one of
the divisions who are crisscrossing this huge pocket and I am sorry
that I won't be able to describe everything adequately. I don't
think any of us finally realized before what an incredible number of
people have been carried off to Germany by the Nazis for slave
labor. They (the Nazis) make any and all of the African slavers of
the 18th and 19th century look like pikers. The roads were filled
with screaming refugees from every nation in Europe still wearing
ragged but recognizable uniforms and national costumes which
they were wearing 2-4 years ago when they had suddenly been
impressed by the Gestapo or SS and shipped off to work 12-14
hours a day for the greater glory of the Third Reich. There were
Italians, Russians, Poles, French, Greeks, Czechs, Yugoslavs,

Belgians, Dutch who had been herded together in wire enclosures near factories or work projects for years, grinding away day after day under German supervisors, given miserable food and shelter, no clothing except what they brought with them and denied the use of German air raid shelters during the frequent bombings by our allied planes of the factories and rail centers. A beautiful picture of the New Order! There were soldiers, young boys, old men, women of every age and occasionally what would seem to be whole families on the move westward, I suppose towards repatriation centers. God only knows how long it will take to straighten out the mess of shattered lives, disintegrated families and the whole damn mélange which Hitler has brought about in Europe. Right now these people are nomadic wanderers, some of them listless, spiritless and without hope but there are others who still have courage in their souls to grin, laugh, make the international peace sign at the convoys roaring through. Battered carts and wagons were hauling their few belongings along the road to home and freedom.

The other side of the picture also presented interesting sidelights on the Third Reich. The Herrenvolk are already at work (by American orders) tearing down the roadblocks of huge logs and dirt which they had laboriously constructed before every village and hamlet and then lacked the courage to defend, as the English would have undoubtedly have done if the invasion threats of the Summer of 1940 had been carried out. The Volksturm has been an abysmal flop and so far, at least, there hasn't been a sign of guerilla resistance or sabotage behind the lines. The people seem awed and frightened by the collapse of their defenses but are submissive and almost comical in their efforts to carry out to the letter every one of the individual orders of the military government. Gone are the swastikas, the ubiquitous pictures of Hitler, the innumerable parades of arrogant goose-stepping youngsters and the hoarse screams of "Sieg Heil!" In their efforts at appeasement, most of the towns seem to have torn down every evidence of Naziism including the signs of renamed streets and squares (Herman Goehringstrasse, Adolph Hitler Platz, etc.). The streets which were so often and so characteristically hung with flags have changed in appearance. The flags are still there, but now they are white instead of the blood red of Naziism and over the main square of the larger cities, you might see the stars and stripes flying from the flagpole. What started this craze of white flags, I don't know but practically every home or building which is still inhabited has one hanging from a pole or window. All very much in the Germanic tradition but this time, thanks to the madness of their chosen leaders, the German people are not escaping the ravages of a war being fought on their own soil.

At intervals, we might encounter a pocket of resistance, usually by an SS unit, but the fighting was brief and decisive and ended with another unit being shipped to the rear under light guard.

You couldn't imagine without seeing for your self, the panorama of horror, destruction and devastation which is Germany today. For the first time, I had been able to see the results of the bombing of a vital center (Frankfurt)—huge railyards smashed into twisted wreckage, rails, cars and locomotives, flung around like toys. A plant which must have once extended over acres of land was so completely destroyed that the only thing which I could recognize was the side of a huge gas storage tank leaning at a crazy angle over the vast expanse of craters and rubble. It is really unbelievable and as I have said before, the real re-education of Germany is well underway right now. I doubt very much if the German people will be anxious for another war no matter how many Hitlers appear in history.

April 3, 1945—Near Nuremburg

A rather amazing and illuminating incident occurred today. An SS Lieutenant of the batch that the men have been rounding up around here lately, was being interrogated and was answering all questions willingly when he suddenly came in with a couple of his own. First of all, he wanted to know why he couldn't be sent to an American military hospital instead of a captured German hospital (he was slightly wounded and we had been sending Germans to their own hospitals, staffed and run by Germans under American guards and supervision, whenever possible) and then he wanted to know if, when his wound was healed, he would be able to join the American Army and go off to fight in the Pacific. All of this from a man who a short time before had been leading a last ditch gang of SS with the intention of ambushing or killing as many Americans

as possible. What the hell could you ever do with someone like
that? He was an officer and therefore it's logical to assume he had
some basic level of intelligence. Through the very efficient Nazi
system, he had been made a complete moron in everything but the
use of weapons and the employment of military tactics. These SS
troops are cold blooded, brutal and efficient killers but beyond
that, there is a complete blank. Their fanaticism is not patriotism
or defense of their homes. They do not really give a damn whether
or not all Germany is levelled to the ground, as long as someone is
around who would build up their animal ego by telling them that
they are elite troops. In that, they are completely blind. Even
when their division is outmaneuvered, cut to pieces and captured
by a numerically inferior unit of Americans, they can still tell
themselves that they are the best soldiers in the world since the
Nazi leaders have told them that for so long that they really believe
it, even when they are holding their hands over their heads and
screaming, "Kamerad."

There is nothing harder than trying to maintain an intelligent
perspective in war and it's getting harder all the time. You have
probably read by this time of the German hospitals which have
been overrun and where wounded American prisoners were found
lying in filthy bedding, untreated for days and weeks, with foul
festering wounds, covered if at all with a dirty rag. That may not
be true everywhere, but it's widespread enough so that everyone is
appalled and infuriated. It's particularly maddening when we treat
(and will undoubtedly go on doing so) German wounded with all
medical knowledge and equipment available. I no longer give a
damn whether any one of them lives or dies but I also know that
reaction will not influence my treatment of them. Most of us would
like to throw them out in the field to rot but we can't do it and
maintain any self respect. It will be wonderful someday to get out
of this whole atmosphere.

April 4, 1945—To Friedberg

My recent letters to you are just gathering dust. The mail clerk has
neither the time nor transportation in the midst of this continued
offensive to attempt to find our incoming mail or even take our
outgoing mail to an APO. There are invariably disadvantages to

sweeping drives such as are going on along the whole front right now, but no one is complaining, obviously. Much as I miss the mail and dislike K and C rations, all those details necessarily accompany rapid movement so, in that sense, they are things for which we should be grateful. Incidentally, I suppose we should also be grateful to Adolph for building all these beautiful Autobahns for us. I suspect they didn't have the Americans specifically in mind when he put the Todt organization to work on the roads but it certainly makes things easier than trying to move an Army over the cowpaths of Normandy or the wilderness trails of the western Rhineland. You can really wheel a convoy along, keeping tanks and trucks in the right lane and faster convoys towards the center. There is no longer any need to groan when we catch up with an armored or heavy ordinance unit on the highway, and MUD, the major headache, is a thing of the past, at least while we keep on the main drags.

During most of the fighting, we had served as a mobile surgical hospital unit to the troops of the Fifth Infantry (Red Diamond) Division and of the Fourth Armored Division, which often worked as a team, and I got to know many of them quite well. They were both superb units and Patton used them as spearheads for most of his major offensive action.

I had spent some time in Munich during the summer of 1938, and had hoped to be involved in its capture, but that was not to be. As I understood the situation at a later date, the first American light armored troops encountered Burgomeister and the city council (or whatever it is called) on the road with white flags ready to surrender the city. A unit of SS troops began firing, however, and the Americans drew back and awaited the arrival of heavy armor and artillery. It then took only a short time to enforce the surrender of the SS and the city was occupied. I did come to Munich during the Occupation, however, so I did not miss out entirely on the reminiscences and observation of the shattering damage that had been done to a once lovely city.

By April 6, 1945, we had reached Friedberg, where we were scheduled for a rest period out of active service. After spreading our personnel thinly across Germany, leaving small groups of postop cases behind with holding units, we finally regrouped in one spot. Along with other units being rested for the moment, we rolled into one of two moderate-sized adjoining towns (Friedberg and Bad Nauheim) off the Autobahn and moved the whole unit into a series of adjacent buildings. In a sort of dual celebration of our newfound freedom and relaxation and of Bill Higgins' birthday, we held a small party. In the afternoon, Dave and I went over to a nearby brewery and purchased a couple of kegs of light beer at a remarkably small outlay. (Wehrmacht, Nazi party, or government material, we *took*; any privately owned goods, we *bought*. Otherwise, it would have been just out-and-out looting.) The two small kegs got the one small party off to a good start with the help of a number of the infantry officers of the Fifth Division, with whom we had functioned for most of our action during the past few months and who were resting with us. It became moderately raucous.

We had been on the seven-day-week routine for so long that it was a little hard to get used to the idyllic life we were then living. We all had the feeling that there must be something we should be doing, and it took a little time for the realization that there wasn't to sink in. We went on to a two-meal-a-day schedule—a large breakfast at 9:30 A.M. and a large dinner at 5:00 P.M.—a system ideal for that type of life. We often supplemented this with midnight snacks made up of various food packages from home.

After breakfast and a haircut on our first day, I came back to our rooms, stretched out on a comfortable chair with a stack of books and magazines beside me, and read on and on for hours—*Annals of Surgery, New England Journal of Medicine, The New Yorker*, a book of sonnets, and *So Little Time*. To enhance our sense of leisure after our early dinner, we went over to an adjoining unit in the division for a movie, *Roughly Speaking*. After this came the crowning glory of the day—a steaming-hot tub bath. Altogether, a very hard day at the office!

The party of the previous night apparently went on for some time after Dave and I left, and several of our compatriots were not faring well during the early part of the day. Rafe was very funny in the dry way he had when he tied one on and barely made even the late breakfast before the kitchen ranges were closed off. He wandered in looking slightly hazy and Mike said, "Rafe, if your trousers didn't have such a sharp crease, I would have said that you probably slept in your clothes"—to which Rafe opened one eye and replied, "Just didn't move, that's all!" Bill Higgins and several others never even made breakfast. And that is about all there is to the postmortem on the case of the First Surgical Unit trip into the land of grain, grapes, and hops, except that the following night was very quiet and peaceful.

April 8, 1945—Friedberg, Germany

This has been about as much like a Sunday as any that I've spent on the continent to date. We had breakfast at 9:30 and then drove over to the next town about 4 kilometers away where an American chaplain had Mass in a local church at 11. It was a larger, moderately attractive church in what had been a German resort town— one of those spots centered around mineral springs and baths and consisting mainly of hotels but now turned into a German hospital center. Being what it is, it is classified as an open town and German doctors and the convalescing wounded are still wandering around by the hundreds. The soldiers (Americans) filled up the whole center of the church and the civilians took places at the side or stood at the rear since this was in fact a Mass said by an American chaplain for the troops. Except for some beautiful singing by some officer, there was nothing unusual about the Mass itself. We came out of the church into a magnificent warm sunny Spring day so a few of us decided to walk back through the country to our own town which looks fairly medieval as you approach it along a country road with its battlements and the towers of the old Schloss standing out against the background of a bright blue sky. Differing from some of the little walled towns of Germany, however, the illusion disappears when you approach a little closer and find the town itself is built up in a very squalid modernistic way. Very little evidence remains of what must have been a charming little feudal village once upon a time. The usual painted slogans, "Antwort der Nation," "Lieber Tot als Schlaf," etc., bring you back to reality very quickly as does the universal roadblock which we find at the entrance to every town. These blocks were built by the civilians under Nazi supervision and supposedly were to be defended by the Volksturm. Except in a few rare instances, however, the whole thing was a farce and the Volksturm either never appeared at all, or melted away quickly when the first American reconnaissance elements appeared. The Nazi party took the Volksturm very seriously and had everybody out for regular drills and military exercises but the Burghers themselves soon decided that discretion

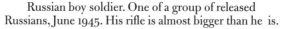

Russian boy soldier. One of a group of released
Russians, June 1945. His rifle is almost bigger than he is.

Four Russian officers. l-r: a captain (doctor),
a major (doctor), and two lieutenants. June 1945

was the better part of valor. The Werewolves was another one of
Goebbels' brilliant ideas which was a trashy comedy in itself. I
suppose there will be a few murders here and there, and some of
these fanatical Jugends will get themselves killed, but the German
people aren't built for anything like that. They have very much the
bandwagon attitude towards life. They'll scurry along enthusiastically behind any militaristic movement which promises to be a
success and which has the necessary accoutrements of shining
brass, dress uniforms, flags, bands, and a few pompous slogans
which make their chests swell out; once the bottom drops out of
the bandwagon and the brass becomes a little tarnished, they'll
retire to a thoroughly peaceful domestic career—until the next
demagogue appears. Where a few years ago, I was maddened and
infuriated by their rampant militarism, their brutality and cruelty
and by their insufferable egotism, now I'm just disgusted by the
sham hypocrisy and stupidity of the whole performance. Anyway,
it was a beautiful day no matter what country you were in and a
pleasant walk.

I should mention that on the way back to our billets on Sunday,
we were passing through a large completely devastated German

city when we suddenly came across a remarkable cortège—a large wagon, pulled along by several men and heaped high with all pieces of luggage. That in itself is an extremely common sight. What added color to this particular wagon was that it was topped off by a large Russian flag, was surrounded by a singing, dancing group of people of all ages and sex and perched precariously on top of the pile of swaying baggage was a very happy and very Slavic looking man playing a Balalaika. The party was obviously a group of Russian prisoners who had been recently freed and were on their way somewhere. They cheered and shouted vigorously when they saw us. When they noticed that I was taking their picture, the wagon came to a screeching halt and, to a man, they all turned around to face the camera, grinning, waving and giving either the V sign or the clenched fist. The whole scene, set against the background of a devastated city and the glum looking German civilians passing by, should make quite a picture.

April 12, 1945—Friedberg, Germany

These are fantastic days! The war goes on but thank God, it is not the war which the infantry sweated out last Fall and Winter. I suppose you could pick today or any other day about this particular time in history and say that Germany has been completely and shatteringly defeated and you would be correct to all intents and purposes. There is no longer any semblance of a continuous line defending Germany and as one radio commentator pointed out, the allied armies were attacking in all directions at once—eastward towards the junction with the Russians, southward into Bavaria, northward towards Bremen, Emden and the North Sea and westward into the Ruhr pocket and into Holland. Now it's a matter of a fight to the finish with the remnants of the once powerful Nazi state and party who apparently have no longer any idea in mind but to drag as many Germans as possible down with them in the final death throes. As more and more wild orders and proclamations come through from Nazi headquarters—threats of death for any German who doesn't fight to the end in this village or town, the "trial" which condemned in absentia the German general who surrendered at Koenigsberg and threatened reprisals against his family, the reported murder of over 1000 officers in the Luftwaffe

for defeatism, the hasty formation into battalions under the whip of
SS troops, of clerks and technicians; "limited service personnel"
(the average life of one of these battalions between formation and
complete destruction and disposal by surrender or desertion in
combat has been figured at two days), the attempts at a "scorched
earth" policy (which wouldn't interfere with the allied armies in
the slightest sense since we do not live off the land in any way, but
would serve to increase remarkably the misery of the German
people), and the evidence that scattered suicidal last stands would
be made—this whole thing takes on more and more the semblance
of a schizophrenic dream. Apparently in their fury of frustration
and defeat, Hitler, Himmler, Goebbels and a few top Nazis have
determined to kill and kill until they are finally run to earth. With
the already crushing superiority of the Allies increasing hourly and
as more and more German airfields, war industries, supply dumps,
natural resources and military divisions are overwhelmed and
captured, there will be mainly Germans who are condemned to
death in the weeks to come but that makes no difference to the
Nazis. As long as they can't control Germany, they seem to want to
insure there will be nothing for any of the potential German liberal
groups to build upon some day. On a personal guess, I would say
that over 95% of the Germans are so completely crushed by now
that they want nothing more than peace at any price. The complete and brutal control of the country by the top Nazis and the
frighteningly efficient and terroristic organization of the people
under the SS and Gestapo which was a source of German military
power in the course of their initial swift victories is now a weight
dragging the nation deeper and deeper into a morass of famine,
destruction and death. By their debasement of all the principles of
humanitarianism and Christianity and by accepting and condoning
the Nazi myths of Herrenvolk, anti-Semitism, "Furor Teutonicus"
and the New Order, the German people so insulated themselves
that now they cannot free themselves even to escape death. With
the murders of the Dutch at Rotterdam, the Czechs at Lidici, the
Americans at Malmedy, the Jews and the Poles in the ghettos of
Warsaw and the slaughter of millions of men, women and children
of all nationalities and in thousands of places over Europe hanging
over them, they can do nothing but cringe hopelessly, driven
against the onrushing weight of the Allies by the dwindling but

efficient ranks of SS troopers and cower under the tons of bombs concentrating on an ever decreasing area—all because over the past decade they sold their souls to Hitler and willingly or not, must go down with him. At this point, I neither waste sympathy on them nor do I wish them any further suffering but I'm sorry that some Americans, English, Russians and other races will still die in Europe during the coming weeks. I suppose in the larger sense of the war, a casualty now is no different than one at Dunkirk or Normandy but it seems particularly sad and ironic to hear, as we all have in the past few weeks, of the death of friends, acquaintances, classmates, etc. As you probably know, we can never mention names of any casualties until well after the relatives have been notified as we never know just when notification has been received. It's better just to write nothing.

While writing this letter and just at the end of the last paragraph, the sad news came to us over the radio that President Roosevelt had just died. Everyone stopped what they were doing, those . . . who had turned in early got up again and we all sat around the radio waiting for any further information and speculating on just what it would mean. I feel like all of us here that we've lost a great American. While many have disagreed with him at various points in his long career of statesmanship, it would be hard to deny that during this struggle, he has been a symbol to the world of hope, of freedom and of everything for which America stands and for which her armies are fighting. I am sorry he could not have lived to see the final victory and to participate in the foundations of the peace. At this stage, I doubt if his death will affect the conduct of military operations in the slightest and how it will affect immediate postwar plans, I don't know, but if you believe in the fundamental tenets of democracy, you have to accept the premise that no man is indispensable and that our government does not formulate principles at the will of one man but only directs, reflects and coordinates the varied strata of thought in the nation. I will be most interested to hear the reactions at home.

April 13, 1945—Friedberg, Germany

More mail came in today and I was highly amused by one of your letters in which you drew the association of two great dates in

history—your husband's birthday and the capturing of the
Remagen Bridge! Makes it very handy for future generations of
school children, don't you think? Anyway, the optimism in that
letter was certainly justified. Just how costly the other crossings
would have been without the Remagen Bridgehead, no one will
ever know, but there is no question but what that took the pressure
off the other later crossings to a great extent. Even without that,
however, I do not think that the Rhine would have been the bloody
barrier which we all imagined because the Third Army crossings,
at least (the only ones I know much about), were beautifully
planned and executed, combined operations (Army and Navy) and
went like clockwork, while the Germans were still disorganized
from the crushing defeats west of the Rhine at the time of the
demolition of the Siegfried Line. Even at that, the speed surprised
me a little for we were naturally a little wary. Since the boys of the
division which we had been with have established every major
Third Army bridgehead across France, Luxembourg and Germany, we had a pretty good idea from them of just how rough a
river crossing can be—particularly in the teeth of the Siegfried Line
as in February and early March. The Fifth Division (Red Diamond) have gotten a good share of the publicity, I guess, but they
are a damn good outfit and I'm not sure that the amount of credit
which is due them for the success of the Third Army's operations
is very widely known. It is very much like football with the
Infantry functioning as the line and the armored divisions as the
backfield—although occasionally the infantry are put on wheels,
and do a little running with the ball themselves.

    This would seem to be a night when I'm full of unoriginal, pre-
digested thoughts but I want to pass on one more and then I'll quit.
Robert Capa (of *Life*) who jumped with the 17th Airborne Division
across the Rhine had his initial impressions printed by *Time*
magazine—a series of disjointed observations made on his return
to the Paris apartment of *Time* magazine's chief military correspondent in the ETO. The one which amused me was this—"and
much as I hate to make primitive statements, the Germans are the
meanest bastards. They are the meanest during an operation and
afterward. They all have a cousin in Philadelphia. That is what I
like about the French. They do not have cousins in Philadelphia."

Towards the end of our stay in Friedberg, our commanding officer, Mike Mulligan, arrived back from a trip to headquarters full of descriptions and tales of one of the German concentration camps that had been overrun by the Third Army. While there had been recent articles along a similar vein, his description was fascinating. What Mike told us was a preface to our later experience at Ebensee. This particular camp was large, holding about thirty thousand political prisoners, some of whom were German and the rest of every possible European nationality. They were jammed into barracks that were nothing more than a roof over tiers of bunks so arranged that there was just enough room between two tiers for a man to crawl in. They were given no covering, even during the winter, and managed to survive without freezing to death only because they were packed in so tightly that they kept each other warm—or at least above the freezing point. One meal a day was provided for them, consisting of two slices of bread and a bowl of soup, the latter being only water that had been boiled for a few minutes with potato peelings or cabbage leaves. The Nazis saw to it that they were kept busy. They forced them to build a factory in which they were made to work all day every day, making and assembling parts of light artillery guns—under close supervision, of course.

The Nazis in charge established a system of credits and demerits according to how they thought each prisoner was working. If they considered that a man was not producing satisfactorily in the factory, he was given twenty-five lashes and sent back to work. The second time one of the guards singled him out for any reason as unsatisfactory, he was turned loose *barefoot* in an enclosure that had been prepared with a close crop of hard stubble in the company of several vicious, wild, and half-starved dogs. If he survived this, he went back to work again. The third time he incurred the displeasure of the superrace, he was taken into a small room, beaten with clubs, and left hanging from the ceiling by a meathook under the jaw for the enlightenment of those who followed him into the chamber. When he died, he was removed to one of the usual efficient crematoria, where other prisoners were forced to place their comrades' bodies on a conveyor belt or shovel them directly into the furnace.

For doing good work in the factory, a prisoner could obtain one credit a week, which he could use to enjoy the weekly entertainment provided by the Germans—"entertainment" in the form of women imported into the camp for this purpose, who were the wives, daughters, and sisters of men in other similar camps. The implication to the men at this camp, of course, was that the women in their families were being forced into similar performances elsewhere. The whole scheme constituted a peculiarly diabolical form of mental torture for the men who knew that their families were prisoners of the Nazis. Whether or not any of the prisoners actually lay with these women or the families of other prisoners elsewhere, I couldn't say, but I suppose a few of them had been sufficiently brutalized to commit officially sanctioned rape.

Prison officials had been making plans to gas the total population of the camp, but the unexpectedly swift advance of the American columns interrupted this little project and the guards were either killed, captured, or fled in civilian clothes. They managed to murder some of the prisoners, however, for a few score were found stacked up with pistol bullets through their heads. The Americans had no time to round up the escaped guards, so they armed some of the stronger prisoners, who scoured the surrounding countryside for the guards, whom they knew by sight only too well. The first night, they dragged in 150 of the miserable whining bastards, and smaller numbers during the succeeding nights. They became prisoners in their own camp, guarded by released Russian prisoners—a very satisfactory end to the story.

The Nazi doctor at the camp, a true and humane scientist, inoculated twenty-five prisoners with virulent bugs of typhus in order to make some antiserum from their blood. All but one died from raging typhus fever. This kindly physician escaped with the guards but was rounded up with the others by the armed prisoners. Unfortunately, he was killed in the process of being captured, undoubtedly by the "accidental" discharge of some of the prisoners' guns.

A whole American evacuation hospital was assigned to treating the surviving prisoners, but the results of disease, malnutrition, tortures, and filth were so horrible that the American nurses were left behind and not allowed to see them initially. Apparently it was a frightful spectacle.

Some American commanders made whole German populations from surrounding towns and villages go on tours of the prison camps to demonstrate what Naziism meant to the world. At the conclusion of one of the tours, the mayor of one of the villages hanged himself.

Having seen men at war, I could imagine almost anything taking place in the heat of battle—but how any human without the provocation of the intense emotional surge and the wild impulses and rage of actual combat could sink so low as to carry out these cold-blooded tortures and murders was impossible for me to understand. It wasn't a question of isolated cases, but a universal scheme of torture, killings, and brutality, involving thousands and probably millions of Germans directly. Yet when they are wounded or captured, they all "have a cousin in Philadelphia," as Capa wrote, and as each city or town is taken, the universal wail is "There's no one here but us anti-Nazis" or "It must have been two other guys." You would swear that there had never been a Nazi in Germany if you watched or listened to prisoners and the Germans behind the lines. A *few* of them probably were and always had been sincere anti-Nazis, but how could anyone tell? That was not our job , thank

God—we were there to defeat the German army, to stay away from any contact with the people, and to police the country until we were finally shipped home or elsewhere in the Pacific.

This episode of April 20, 1945 was the first direct description we had heard of concentration camps. Some articles had appeared in the press, but obviously our units had neither encountered nor even heard very much about such camps, and no one understood how they related to the Holocaust and whether Jews and "political" prisoners were confined together or separately. I was never sure which particular camp Mulligan saw, but I believe that it was Belsen, since the British had captured Belsen shortly before this. Whatever its name, the camp was certainly similar in description to Ebensee, which we liberated later.

Over the past several decades, questions have been raised continuously as to how much was known outside of Germany—and even inside Germany—about the existence of the camps. Certainly, aside from a few brief preceding articles or radio broadcasts, until this particular recountal by Mike I had absolutely no knowledge of the degree of this particular and peculiar form of atrocity, and I am still unsure of how much members of our and other Allied governments knew about the facts.

I am almost ashamed to recount how high we were living at that point. We obtained some more captured Wehrmacht stock, so with that and a little of the lemon powder that came in the rations, we had some excellent sidecars before dinner. The hors d'oeuvres that were laid out to go with the cocktails were not the usual fare of the ETO—anchovies, shrimp, smoked oysters, pickled onions, sardines, lobster meat, served with crackers and various dressings (mayonnaise, horseradish), all from packages sent from home. After dinner, there was a choice of cognac—Remy-Martin, Martel, Salignac with a dash of Cointreau to smooth it out a little. Sounds magnificent? It was! Our predinner gatherings almost took away our appetites—but not quite. It would have taken a remarkable amount of hors d'oeuvres to destroy my appetite when I was only eating two meals a day. (We usually managed to scrape up a midnight lunch of sorts, so we were hardly starving.)

A December *Time* magazine reached us containing an interesting story about a medic in the Fifth Infantry Division, entitled "Foxhole Surgeon." Even though *Time's* anatomy was somewhat inaccurate and the operation was not exactly "risky," the boy showed a startling presence of mind and a remarkable courage of his conviction that a tracheostomy was the correct thing to do. We always describe the how and why of the procedures to aid men in lectures, but I never expected anyone to actually crash through and do one, and thereby save a life. A damn good job! He came back to our unit and was tidied up so that Dave Dunn got a byline in the article.

On Thursday night, April 26, word came through that our life of luxury and ease was over. After eating breakfast with my eyes still shut, we pulled out at about 5:30 A.M. My eyes had opened to two narrow slits at that time but it doesn't take very long for them to open the rest of the way when you are crammed into a jeep with two other officers and a driver plus a load of personal baggage—it made a seat on the subway at rush hour look like a drawing-room reservation. By the time we reached our destination, Denkendorf, a little before midnight, I was sure I would never be able to straighten up again and my tail felt as if it were worn down to the bone. The scenery in northern Bavaria was much the same as elsewhere—intact villages and suddenly several in a row piled into rubble where there had apparently been some resistance. The army didn't put up with much nonsense in the way of sniping anymore. Rather than attempting to dig out small individual groups by the slow and costly process of clearing streets and houses one by one, the advance units just rolled along until they met some resistance, at which point they pulled back, waited for heavier armaments to come up, and then battered the town to the ground with tanks and artillery and swept on through it. This practice undoubtedly discouraged a lot of Germans from shooting men in the back as they went through a town and then disappearing or changing into civilian clothes, which was a pattern we encountered from time to time, mainly in the offensive.

The larger towns and cities all presented a familiar pattern resulting from the repeated bombings of factories and railyards at strategic points. After a time, each trip was like a merry-go-round with the same themes repeated over and over again—the same dirty little intact villages, the same battered points of resistance, the same bombed-out cities, the same happy released prisoners (dispossessed persons, as the army called them), dazed civilians, truckloads of German prisoners, the same roadblocks, burned vehicles littering the route, and dead horses in the ditches. We ultimately bypassed Munich.

While this type of warfare was directed against disorganized opposition, casualties were relatively minimal as compared to Omaha Beach, the breakthrough in Normandy, the Bulge, and the drive through the Siegfried Line into Germany. Nonetheless, when no one knew with any degree of certainty where the lines were, what areas were still held by the Germans, and where our own advance units were at any given moment, there were unpredictable risks. For example, one of our mobile surgical units was cut off and captured and lost several officers and men in the fracas. The survivors were recaptured within a day or two.

Events piled one on another during the latter days of April. Hitler had delivered his "scorched earth" proclamation from his bunker in Berlin, ranting and raving that "if the war is lost, the nation will also perish" and that "those who will remain after the battle are only the inferior ones, for the good have been killed."

Outside of Salzburg, en route towards Munich. Shell bursts ahead

On April 30, two days after Mussolini was captured and executed, he committed suicide.

In the ground offensives, the Americans and British awaited the Russians in northern and central Germany on the line of the Elbe. The Third Army moved into Pilsen in Czechoslovakia and down the Danube towards a meeting at Linz with the Russians who had captured Vienna on April 13. Obviously, the end was near!

We were also heading in a southeasterly direction through Bavaria towards the Danube, which we crossed at a snail's pace on April 29. The roads to the Danube were jammed with armored and infantry divisions moving as rapidly as possible to meet the Russians and convoys of prisoners were being brought to the rear, so there were inevitably bottlenecks at bridges that had been demolished and rebuilt by the engineers. With everything on the

Capture of Pilsen, Czechoslovakia

move, it was hard to make contact, but near the end of our trip we finally got some information from higher headquarters. By that time, it was pitch black and we crawled on through a wild country of narrow roads and treadway pontoon bridges for several more hours until we finally hit the town of Erding, where we were to await orders for our new assignments, this time to the 3rd Armored Cavalry Division. It was almost midnight and everyone was tired, so we were merely handed out a couple of blankets apiece and rolled up on the floor of a schoolhouse, scattered through various rooms. This auxiliary surgical group had been somewhat dismembered, so there were only five officers and an indeterminate number of enlisted men to carry out whatever function we would be assigned under the aegis of the armored cavalry division. Despite being hungry (one chocolate bar since breakfast at 5:00 A.M.) and wet (it had drizzled steadily since late afternoon), we all promptly fell asleep. The next day we fell out of bed, or rather out of our blankets, and moved off a short distance to a field on the outskirts of town to set up tents—all in thoroughly miserable weather. It is invariably true that whenever you have a comfortable setup, the sun shines all the time, but as soon as you begin to move frequently and live out of sleeping bags, you never see the damn sun for days on end. The rear elements of our unit finally caught up with us; we got everything unpacked and just as it looked as if we could relax slightly, a call came in from headquarters to send a surgical team to another field hospital about fifteen miles away that was overburdened with work. Mike sent Gish, Higgins, and me and two enlisted men from his team. When we arrived, we found that Barney Sinner (who had been with us temporarily in Luxembourg) was in charge of the team we were supposed to relieve—and he really needed relief. There was only one team and Barney had been operating steadily for over twenty-four hours and was exhausted. Needless to say, he was delighted to see us and demonstrated it by falling into bed while we started to work. By the time we had cleaned up all the remaining cases, Barney was back on his feet again after a long snooze and we relaxed with several hoots out of a special bottle of VAT 69 that he had been saving. He wasn't too happy in his present setup and wished that he were back with us. It didn't take very many hours there to convince me that I was damn lucky to be in my particular unit—as if I hadn't known it before. If I had to be overseas, I couldn't have asked to be with a better group.

It was a pleasant surprise to turn on the radio that night and find out how fast everything was moving everywhere. Of course, we had heard the usual rumors, but you don't have to be in the army long before you discount every damn one of them. Anyway, as long as you could see and hear firing and were working on men who had been hit with everything from bullets to shrapnel, it didn't take a genius to figure out that there wasn't much behind a rumor that Germany had surrendered unconditionally after an initial attempt to split the Allies. I suppose when it was so obviously near the end of the war, it was natural for everyone to jump to conclusions.

If ever a nation thoroughly degraded itself in defeat, Germany was outdoing itself this time. The Wehrmacht, or rather the SS, in retreat was probably worse than it had ever been in conquest, the main difference being that it was now Germans who were bearing the brunt of their own army. The SS troops in their flight to nowhere were pillaging, looting, and stealing from the very people whom they were theoretically defending—food, horses, clothing, wine, liquor, beer, anything that happened to meet their eye. Their senseless demolitions were wrecking their own country and people without stemming the advance for more than a few hours at the most. Sniping at trained reconnaissance units accomplished nothing beyond bringing about the complete destruction of the town from which the firing came. Townspeople frequently gave away the positions of the SS troops to save their homes from being battered by artillery, and one lieutenant told me that he and his men had a job on their hands to prevent a lynching. An SS captain and a few of his men had holed up on a farm and refused the pleading of the people to come out and surrender. The lieutenant had no intention of sending his men on a frontal attack, so they set fire to the buildings with tracers, at which point the SS trotted out with their hands over their heads The buildings, of course, burned to the ground. The civilians wanted to hang their own soldiers on the spot. Needless to say, they didn't, but it might not have been such a bad idea.

After three solid days of K-rations or less, even the C-rations which we had for dinner looked good—at least they were hot. When you're hungry enough you lose any semblance of ordinary taste.

While we had comparatively little surgery compared to the heavy casualties in Normandy, at the Bulge, and on the Rhine, the process of packing, moving, and setting up again was more than enough to keep everyone busy. We were in a pretty good location in Erding in a building that could house an entire functioning part of the surgical unit and in several scattered buildings that were occupied by personnel and by division troops. Not more than a few days earlier, this had been the nucleus of a large German camp—in fact, the Germans were still occupying the camp that morning and when we rode in that afternoon, hundreds of prisoners were being marched out. These prisoners became our problem; there seemed to be an endless stream going back to the rear areas all the time. I would swear that even over my limited route of travel, I must have passed the whole damn Wehrmacht at least once—but it was obvious that I had seen only a small percentage of the total prisoner-of-war bag. When you add to this the problems presented by the release of thousands of Allied prisoners and by the liberation of millions of slave laborers, you could see that the army had more on its hands than just fighting the Germans.

The released workers and prisoners made things difficult because their bitter hatred of the Germans was hard to control. Few of them had the slightest compunctions about taking from the Germans anything they needed in the way of food or clothing. Occasionally, they went to even greater lengths, particularly with the SS. A young rifleman told me that he and a friend had captured three SS men and as they were taking them back to battalion headquarters, they were suddenly jumped by a crowd of Russians and Poles, who took away their guns, shot the SS troopers, and then politely handed back the weapons. They had cherished the thought of revenge for four or five brutal years, I suppose. Now when the opportunity presented itself, it was not surprising that a number of them would take advantage of it. Knowing what most of them had been through, you couldn't blame them, although you still had to control them and establish order. The MPs had to forcibly restrain large groups who were heading for German towns with the avowed intention of burning them to the ground.

On May 2, we were still in Erding and I had just spent three hours in what to me was a fascinating conversation. I had just finished up my shift in the OR, had a late supper, and then came back to an empty preop ward to write where there was some light and heat. I hadn't even started when a ragged-looking soldier came in carrying a pack made of an old army shirt and asked if we could put him up for the night. It turned out that he was a staff sergeant in the air corps who had been a prisoner for over a year and had just escaped and gotten back into American lines. Except for a cold and tonsillitis, he was in fairly good shape, and he sat down and talked about his experiences endlessly.

It all started when the Fortress in which he was a gunner was shot down over Berlin. He bailed out and landed on the roof of a house on the outskirts of the city. A mob of civilians captured him. They beat him up pretty badly. One or two jabbed at him with pitchforks and finally they stood him up against a wall while several of them with guns of various sorts screamed at him and threatened. He thought they were going to kill him but for some reason or other they didn't and eventually he was taken to a nearby airfield where several other airmen had been taken. There they were all lined up while the Luftwaffe officers stormed and bellowed at them in German, stopping every so often to beat them about the heads with a heavy Mae West life jacket or belt. The sergeant ended up in a Stalag near Danzig, where he remained for some nine months. They were treated harshly and at times brutally, but the conditions were never like those in the concentration and extermination camps we had been hearing about where the Germans kept their so-called "political" prisoners and Jews. He escaped twice but both times was recaptured by civilians.

He told us various stories of life in a Stalag, including one about an American airman of German birth who collaborated with the prison authorities and among other things tipped them off to several escape plots before the other prisoners discovered him. The prisoners eased their lot somewhat by bribing the guards. This boy said, "They'd sell their souls for cigarettes or soap, and a good portion of the Red Cross packages provided them with extra food, warm clothes, tobacco, soap, etc." In January, the Germans decided to move the prisoners because of the approach of the Russians and started marching them west. When the rapid Allied offensive in the west forced them to turn south, they walked hundreds of miles over Germany before some of them finally escaped. The sergeant said that it had been horrible in Germany for almost two months, since the Allied air forces had been everywhere, night and day, bombing and strafing practically continuously.

Perhaps the most interesting part of his story concerned the gradual change in the attitude of the Germans in general and the guards, or "goons," as the prisoners called them, in particular. A year earlier, this boy had been beaten and clubbed by an arrogant Nazi, by civilians, and by guards, but for the past few weeks, the slow transition had reached the fantastic point where the "goons" were pleading with prisoners to remember how good they had been to them. Not long before, a few of the guards were still clubbing with rifle butts any of the prisoners who straggled, until an American medical captain stood up and announced that he personally would see to it that any guard who mistreated a prisoner was killed as soon as the American columns caught up with them. Almost immediately, he was surrounded by guards who begged him, "Doctor, please remember that I have always been a friend of the Americans." After the sergeant escaped, he was hidden from wandering SS troops by civilians—a remarkable contrast to a year before when he was nearly pitchforked to death and was brutally beaten up by some of the stellar characters of the Third Reich. The whole thing became a chaotic fantasy, with Germans wandering around pleading to be taken prisoner by American troops who were too busy moving forward to be bothered with them. One German tried to surrender to the air corps sergeant while the sergeant was making his way back to our lines and when told to stop bothering him, burst into tears, saying that he had walked eighty kilometers to surrender and now they wouldn't take him. Civilians waved at the sergeant as he passed through towns not yet occupied—a far cry from the days when civilians spat in the faces of him and his fellow prisoners as they were marched through the streets by gloating guards.

All through this recital, we kept hearing the news reports of the unconditional surrender in Italy, the end of fighting in Berlin, etc. The whole damn mess was almost over, but the final chapter left me a little cold, without the tremendous enthusiasm and emotional satisfaction that I had imagined I would feel. I guess most of our enthusiasm and exhilaration was spent in the days when the victory was actually won—the days when the Siegfried Line was broken after a long, bloody, and tortured struggle and when the armies roared through to smash and destroy German armies on both sides of the Rhine.

More and more escaped prisoners straggled in. This was fast becoming a sort of stragglers' overnight camp, but obviously everyone was delighted to do everything possible to make them comfortable on their way back to the rear echelons. None of them were quite as vocal as the young sergeant who arrived first, but they were all happy—and for good reason. It's hard to imagine a more consistently discouraging, depressing, and miserable life than the one they had led for varying numbers of months, and now they were on their way back home.

13

V-E Day

From Hitler's suicide on March 30 until the final capitulation at midnight of May 8–9, the train of events was thoroughly confusing to us in ETOUSA and equally if not more so to those at home, I suppose. The negotiations between Stalin and the West were as difficult to understand and interpret as those between the German leaders and Eisenhower. Apparently, Himmler had entered into discussion with the Allies while Hitler was still alive, but the ultimate accession of Admiral Doenitz to leadership finally provided an individual with whom the Allies could deal.

On May 7, generals Jodl and von Friedeberg met with General Eisenhower and Allied representatives at his headquarters in Rheims and on behalf of Admiral Doenitz, signed a document agreeing to the unconditional surrender of all German armed forces. This surrender was to take effect at midnight of May 8— the day for which so many millions of people had prayed for so many years. And thus ended World War II in Europe.

We hardly gave a second thought to the May 4 news flash that the Germans in the north, in Denmark and in Holland, had surrendered unconditionally. For over a month, it had been a foregone conclusion that V-E Day was only a matter of days. Everyone, after endless months, had set V-E Day as a goal, as the climax for which they had been hoping and praying; and it wasn't until it was imminent that the realization dawned that it was not the finish line after all. The resulting uncertainty and speculation were a letdown that was hard to fight off. It should have been obvious that, while the victory in Europe was only a part of the global war, Japan had been brought halfway to her knees during a period when Britain and the United States had more than half of their forces and efforts concentrated in Europe. A pessimist could point out innumerable difficulties; but only a year earlier we had been moving into concentration areas for the initial instructions and shakedown inspections preceding the Invasion. At that time, we faced a country geared for modern warfare to the highest degree, drawing on the resources of a highly industrialized continent and fielding an army of more than three hundred magnificently trained and equipped divisions sitting behind two successive lines of the most ingenious and thorough defenses that modern military science could devise.

So much for the Silver Lining Department! Now we faced the problems of Japan and the Pacific Theater.

May 6, Erding, Germany

I just sent off a German parachute by mail. . . . I'm very skeptical about it reaching you since I'm afraid that the mail is pilfered from time to time [but] at least it's on its way. What you can ever do with the yards of white silk, I haven't the vaguest idea. You can always burn it or just stuff it away for some future use such as diapers for our offspring—or isn't that very practical? I wouldn't know not being very versed in anything but the more theoretical side of pediatrics. One word of advice, then I'll leave the subject of German parachutes—if this one does reach you, you'll find that it will arrive stripped of all harness, strapping, gadgets, etc. and the ripcord removed and replaced by a wire holding the release flap. Once you cut or unwind the wire, the pilot chute will spring out and then voluminous folds of silk from the main chute will billow out over the floor. It's practically impossible to repack it in the original canvas container so don't open it on a streetcar or in a taxi or you will find that you are confronted with quite a problem. Not that any of these eventualities are very likely but I thought it might be helpful to pass on a hint or two on "parachutes, opening of." . . .

The news broke today that Himmler had offered to surrender to Britain and the United States—this certainly presages the end within a few days. I'm sure that when the day actually comes, there will be much more unrestrained enthusiastic response at home than over here in the armies but actually that's understandable because I think that the intimations of the end have been made apparent to us so gradually and over such a period of time that the finality seems to us a steady succession of events taking shape before our eyes rather than one dramatic breathtaking announcement. That particular revelation was made such a short time ago that we'll just have to await results.

The formal announcement came over the radio on the morning of May 8 by representatives of the German government and army (such as it was) of the unconditional surrender by Admiral Doenitz of the remaining German troops; followed by the interesting announcement that the surrender would not be officially announced until the following day. After much deep thought, it was decided the only sensible thing to do would be to have two celebrations—one for the eve and one for the day itself. That solution was very satisfactory all around, in fact, since we still had a half dozen patients in postop and some of us would have to remain strictly sober. We opened up a couple of carefully hoarded bottles of GI bourbon (Old Granddad) and made some hors d'oeuvres and sandwiches out of packages from home. After dinner, we came back to quarters and sat around for some time in general conversation while rolling each sip of bourbon over our tongues. Finally, a poker game started up and wound up a little after midnight, at which time we folded up quietly to write a note home or go to sleep. We even kept up the blackout since no official order came down to raise it.

It didn't really seem over but I guess it was. In the days of winter, when there was no element of time except whenever you happened to eat or sleep, when the crashing of guns and the drone of motors overhead were part of the routine of life and the ambulances and jeeps rolled up one after another with their loads of frozen, shattered youngsters, it didn't seem possible it would ever end, but would go on and on forever. Now that it was over, there wasn't much left to say except to thank God that at least out of the worldwide mess, part of it was cleaned up and we were well beyond the halfway mark At least it did somehow seem to bring home a little closer.

May 9, Erding, Germany

We sat around yesterday with little to do except routine care of our postop cases. I waited for the official announcement by Churchill. He wasn't up to his old lyrical standards by any means although it's true it was not intended to be more than an announcement and he was apparently planning on making a real speech on May 10— which may turn out to be full of his old spark and fire. At any rate, after the announcement which was broadcast in late afternoon, we settled down to serious drinking and planned a joint party. Since we were dividing the two days of the announcement between the work shifts, things hadn't really gotten under way very much, however, when an emergency order came through for us to join with the Third Cavalry in a move to take over the liberation and the medical and surgical care of a concentration camp full of political prisoners at Ebensee in Austria. It was to be a long trip so there was no recourse except to get up again at 5 A.M. Plans were

Department of Shattered Illusions: W. V. McD.
the day after V-E Day, on the way to Ebensee.

made accordingly and we started to pack. By the time everything
was ready, I was tired as the devil and became progressively more
so as I kept thinking about the 5 A.M. ETD (estimated time of
departure). The upshot of it was that I eventually fell into my cot
quite late and without a word written to home on V-E day. I had
planned on writing when the party broke up and on sleeping late in
the morning but something about the "best laid plans of mice and
men—" might be appropriate and I got very little sleep, had a
reasonably large hangover and there was no letter home. It is a
thoroughly ridiculous hour at which to arise and I felt thoroughly
miserable as I had to fall out of bed at such an ungodly hour. Life
brightened up considerably as the day wore on, however, because
of an interesting if long drive. The sun was shining warmly and
brightly out of a clear blue sky and the section through which we
passed in Austria was magnificently beautiful with the route
running through part of the Austrian Alps. We wound along
through a succession of fertile green valleys, flanked always by
towering snow-tipped peaks which rose precipitously at the edge

of the valleys. It really was glorious country and just too damn bad that it was ever a part of greater Germany. The Germans most certainly did not deserve all that beauty.

There are a couple of other interesting things about the journey today. One of these was the picture of the southern German Army struggling along the roads to POW cages. They have no guards since all of them (the Germans) had formed an intact force up to the surrender and a number of them were semi-organized units with all their transport and equipment. Down the road they came in a disorganized mob—walking, riding bicycles, motorcycles and horses or piled on to any available vehicle which still had enough gasoline to run—ambulances, horse-drawn wagons and artillery caissons, Volkswagens, trucks, civilian cars. There were all types and ranks—generals riding in groups with clean pressed uniforms and shining brass, officers crowded in groups in the various kinds of cars, sullen looking SS troops; beaten, ragged, dirty and un-shaven Wehrmacht, men trudging along alone or in groups. Where this motley procession was heading, I had no idea but I supposed there were other collecting points in the rear echelons where they were imprisoned, interrogated, numbered and classified. This must be an enormous problem in itself since the last figure I heard quoted on the radio was that there were 5,000,000 German prisoners in the western front alone. Then, you can add to that millions of DP's, the last allied political prisoners and slave laborers, and it makes your head swim. At least, we no longer had to fight a war on top of everything else. It was still a stupendous problem when you consider a comparatively few allied troops who will have to feed, organize, treat, house, and eventually repatriate the sick, miserable enslaved herd and at the same time handle all the German prisoners and rule the German civilians.

At times one would see small arms (pistols, etc.) being tossed out of an occasional small car usually bearing officers. We sus-pected that, as we approached, the Krauts might think that we were infantry. Some showed disdain when they squeezed by on the crowded road and discovered that from our Red Cross flag, we were nothing but a lowly edentulous medical outfit. One or two overladen cars tipped over into the ditch in their eagerness to give us plenty of room on the road, so even a harmless medical unit was given some respect.

The other thing which particularly interested me was the sudden revival of the Austrian National Flag—Red, White and Red. Practically every damn house had one flying in an attempt, I suppose, to convince the Americans that they were liberated rather than a conquered country. I recognized the fact that generally speaking, these Austrians were on a distinctly higher level than their brethren to the north but all this flag waving didn't impress me very much. They accepted the Germans and, therefore, they are Germans and while it is true that Naziism may have been more or less thrust upon them, I'm not entirely sure since I have seen nothing as yet to convince me that many of them had any serious objections. At the very best, they condoned it and a helluva lot of them were just as enthusiastic as any Prussian.

They all knew what Naziism was, what the Nazi creed and philosophy implied and many knew at first hand the horrors of the concentration camps. (More about this later since our mission after we arrived would be the reorganization and treatment of the prisoners in a concentration camp). There was no suggestion of the Austrian underground to my knowledge or even of any general-ized passive resistance. It will take more than red and white flags to convince me when they still gather in groups to wave and shout at German troops on their way to prison camps. If they were good Austrians or good Germans, they can begin right now to try to prove it to us but it will take more than a flag and a little soft talk. The bandwagon is a great institution and no one seems to be more conscious of that than the Germans. Austria was a great country— nothing but anti-Nazis! It makes you wonder if the world has been shadow boxing all these years. Why, everyone except Hitler, Goebbels and a few SS men were all gentle, friendly, democratic souls who would not murder anyone, even a Jew, much less one of these nice Americans! The programs, the mammoth party rallies at Neuremberg (which I saw before the war), the 99% Plebiscites must have been pure figments of the imagination. A lot of goddamn hypocrisy!

The end of this long jaunt was a picturesque little Austrian town called Ebensee, situated in the most magnificent natural scenery imaginable. Just across the Danube from the Russian lines, the houses were clustered at one end of a small mountain lake with tall, craggy peaks towering precipitously on all sides of this natural saucer. The streets were neat and clean and the houses built in the tradition of the ancient Austrian chalet. The lake was a pure blue and the mountains were so sheer that they seemed about to topple into the valley, a mélange of brilliant greens topped off with snowy summits. Gmunden, at the other end of the lake from Ebensee, was where Schubert used to sit on the bank and write lieder.

As we rolled through the town of Ebensee on May 10, we came to the gates of the concentration camp, where the French prisoners had hung a large sheet with the words—*"Honneur à nos liberateurs!"* As we entered the gates, we faced a horror story. Words couldn't approach the actual facts that hit our eyes, ears, and noses.

The camp itself was located on the outskirts, at the foot of a huge cliff that formed a sheer side of one of the surrounding mountains. This put the prisoners in immediate proximity to their work, which consisted of blasting, digging, and chipping away in the solid rock to form a series of subterranean chambers and corridors in the depths of the mountain. When finished, this was to have been a part of the Nazis' southern redoubt about which so much has been written—the "Festung Europa."

The general arrangement was not remarkable—there were innumerable draughty one-story wooden barracks spread over a wide area of many acres surrounded by a high barbed-wire fence with sentry towers at close intervals and strong floodlights around the perimeter. So far, it sounds very little different from any prisoner-of-war camp anywhere, but if ever there was a place created with calculated sadism, frightfulness, and horror, this was it! Ebensee was technically a death camp for Mauthausen, the largest of the concentration camps in Austria. No one who entered the camp was supposed to survive, but while they lived, they were forced to work on excavations in the mountains during all daylight hours. The prisoners were all "political," that is, nonmilitary, but there would seem to be no rhyme or reason to explain why they were here—some were members of the underground in all parts of Europe, some were Jews, some were editors of newspapers (*Paris Soir,* for example) and they were of every age, nationality, and occupation with what seemed to be a very high percentage of men in the upper intellectual bracket—lawyers, editors, doctors, professors, businessmen, etc. On entering the camp, everything was taken from them and they were given a thin shirt and trousers with prison-stripe design and a winter "overcoat" of equally thin texture. Each man was assigned one-half of a double-decker bunk in one of the barracks. The bunks were so jammed together that hundreds of men slept in one small building, under the command of a "Kapo"—a prisoner who had been subverted by the Germans with special privileges to maintain order and to brutalize his own compatriots—unbelievable! There was no water, no heat, no latrines, and no cooking or eating utensils or facilities. The prisoners had no shoes and went barefoot even in winter. Rations consisted of six ounces of bread per person per day with some potato-peeling soup, which they fished out of a container with anything they could find or make. A man does not survive long on that diet although some managed to stretch out their life span a few months by various means including eating roots and grasses.

The prisoners were worked all day every day until they were too weak to climb the steps of the excavations, at which point one of two things happened. Most were sent to the "hospital" (several barracks in which a selected number of doctor-prisoners were allowed to work, but with no equipment), where the Germans put them on half rations in order to speed up death. If someone lingered too long, he was disposed of either by the SS or by a fellow prisoner, whom the Germans had bribed to kill by means of a promise of extra rations; a sadistic method of further degrading the prisoners, since the Germans certainly had no compunctions about murder. Gas chambers were constructed to resemble a shallow room. The doomed men were given a small piece of soap and told to take a shower, and then the door was closed behind them and the gas turned on. The eventual disposal of all bodies was theoretically carried out in the crematorium. The German genius miscalculated, however, because the crematorium could only handle two hundred bodies per day. When we arrived, we found a large room next to the crematorium in which hundreds of bodies were stacked like cordwood up to the ceiling, and outside were several mass graves in which thousands of prisoners had been interred.

When we arrived, we took charge of the "hospital area," in which several thousand of the worst cases were incarcerated. The military government handled the rest of the camp. The sight of any one of the prisoners would have horrified anyone; what the several thousand "hospital cases" were like was beyond imagination. Doctors become more or less accustomed to the sight of illness, suffering, and death, but we were all physically sick after our first view of the camp. These men were walking skeletons, every bone of the skull and trunk standing out sharply. Their bodies were bent, twisted, and shrunken by disease and torture. They all had horribly diseased skin, huge running sores, areas of osteomyelitis where wide sections of bone were exposed and discharging pus, and a number of large open empyemas draining from their chests. A few had their wounds covered with paper bandages that the Germans had kindly given to the doctors. I can't begin to enumerate the prevalent diseases. There were cases of typhus, tuberculosis (men racked with coughs and bringing up blood), dysen-

Ebensee. Pile of bodies with American G.I.

tery so severe that the men were completely incontinent. Almost every one of these thousands had at least several terrible conditions and all, of course, had some degree of dysentery and were wasted by starvation, so they presented the grotesque picture of a distended abdomen and feet and ankles swollen by nutritional edema with the rest of the body shrunken literally to skin and bones. Any one of these cases would be unbelievable, and, when they were lying, crawling, or walking around by thousands, it surpassed anything the human mind could imagine. Those who were too sick to move were lying in barracks, six and eight to one double-decker wooden bunk, in conditions of indescribable filth and covered with millions of lice, bedbugs, and flies. We could smell the camp before it came in sight!

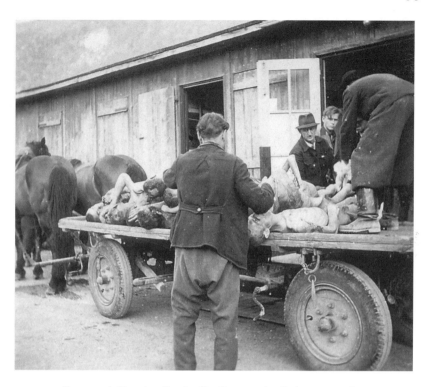

German civilians loading bodies from stock-pile in crematorium,
for transportation through town to special cemetery.

These men had been normal, healthy, happy human beings once upon a time but the majority of them were worse than animals now, without any instinct of cleanliness, pride, modesty, or shame. Driven to their desperate state by months of insensate brutality, they groveled and pleaded for food, which they wolfed down like beasts. When we began feeding them light meals, they would cluster around the containers afterwards, scrape the sides with their fingers, and gnaw at their nails to get what had collected there. I set down a box of soap for a few minutes and when I came back, half of it had been eaten! It was impossible to hand a cigarette to one of them, for he would be almost torn to pieces by hundreds of his fellows in their attempt to take it away. It was an endless panorama of mass brutality and calculated sadism such as has never

German civilians digging individual graves in cemetery
planned for bodies found in concentration camp.

before taken place in this world to my knowledge—and this was
only one of hundreds of camps that had been in existence all over
Germany, as far as we could tell by reports.

Medically speaking, we were faced with an impossible situation. You could watch men die by the dozens as you walked
around. Five fell dead while they were waiting in line for the first
meal we served. There were not enough medical supplies, vita-
mins, plasma, or doctors in the world to give all these men all over
Germany what they needed in the way of immediate individual
treatment. They were dying by the hundreds and would continue to die at a diminishing rate for a while. All we could do was
gradually improve the living conditions, sanitation, food, and
cleanliness and slowly begin medical treatment.

Atrocity graveyard at Ebebsee

On orders from army headquarters, all the Austrians of the whole district were put to work in the camp—scrubbing the barracks, cleaning up the filth, washing the bedridden patients, etc.— not only because we needed the workers, but also to impress forever in their minds the true frightfulness of the regime that they had fostered or condoned for twelve years. They were made to load the hundreds of beaten, wasted, and bloody bodies on to flat horse-driven carts, bring them through the main street of the town, and dig individual graves in a large plot on the outskirts, which was to be prominently marked "German Atrocity Cemetery," with each grave individually identified whenever possible by name, number, and cross or Star of David.

For us, even though we had read and heard of such horrors for

the past few weeks, the reality was a staggering blow. For them—
or at least for those who could still react in any way—the liberation was a miracle in a world of despair, and all Americans were
and will always be a race of mortal gods. When I walked into one
of the frightfully crowded barracks on the first night, there were
three pitifully weak cheers for the American Army. A few who
were apparently ex-soldiers struggled to their feet in an attempt to
salute and someone tried to sing "Over There." I thanked them as
well as I could and fled precipitously before I broke down completely. This was such a sad commentary on a race supposedly
civilized and exposed to centuries of Christianity, but I had given
up even attempting to answer the question of how human beings
could do all this. The whole damn country was pathological, and
I am no psychiatrist.

All three units of the hospital were finally working together on
this frightful and discouraging project. A camp like Ebensee would
present an enormous problem even to a huge three-thousand-bed
civilian hospital already permanently established in buildings with
tons of medical supplies, beds, blankets, food, soap, towels, laundry facilities, medicines, and surgical facilities, and a large staff of
doctors and nurses. Even with all three platoons acting for the
first time as a unit, it was a matter of constantly butting our
heads against a wall. We had to run water into the camp, set up
outdoor showers and delousing stations, scour the countryside
and captured German depots for clean clothing, blankets, dressings, etc., set up all our tents, get the barracks emptied, fumi-
gated, and scrubbed, burn all the prisoners' old blankets and
clothing, set up hundreds of latrine facilities and dressing stations, isolate typhus, tuberculosis, and other infectious diseases,
and separate various types of cases into some sort of ward system by medical category. It boiled down to three small specialized surgical units trying to run a city in which there was no

elementary sanitation, housing, clothing, or food, and whose inhabitants were all in the last stages of starvation and typically had one or more horrible diseases. We began to organize things fairly well but medically and surgically, we really didn't scratch the surface. Fortunately, a much larger evacuation hospital was moving up. It was not only an exhausting business but the whole atmosphere was so depressing that you were completely worn out by the end of the day.

We all needed a little relaxation and someone had the bright idea of taking over a large boat for a cruise around the lake. We left just after dinner and as it stayed light until well after 9:00, it was a really beautiful trip. The scenery was as magnificent and glorious as the concentration camp was horrible and filthy—"where every prospect pleases, and only man is vile." The weather was superb and with a slight breeze blowing across the lake, you couldn't ask for a better setting. I could even forget the camp for a short time. Two comparatively healthy ex-prisoners who had arrived at the camp just before we did wanted to come along and provide some music, so we dug up a violin and an accordion from the village and they sat up on the bow of the little steamer and played the whole time with great relish. Both had studied music in Paris and were excellent musicians, so we had variegated selections—Beethoven, Brahms, Tchaikovsky, Strauss, Gershwin, etc., right down to "Tiger Rag." Very pleasant!

It was a cavalry unit, which had the job of rounding up the SS guards who had escaped, and militarily speaking, liberated the camp. Most of the guards were rounded up and shipped back under special guard for eventual criminal trials. Some of them who tried to smuggle knives or guns with them were shot. The ex-prisoners were kept enclosed during the process of rounding up the guards—I'm sure if enough of them had had the strength, they would have torn the SS troops to shreds.

After a few days, an evacuation hospital arrived and took over our job at the concentration camp. The hospital had so much more in the way of facilities, equipment, personnel, and stores for the job that they could handle it much better than our little group of surgical units and teams.

My God, what a relief it was to get out of that sordid atmosphere! It kept us in a state of pity for the poor bastards who had suffered so horribly, in a mood of hatred and disgust for those responsible, and in a depression that such inconceivable things could happen in a supposedly civilized world. After a few hours in the camp, you found yourself wondering on just what basis man set himself up to be above the level of the so-called lower animals.

The whole continent was a shambles, what with millions of wanderers, enormous destruction, looting, killing, and general lawlessness. Gangs of SS and Gestapo roamed at large, armed terrorists released or escaped from concentration camps burned, murdered, and looted. A human life was worth just about the 6x2x2 plot of earth that it took to bury the body. The American Military Government did a good job with what it had available, but even a few million Americans can't run a whole continent in such a frightful mess—thanks to the "New Order."

It was somehow typical that practically the last organized flight of the Luftwaffe had the mission of bombing a liberated concentration camp. Senseless, sadistic madmen! Dave's theory was to clean out central Europe completely and turn it into a game preserve or bird sanctuary, which at the moment seemed to be one of the most sensible ideas which I had heard.

At times, when we heard the crackling of rifles or machine-gun fire that broke out spasmodically, we wondered if the war was really over. Usually it was SS men or released Russians, or both, shooting and looting German civilians or each other. They both stayed strictly out of the way of the American troops, so, except for the fact that our patrols were bothered with rounding up one gang after another, it didn't affect us too much personally.

Except for that business of a few loose Germans and Russians playing cowboy with each other back in the woods and mountains, May 15 was a pleasant, lazy day, with a trip back to a mountain peak via a little car that travelled hundreds of feet above the ground suspended from a couple of cables, a little boating on the lake, and a movie (open air). There was a tangible atmosphere of tenseness and speculation among officers and men alike about what would happen next, who was going home, how and when. There was too much talk for weeks by everyone, especially the *Stars and Stripes* about demobilization, points, and whatnot. No one in the ETO wanted to get home more than I did, but there was still a war on and I thought the whole business was nonsense. It didn't take much time in the army before you developed some degree of fatalism about the immediate future, and I thought all along that a simple announcement that men would be discharged as quickly as feasible and as fairly as possible and that an attempt would be made to get men who had been overseas for a long time home rapidly would suffice. As it was, everyone sat around figuring out points and, as invariably occurs when you announce any kind of a system like that, no one was really satisfied—this should count more, that should count less, and all that nonsense. Except for the men who had very high numbers of points (who undoubtedly would have been rotated home anyway), going home would be purely a matter of luck. One of the boys made an amusing crack in a letter I censored: "V-E Day has caught me with my 'points down'."

So much for points and plans. There was still a war in the Pacific and some of the troops would go directly there rather than back to the United States. We just had to wait and see what the luck of the draw would bring.

On May 16 we received orders to move on to another job in two days, this time without the other two platoons.

We were right at the Russian lines. The bridge at Linz over the Danube was immediately adjacent to Ebensee and formed the communication structure between the advanced units of the American and Russian armies. There was a little communication back and forth about Russians in the camp but they had remarkably little interest in retrieving their countrymen. Before leaving the next day, I was out of bed early to get off on a fishing expedition. It was all very primitive since we started off with nothing but some lines, two hooks, and a glass full of worms. It was a glorious spring morning and after a long hike, we hit the mountain stream on which we had had our eyes set since seeing it from a peak a few days earlier. We cut off a couple of branches, fashioned a very unfashionable pair of rods, took off our boots and shirts, rolled up our trousers, and started to fish the pools. It was an ideal trout stream, with dozens of small waterfalls falling into deep pools, which in turn cascaded into a series of rocky rapids. The water was ice cold, of course, and made the ocean at Marblehead seem like a steam bath; so I didn't do much standing around in the approved fishing style, but hopped up on the rocks whenever possible. We landed seven moderate-sized trout, picked up a good sunburn, and were not ambushed by any wandering guerrillas. Shortly after noon, we started back, wangled a frying pan, lard, and corn meal from the kitchen, and prepared an excellent lunch of trout, fried onions, hush puppies, and beets. I hoped that it would be the last wedding anniversary I would celebrate in any such way.

After the fishing expedition, it was about time to crawl into the sack, which was hardly in the same class as Dave's arrangement across the room. He had lined his bedroll with a huge piece of parachute silk. Very sensual and carried with it the atmosphere of *Salambo* or *The Arabian Nights.*

The next night we were back in tents again, in Traun, Austria after a few hours on the road. The eight officers who remained with the unit were now living in a ward tent with plenty of room and electricity we usually didn't have to use our portable generators in Germany, but merely tapped into the local line when it was working. Supposedly, we were to function as a "Typhus Diagnostic Center" with wards set up for observation, study, and treatment—an interesting job for a group of surgeons! We all dug out books from the hospital library and started to read up on typhus and Rickettsia diseases. Personally, I hadn't thought about them since days at medical school and Zinsser's book *Rats, Lice and History.* He was our professor of bacteriology and he achieved most of his fame for his discovery of a typhus vaccine and for his work on the Rickettsia (small organisms not yet definitely classified as bacteria or viruses), one of which is the causative organism of typhus—and that pretty nearly exhausted my available fund of information on the subject. I suppose we were assigned to these odd jobs because we were such a highly mobile unit and could cover considerable distances relatively quickly.

Traun was nothing like the magnificent country we had left—flat, almost dismal-looking farming country with drab villages and farms. I did locate a good trout stream fairly nearby so that if we were not too busy, I might be able to squeeze in a little more primitive angling.

Blackouts had been a source of constant irritation for so long that almost everyone's first reaction to the announcement of the cessation of hostilities was how wonderful it was to forget about them. It was a remarkable feeling to be able to go out into lighted streets, see the glow of windows all around, drive with headlights, and walk outside at night without fumbling and crawling around in pitch black, with the dubious assistance of a dim glow from a covered flashlight.

It was a relief not to wander around with an ear instinctively cocked to the sound of a plane's motor or to the sudden eruption of artillery or mortar fire. The major relief, though, was to be able to turn on a bright light in a room without nailing up blanket or boards tightly and to be able to read or write in a tent at night with all the flaps open.

Before actual work for "Typhus Diagnostic Center" began, friends and I investigated the countryside's hunting and fishing possibilities, then set out with three ancient shotguns to scour some likely-looking fields for game birds. We couldn't get enough birds to feed a whole outfit but we had a good time, handed the bag over to the kitchen to distribute as the codes saw fit, and ordered partridge for lunch. I suddenly realized that I no longer had any interest in hunting, probably because I had lived with so many young men who were wounded or killed by shooting.

That pompous ass Major George Fielding Elliott wrote a lengthy article for *Look* magazine on what Germany would be like immediately after V-E Day, painting a picture of a fabulous underground, bands of organized cutthroats terrorizing American troops, V bombs flying all over the world from secret hideaways, and all sorts of drivel. Central Europe was hardly a tranquil twentieth-century version of the Garden of Eden and most of us carried a gun when we went anywhere, but except for a rare group of unreconstructed SS men, most of the trouble came from wandering Russian DPs with a penchant for throat slitting and looting— and they avoided American troops as much as possible. The Germans themselves, now that their organization had been thoroughly broken up, were the best individual skin-savers you ever saw. There was certainly no evidence of the "Furor Teutonicus" with which they liked to intoxicate themselves.

In the large field which we were now occupying, we were enjoying the hospitality of the late great Hermann Goering. He and other top Nazis really made a good thing out of the racket they ran there for fifteen years. The industrial plants, estates, acres and acres of farms and farmland, art treasures, etc. that Goering managed to acquire might make even the Henry Ford holdings seem like selling apples on a street corner. Our own public servants of the Curley, Kelly, and Nash ilk were cherubs by comparison.

Our first batch of patients turned up, twenty-five ex-prisoners and Austrians, all suspected of having typhus fever. Our job was to confirm or disprove the diagnosis by observation and laboratory studies. If they had the disease, we were to carry them through the acute phase—if not, we were to evacuate them to a rear echelon. It was not a bad job under the circumstances. Obviously, it entailed no surgery, but on the other hand it didn't entail too much work and promised to be interesting, since all I knew about typhus was the small amount of standard stuff about the more obscure diseases that is fed medical students.

By May 19, our motley crew of typhus patients had increased enormously. Dave and I both sweated into late evening over several laboratory tests that we had planned to do on each patient. Fortunately, we finished up with the last two a few seconds before a wild thunderstorm broke, because the laboratory damn near came down about our ears. By dint of much pegging and bracing, all the tents survived the sudden storm.

Soon our Typhus Diagnostic (and apparently treatment) Center began to fill up by leaps and bounds, and we were really kept busy during the day.

We had a pleasant surprise one day with a visit from a chaplain whom we knew from training days in England. He was a great person, very amusing, and we all liked him tremendously. He had been chaplain in a camp at Penzance where a number of the half-track and anti-aircraft units went for firing practice during one of the phases of pre-Invasion training and maneuvers. It was a bleak, barren, desolate spot on a rocky Cornish coast near Land's End, on the supposed site of King Arthur's castle. We stayed there for about ten days and had a fairly pleasant time (despite that miserable damn climate!), due in a large part to Father Flatley's personality, enthusiasm, and efforts. His arrival in Traun made me realize how much had happened since I had last seen him—which under the circumstances seemed like centuries. In the fifteen months since Penzance and Cornwall, we had gone through maneuvers at Blandford and on the Salisbury Plains, taken up action stations at 9th Air Force Fields in East Anglia, returned to the First Army for the intense period of the concentration, marshalling, and staging areas, come into Normandy on Omaha Beach, been transferred to the Third Army for the breakthrough and race across France, been thwarted on the Moselle crossing; then bounced back and forth during that long, depressing stalemate at the German border that was finally broken during the Battle of the Bulge and the subsequent bloody grind through the Siegfried Lines (during which I was transferred). We had rolled across Germany and Austria, had waited for the announcement of V-E Day, and finally had taken up the postwar concentration camp and typhus problems. When I thought of how many days and weeks seemed to drag by depressingly without activity or apparent progress towards home, that was a remarkable amount to have happened in such a relatively short period.

Another farewell celebration was brewing, since George Gish and Bill Higgins were going back to the 4th Auxiliary Headquarters Center in the morning and Dean Bohrer and his team had left a few days earlier. Our little group, with only four of its original senior officers left, was slowly but surely turning into a shell of its former self, and this would be our last night as the surgical unit that had worked together for so many months. Very sad! It had been a lot of fun.

Higgins, the great raconteur, left us with this story: "Shortly after an elephant escaped from the zoo, the director received an excited call from an elderly maiden who screamed over the phone that there was a huge monster loose in her garden who was pulling up cabbages with his tail. When asked what the monster was doing with the cabbages, she replied, "'If I told you, you wouldn't believe me!'"

We all knew that, come V-E Day when there was no longer a large volume of surgical work, we would all be broken up in this way, but we had worked together for so long in such a congenial group that it was somehow hard to realize that we wouldn't continue as one surgical unit until we all scattered to our various homes when everything is finished. We will undoubtedly never be together again as a group but it was good fun while it lasted. They were all damn decent, interesting, and amusing and each of us was sorry to see the inevitable breakup finally arrive.

Having heard that Joe Krimsky, a colleague and officer from one of the battalions with which I left America, was in the area, I took a jeep and drove some fifteen kilometers. It was good to see him after all those months and we sat around bulling for about three hours over a bottle of scotch that he produced for the occasion. That in itself was remarkable, since no one in our unit had had anything on a higher scale than ethyl alcohol for some time. It was from Joe that I learned that my old friend and staff sergeant, Pat Gavin, had been killed shortly after I left the battalion. I felt very badly. I always liked Gavin—a big, capable, genial, courageous Irishman. Except for that piece of bad news, we had a very pleasant evening. Joe wanted to hear at length about Blanche and told me about Maxine and her writing career in New York.

May 24 was a banner day; an order reached us that the wearing of steel helmets and helmet liners was no longer required. Out came the garrison caps and overboard went another of the chronically irritating customs associated with the war. We used to think when we first hit England that we'd never get used to wearing a helmet constantly—and we never did, the damn things were always annoying. But after a month or so of wearing them constantly in France they became bearable and we didn't have to take them off every half hour to relieve the headache. It was nice to dispense with them for good.

More talk in *Stars and Stripes* (as well as everywhere else) on the point system—dozens of letters all of course bitching about the whole thing; too many points for children, too few for children, not enough credit for overseas time or too much, too little for total, too much for decorations, etc., etc. The best letter was one that read, "I personally don't like the system because I haven't got enough points"—which summed up everything. I could observe the whole thing with some detachment, because I knew that young medical officers would be considered necessary and probably would not be released early. Even the Bronze Star, which I received en route, the Distinguished Unit Citation, and a total of six battle stars would not get a medical officer out very early.

14

Transitions

RETURN TO EBENSEE
SCHLIERSEE (NEW MASH UNIT)
May 27–July 23, 1945

When we finished our mission at Traun we closed up shop and moved about three miles to Neubau to take over another job—the supervision of a large German hospital staffed with Wehrmacht medical officers, which had been turned over for the care of 1,600 displaced persons. Each of us acted more or less in the same capacity as the members of the visiting staff did in an American hospital, with the German medics doing all the routine work under our direct supervision. It was a good system as there were just not enough American doctors and hospitals to handle the enormous medical and surgical problems that existed in Europe.

On the whole, everything was now running smoothly. Our relations with the Germans were courteous but cool and distant, with no hand shaking or exchange of ordinary amenities. The first day we arrived, I heard that one of the Germans had told a patient who complained about some item of food (the diet was not remarkably palatable) that it was because of the Bolsheviks. I

l-r: W.V. McD., Dean Bohrer, Charlie Hargrader. Camp occupants
undressed for exam and treatment. Crematorium in the background.

immediately called a general meeting and strictly forbade any
mention of cause and effect or anything vaguely resembling a political discussion between the Germans and the patients. After
that, there was no trouble in that line. All the Germans shared a
tendency to whine over present difficulties and shortages, but every one of us cut the subject short—"You should have thought of
that some years ago." Nor did we allow any explanations that they
were all anti-Nazi at heart.

Everyone, even the Germans, seemed to expect the Americans
to solve their problems for them. What would happen over the
next few months, God only knew. We certainly couldn't feed,
clothe, and transport the whole continent, and that's what the
problem looked like. The immensity of the DP problem even
dimmed our original fury at the Germans for creating it—faced
with trying to find solutions, we had no time for recrimination.

16-year old boy after several months in camp at Ebensee.

None of our patients could stand seeing one of their comrades get something they didn't. Poor Mike went crazy trying to coordinate the four hospitals and hunting up supplies, transportation, clothing, etc. At Ebensee, one misguided officer tossed a pack of cigarettes to a group of sad and miserable ex-prisoners, and within thirty seconds a good-sized riot developed. I had to wade in to the midst of a hundred screaming, struggling men and take away the pack or someone would have been killed. We didn't have enough for all and therefore we couldn't give anything to anyone individually.

March orders came again. On May 23 extra trucks arrived unexpectedly and we headed back to Ebensee. Apparently, the high-priced help felt that the hospital at Neubau was sufficiently well organized that it could be run by a large German staff under the supervision of one or two Americans. Good Luck!

The conditions of Ebensee showed considerable improvement. I feared that we would still have about two thousand sick patients but now we had all three platoons working together as a unit again and the patients were on the whole in much better shape than the mass horror that had faced us three weeks earlier. The area was so jammed with American units that we had a major problem finding anyplace to live, particularly since we were the last unit of our particular group to arrive. We finally settled the men in but then couldn't find a place for ourselves. Putting up tents in this mountainous area was impossible and we were reluctant to evict Austrian families indiscriminately. We went down to the military government, lined up a good Nazi party member whose house suited our needs, and the Burgomeister sent word (with some relish) for the family to be out in two hours. After dinner, we moved into our comfortable quarters.

Rafe Jones and Liza, our Red Cross girl, were off on some special service mission, and agreed to drop off a German civilian on the way back after the military government requested it as a favor. Their passenger turned out to be Hitler's sister, apparently a gentle, timid, kindly elderly woman, who invited them in for a cup of coffee (they refused), patted Liza's hand when they were leaving, snivelled a little, and thanked them for their kindness. The language difficulty combined with her motherly, timid attitude stalled Rafe and Liza off from asking any personal questions, so that was the end of the story. (Hitler had been brought up in Linz, very near Ebensee).

On the evening of our arrival, Lieutenant Colonel Sanford, Dave, and I were invited to dinner at the French Officers' Mess. It proved to be quite an international gathering—three of us, three French officers (two male, one female), a Scot, and a French ex-aviator of the last war who was serving with UNRRA and was covered with decorations. Other women were a Swiss girl with UNRRA, a middle-aged French widow working with the French Army on DP problems, and two French nurses. After an excellent long meal with much good red wine (they must have brought it from France), we sat around drinking cognac, talking, and singing while one of the French officers played his accordion.

Colonel Sanford took me aside and described what the army planned for the type of unit in which we were now serving. Basically, it would eliminate the old field hospital and the attached auxiliary surgical units and make a series of very mobile flexible surgical hospitals, called "MASH" (mobile auxiliary surgical hospital) units and designed to go onto the beaches in the invasion of Japan and stay closely involved with combat units. He wanted Dave and me to serve successively as commanding officers, and stated that he would try to block any transfer out of the unit in order to provide for our transition. For Dave, the situation was quite understandable because he had a long service, three and a half years of which had been spent overseas, but I hadn't been in the army even two years and had less than a year in grade as a captain. The job would entail being in command of officers who were not only considerably older but had much longer army service. Promotion to the rank of major at that point would have been extraordinarily out of line with the usual elephantine progress of army promotions. Well, I was a skeptic and intended to take it all *cum grano salis.*

I was very saddened to learn in a letter from Blanche of Bob Hurlburt's death on a destroyer off the coast of Japan. Bob was several years ahead of me in the residency program at the MGH. His death was no different from that of an eighteen- or nineteen-year-old killed in France or Luxembourg, but it seemed particularly tragic to me and to anyone else who knew him. In some ways, I felt less sorry for the men themselves who were killed than for their wives and families. It's a helluva war and a helluva world when we let things like that happen to young wives and mothers. Death itself is important only to those left behind. The dying was over in this theater, but it seemed that in the past few months, more and more tragic cases turned up—men we had known at some time or other who left young wives and several children.

The first anniversary of D-Day came and went without ceremony. It was declared a holiday in the ETO but as far as I could see, it made no difference in the daily routine of anyone except the lads of the APO, who refused to accept even outgoing mail from our mail clerk after his long trek back. We all thought back in various ways to a year before. It was a terrible day for the 1st and 29th divisions on Omaha Beach while we were sweating it out on our LSTs, which were just leaving Southamptom for the beachhead. Having come over a few days later on that section of Omaha Beach, I can't see to this day how their 16th Regiment (of the 1st Infantry Division) ever hung on to its toehold and finally pushed inland to secure the beachhead. It was a horrible place.

Returning to work at Ebensee was discouraging and depressing. The great majority of the original thousands had been evacuated after they had been nourished to a condition where they could travel, so now there was almost adequate room for the two thousand patients (out of the original thirty thousand) who remained. The camp grounds and buildings had been cleared of the frightful filth, stench, and litter of three weeks before. Now it conveyed less horror, but our memories were too strong to make it a congenial place to work, and the patients still there served as a constant reminder. Even a month of adequate feeding and of medical care, their condition was enough to make one gasp. How could these dreadfully sick human beings ever again be completely normal? None of us had any knowledge of the long-term results on the human mind and body of the life they had endured. They were still terribly listless and apathetic, moving and reacting on very basic instincts. Their faces bore a characteristic expression that was hard to define—a sort of blank, "the vacant stare which bespeaks the empty mind." It was all the more terrible and tragic if you recollected that most of those brutalized individuals were once highly intelligent if not brilliant men and leaders in their various professions.

On the way home from dinner to our peaceful little chalet, Dave, Mike, and I had to break up a small riot. It arose when several of the ex-prisoners from the Lager working for various American units as KPs, etc., recognized a German in civilian clothes who had been one of the SS guards at the camp. He had been particularly brutal, had beaten a twelve-year-old boy almost to death because he could not carry a heavy enough load. A gathering mob had him in an orchard ready to hang him. He was already beaten to a pulp (the young boy whom he had beaten was jumping up and down on his face when we broke up the party), but we called an ambulance and shipped him off. I can't say that I had much sympathy for him, but shooting a man after a trial is one thing and lynching is another.

Since the remaining occupants of Ebensee were by now convalescent, the workload was light, and after three weeks Mike decided it would be a good idea if Dave and I had a break. We took off on June 18 towards Berchtesgaden, stopping overnight at the 109th Evac Hospital en route. The drive was through the magnificent scenery of the Austrian and Bavarian Alps, with the fog just rising out of the valleys ahead of us as we drove in the early morning through Bad Ischl, Salzburg, and thence to Berchtesgaden. It was a sleepy picturesque little town, well filled up by the men of the 101st Airborne Division (the "Nuts" group from Bastogne), who were in charge of the "Retreat." We drove up a long, steep, winding road through several guard gates to the plateau below the actual mountain peak where all the main build-

Hitler's Mountain retreat, the Alderhorst, on top of Mt. Kehlstrin.

ings of the area were located. An air attack had taken place a short time before V-E Day, and a better job of pinpoint bombing I had never seen. Every building in the "Retreat" area was smashed, but there was not a scratch on the town itself, which lies far below in the valley.

There was little left to see of the homes of the Nazi bigwigs. We wandered around the ruins of Goering's and Hitler's houses, snooped around the tunnels that connected all the buildings, and snapped pictures at random until it was time for the convoy to form for the trip up the peak itself where Adolph's famous "Eagle's Nest" (Adlerhorst) was located. After crawling in first gear on a road that wound around around the peak in its ascent, and passing through innumerable tunnels that could be closed with heavy doors, we finally arrived at a small flattened area below the peak itself, where the road ended at a parking lot. We had brought up the lieutenant of the 101st, who was in charge of the guard, and he

Johnson, Dean and Lt. Col. Bozalis in the conference room of the Alderhorst.

offered to take our group up in the elevator. The rest of the members of the convoy had to struggle up the fifteen-minute climb to the summit. The lieutenant took us through a set of heavy iron doors and down a long tunnel into the heart of the mountain which ended abruptly at a small, very ornate elevator, mirrored and luxuriously cushioned. This brought us up the remaining 130 meters and disgorged us in the hallway of Hitler's hideaway, a small, one-story stone building on the very peak of Mount Kehlstein with awe-inspiring views of the Alps in every direction.

The "Adlerhorst" had not been touched by the bombing Most of the valuable and ornate furnishings had been removed for safe keeping, but enough remained to give us a good idea of what it must have been like. Besides stone balconies and porches, baths, kitchens, and a few more alcoves and bedrooms, the building consisted mainly of two huge rooms, one a banquet hall and the other a large sitting and conference room with an enormous semicircu-

lar wall almost entirely of glass, with a huge fireplace against the
central end of the room. It was impressive—you lounged in a soft
chair or sat at the conference table and looked out at a 180-degree
arc over an expanse of towering snow-capped peaks, wreathed in
clouds. Being in a spot like that certainly must have been therapy
for adults firmly established in delusions of grandeur, like Der
Führer and his colleagues. All of this stirred up memories of the
prewar era and Chamberlain's visit to Berchtesgaden.

We left the mountain about midafternoon and went to a building a few kilometers outside Berchtesgaden where the 101st was
housing the portion they had captured of Hermann Goering's loot.
Much of it was already classified and crated, but numerous paintings remained, plus a few tapestries and statues. It was incredible
to see how much that fat oaf had looted from every corner of Europe. Three floors of rooms were stacked with paintings, and this
particular collection was not all of his loot by any means. There
were Titians, Raphaels, Rembrandts, Holbeins, Breughels, Van
Goghs, Reynoldses, Gainsboroughs, and Fragonards, to say nothing of a number of Italian primitives (Botticelli, Fra Angelico, etc.).
It all represented an enormous sum.

I've only mentioned the impressive painters, but Fat Hermann
had collected a lot of trash as well. Apparently, he just hauled in
whatever he could get his hands on. In addition, it was obvious
that he was partial to any painting that was sensual enough, regardless of artistic merit; the collection contained a heavy pre-
ponderance of rosy buxom nudes portrayed in the bedchamber,
in the bath, or in the hasty embrace of some equally unclothed
swain. There were innumerable portrayals of Bacchanalian or-
gies, groups in woodland pools, satyrs leering at fat nymphs, pinch-
ing their nipples, chasing them under the trees, and other less deli-
cate pastimes. Some were amusing, some just pornographic.
Hermann was not interested in sylphs—all of his ladies of the can-

vas were exceptionally rotund and cushiony. Tucked away in a corner was a collection of terrible sepia drawings of Hermann and his wife, Emmy (and his previous wife, Karen) in glamorized poses with medieval costuming—ludicrous, particularly of Fat Hermann on horseback.

The chances of my getting to Vienna during this European tour were less than slim. There was no casual visiting between the American and Russian zones, so the chance of my discovering whether or not the Baron and Baroness Pitner had survived the Nazi regime were minimal. No fraternization was permitted with the Austrians, although they were looked at in a little different light from the Germans, but I was sure it would be permissible to investigate the whereabouts of known anti-Nazis who had American relatives. When we were coming through Bavaria, we sent our mess sergeant off on a side trip in a jeep with an officer to see his sister, who lived north of Munich. There were always reasonable exceptions to the rule, though on the whole it was strictly enforced.

The main difficulty with the nonfraternization policy was the fact that it included children and girls. The high command quickly recognized that the American soldier had a natural affinity with small moppets, and an exception was made in the general rule so that it no longer affected young children. Girls remained officially on the black list, but it took no savant to recognize that that would present an increasing problem as time went on. For most men with wives and sweethearts at home, it might make no difference one way or another, but for the young bachelors in their teens or early twenties, a pretty girl was a pretty girl, no matter how much he might hate and despise the Germans. The Austrian girls were very attractive in their bright-colored dirndls and they clearly had no distaste for the GIs. They were a very frustrated lot and a number of them were clearly coquettes, although they too knew the nonfraternization rules. For a young, unattached soldier who hadn't talked to a girl in months, there was a constant temptation, and there were any number of assignations. Ideology and biology do not always run on parallel tracks, and it would take some pretty superhuman arguments to convince young, carefree males and unattached pretty girls that they should ignore each other indefinitely, particularly when a number of Austrians honestly consider themselves "liberated." Even the ex-prisoners at the camp, who had more cause than any of us to hate anything Germanic, were unanimous in saying that the Austrians, with certain notable exceptions (now in the clink or at hard manual labor about the camp), were an entirely different breed of cat from the Germans. Even so, while it is true that the Germans took over the country in 1938, there was no doubt that there was a strong pro-Nazi minority in Austria.

During the initial advance through Germany, the frauleins (many of them young fraus with absent soldier husbands, I suspect) were always very much in evidence in the vicinity of columns of troops and American bivouacs and billets. They sat on embankments on side roads with skirts up to their hips by day and paraded by guardposts at dusk until military curfew drove them indoors. It was a remarkable way to greet an invading army, I thought. I remember stopping at a checkpoint to show our papers to a couple of MPs and one of them pointing up to a hillside above a country road and saying, "Look at that. These damn women come out here, undress, put on their bathing suits and take sunbaths—and we're supposed to arrest guys for blinking at them!" Between hormones and children, I suspected the whole nonfraternization policy would soon collapse like a house of cards.

On June 22 we evacuated the Lager "hospital" of Ebensee and

sent all the remaining patients to German hospitals in the relatively nearby town of Bad Ischl, under American supervision and direction. As far as I was concerned, it was a great improvement all around. Our personnel were not adequate for the numbers of patients and the old Lager barracks were hardly pleasant or roomy, although we had worked hard to clean them up. When a place was as incredibly filthy as Ebensee was for so long, you couldn't transform it into a modern hospital no matter how much work you put in.

Another big event was Mike's transfer out of the unit, which he did not know about since he had gone off on a two-day trip to Czechoslovakia. The news would be somewhat of a shock, for it looked as if in his new position as lieutenant colonel in an evacuation hospital, he would be heading directly to the Pacific. Dave and I, in that order, were slated as the next commanding officer, so Dave took over that post. It was a good break for him (although we were both sorry to lose Mike), since he possibly would get a majority within a couple of months. He would probably be discharged, or at least assigned to some unit heading back to the States. In either case, he would pick up a promotion, which he richly deserved. He had an enormous number of points (going on four years overseas) and if anyone deserved promotion and return to home base, it was he. I suspected that the rest of us would be dispersed in varying directions, some to the Pacific, some to stay with this unit, which was rumored to be up for re-equipment and reorganization to go to the Pacific after a thirty-day leave in the States.

Mike continued to live with us for a few more days until his new unit, which was nearby, moved out. Since Pilsen was in the American zone of Czechoslovakia, he obtained permission to visit Prague, in the Russian zone, and brought back a number of tales and impressions. Obviously, the Russians' attitudes and methods were much different from ours, but on the whole, my opinion was that things in their zone were running pretty well; although I thought Mike was correct in saying that the Czechs would much prefer to be under American occupation. It was unfortunate the Russians maintained so much secrecy about everything they did, because Americans are as bad as any other people about conjuring up bogey men. There was no question in my mind that everyone in Europe, Americans included, was placing far more weight and significance on a few exaggerated third-hand stories than they would have if Russia had lifted the veil of secrecy and censorship.

The story of General Patton's triumphal entry into Boston was fascinating. While everyone chuckled at his antics and mannerisms, there was no doubt but the faith in his tactical ability as a commander of an army was unanimous. It was a colorful army to work in and a good part of the drama and dash was undoubtedly due to his flair and showmanship. He had some damn good divisions to work with. I had seen enough of three of them (traveling across France with the 4th Armored, with the 80th Infantry at the Moselle Crossing at Pont à Mousson, and then the extended period with the 5th Infantry) to appreciate the material available with which he could carry out his tactical plans. I never thought that the Fifth Division received a tenth of the credit they deserved for their work across France, at the Seine, taking Metz, breaking the shoulder of the Bulge, saving Luxembourg City, opening three successive holes for the Fourth Armored through the Siegfried Line, then battling south across the Moselle near the Rhine and finally crossing the Rhine to Frankfurt. Dave, who was with the 5th Medical Battalion until he joined the 30th Field, said that the division public relations officer was very stuffy, toward both higher headquarters and representatives of the *Stars and Stripes,* just after the division came to Great Britain from Iceland. Therefore, the whole unit consistently received a cold shoulder. Patton himself, however, always swore by the Fifth and the boys in the Fourth Armored invariably said that the doughfeet of the Fifth should have received at least half of the credit for Fourth Armored exploits.

I had no objection to going to the Pacific, but I emphatically did not want to go without getting home first. It was good policy to be as inconspicuous as possible and to stay out of the sight of anyone whom you might happen to know with silver leaves or eagles on his shoulders. The out-of-sight, out-of-mind philosophy! For example, Mike wanted me to join his hospital and promised me the rank of major once we had arrived in the Pacific, but he was sympathetic and understanding about my wish to go back to the United States on the way to the Pacific so that I could have at least a brief visit with Blanche. Mike's new unit was leaving Marseilles and heading directly through the Suez Canal to the Pacific. Mike also warned me that another "chicken" colonel who was departing for a brief leave in the States would return here to pick up his eagles and take a fairly fresh evacuation hospital directly to the Pacific. Apparently he had his eye on me, and I was certainly going to try to stay out of sight and avoid that direct shot at the remaining theater of the war.

It looked as if we would be moving out in a few days. The general plan was to have the three platoons set up three separate temporary station hospitals, which was a much better job than the ones we had through May and June. It would probably mean that we would be doing some surgery and functioning in general like a community hospital. Dave, our new commanding officer, left on reconnaissance to pick out our new site, which was to be just south of Munich. In addition to functioning somewhat as a station hospital, it was planned for us to begin training and reorganization for the Pacific in our new capacity as a MASH unit.

Finally on June 29 we headed for our new station in Schliersee.

Dave and I took Mike down to his new unit's troop train, said goodbye, and took off well ahead of the convoy. When we arrived we began planning the distribution of the components of the station hospital that our platoon was supposed to run for the 20th Corps. The other two platoons would have similar missions elsewhere in Bavaria. All of this wasn't quite as simple as it had been in the days of actual fighting, when we could roll into a town and take over any suitable buildings (if there were any standing). Now only certain types of buildings could be requisitioned and, as was always true in a peacetime garrison army, the amount of red tape involved mounted daily. We happened to be in the military government office when a German lieutenant general who had tried to escape in civilian clothes was brought in. His complete uniform had also been found near where he was captured so that was brought along too. What a regalia—blue-green cloth with red facing on the lapels and dripping with braid and brass. It looked more like the outfit of a doorman at a nightclub than that of an army officer. Being in a somewhat juvenile frame of mind, all of us who were sitting in the AMG had our pictures snapped in this remarkable getup.

Our new location was in an SS rest area high in the mountains overlooking Schliersee. Officers were housed in a very clean and attractive Bavarian-style Gasthaus, which was small but spacious enough to give each of us either a single or a double room, depending on the draw. In addition to a small lobby and desk, the first floor had a good-sized Bierstube, which could be used as an entertainment center. For our new role as a station hospital, we had been reassigned nurses, and when that happened, there were always innumerable male officers hanging around like flies around a jam pot.

With the exception of the short periods at Traun and at Neubau, which were dull, flat farmland, our locations since V-E Day had been in the most beautiful and picturesque area of Europe. Schliersee lies some fifty miles south of Munich, in the heart of the most scenic part of Bavaria. The countryside was very mountainous, dotted with lovely little lakes and rich in the native color and tradition that even the inroads of Naziism had left relatively untarnished. The people still wore lederhosen, Tyrolean jackets, and brightly colored dirndls. The villages were small and neatly arranged in the valleys and the outer walls of the sparkling clean

Generalleutnant Scherer
Kommandeur einer Infanterie-Division

Signed postcard of Lt.. General Sherer

chalets were decorated with murals of religious and native scenes typical of that part of Bavaria. I always loved the scenery and the surroundings south of Munich and my feelings towards Naziism and the Germanic psychosis hadn't changed that.

A large Fourth of July wingding had long been planned and the colonel of the whole unit arrived as scheduled to start things off. Various officers from local units came too, plus quite a few from a distance. The two large rooms downstairs were decorated after a fashion. Everyone contributed items from packages to make hors d'oeuvres, sandwiches, etc. and the mess sergeant sent over a large, fancy cake. Macon Leigh, in charge of one of the Fourth Aux teams (which had been with us for quite a while) and I spent most of the morning brewing up punch. The party came off well. The Fourth of July celebration was not accompanied by rockets and fireworks. Although there was enough ammunition and various types of projecting equipment to have a spectacular display, it was obviously *verboten* to utilize firearms. There was still enough scattered gunfire from isolated German units in the mountains to make the casual use of weapons absolutely out of the question.

The highlight of the day after the Fourth of July celebration was my meeting and talk with the Count and Countess Felix von Luckner. I remembered, as a small boy, reading *The Sea Devil,* his exciting account of his activities during World War I as commander of an armed yacht that raided Allied shipping in the Pacific and South Atlantic. His greatest boast was that, in sinking a large number of merchant ships (a total of 186,000 tons), he never took a single life and treated the captured crews royally until he let them off the ship in lifeboats. Then after sinking the merchant ship, he would wire the British the location of the lifeboats so they could be picked up. Eventually, his yacht was run down by the Allies and he spent the rest of the war as a prisoner in New Zealand. Von Luckner assumed almost legendary proportions in Germany, and after World War I was a very popular lecturer in the United States, which he liked so much that he stayed for seven years. When he returned to Germany, he was exhorted by Hitler personally to join the Nazi party and to accept a position in the naval high command. He made it clear that he wanted nothing to do with the Nazi government and retired to his estate near Halle, where he remained under constant surveillance and house arrest by the Gestapo. Because of his reputation and widespread popularity, the Nazis didn't dare imprison him, but during the complete collapse in early May, the SS and the Werewolves had orders to kill him. Fortunately, the arrival of the American troops forestalled that.

Von Luckner and his wife had been staying in Heilbrunn, about fifteen minutes away, and they came to Schliersee to see a local tailor. He had in the past received honorary citizenship in the United States (the Nazis ordered him to renounce it, but he never did). In addition, he had performed some valuable services for the Americans and was now working for military government and intelligence. With all this, we felt that we could invite him and his wife to lunch with a clear conscience. They accepted with alacrity and polished off everything in sight. One little incident was an interesting commentary on living conditions in Germany. After the count had cleaned his tray, Dave offered him another piece of bread and butter. Luckner smiled a little and said, "No, I couldn't eat it right now, but would it be all right if I took it with me to eat later?"—that from a very wealthy man.

The conversation was most interesting. Von Luckner had a worldwide collection of prominent friends and acquaintances and regaled us with stories of people and places for hours. They were really an extraordinarily attractive couple. He was a big, striking-looking man in his late sixties, a thorough extrovert, bon vivant, and raconteur. The countess, who was Nobel's granddaughter,

had been a real Swedish beauty in her day. The count's stories of
the July 21 assassination attempt against Hitler by Count von
Stauffenberg and his colleagues were fascinating. A number of
the conspirators had been his friends, and he certainly would
have been involved (or at least implicated) had he not been
under house arrest.

Signed postcard from the "Sea Devil", himself, Count Felix von Luckner.

Sergeant Tommasette from our unit had some interesting fol-
low-up reflections on the count, which I will quote verbatim from
one of his letters.

> Coming home from the war and attending some classes . . . the
> professor of the class was always eager and anxious to know of the
> GIs' wartime experiences. So, he pressed me for some stories and
> when I got around to telling him of the Von Luckner story, he
> being Jewish, was livid and incensed because I thought the Count
> was such a great humanitarian and a noble person. There was
> nothing I could say about the Count that he would buy and he was
> very cool to me thereafter. Since, I saw first hand the concentration
> camps and the victims, I could understand his indignation and
> why he felt the way he did. I learned that people close to him had
> been victimized by the Nazis.
>   . . . One more story about the Count . . . made me smile and
> reflect a bit. . . . Lowell Thomas who thought enough of him to
> write his biography long before he died, had this daily 15 minute
> news broadcast on the radio for many years. . . . He always had
> this same announcer introduce him and sign off for him at each
> broadcast. The day the Count died, in Malmo, Sweden in 1966, I
> caught Lowell's broadcast by dumb luck, as I really didn't hear him
> very often. Without doubt, Lowell, no slouch himself, idolized the
> Count. He did such a masterful job that, when the announcer
> signed off he said pensively, "I wish I would have met the man."
> That remark gave me a special feeling and I think it would have
> done the same for you.

With so little work to be done in the hospital, and since we had
not yet embarked on a training program, I found that claustrophobia set in rapidly. On the first good day I decided to get out of
there. Dave and I took off in the jeep to wander through southern
Bavaria and Austria. We drove southeast through beautiful mountainous country, through the town of Kufstein with its ancient
schloss and into the valley of the Inn River. Following this towards Innsbruck was reminiscent of the Rhine because of the
number of old feudal castles dotting the banks, but the general

topography was, of course, entirely different, since the Inn cuts
through the Alps. The valley drive was a long, comparatively level
stretch rimmed by the towering Alpine crags. Innsbruck itself
was not particularly remarkable. There was moderate damage from
bombing, but nothing to compare with cities like Frankfurt and
Nuremberg. Both Austria and the part of Bavaria lying south of
Munich had been very fortunate. Innsbruck was the first damaged city I had encountered since seeing Linz in early May. Except for Innsbruck and one other small mountain railway junction,
there was no sign of the usual ravages of war in our whole trip.

From Innsbruck, we cut back over the mountains towards
Garmisch, once so gay and glamorous, now a dead city. The
Alpenhof Hotel, where a wonderful pianist in the smaller bar used
to play for our bacchanalia, was a German military hospital. The
shops were closed tight and the streets, once lined with cars from
all over Europe, were empty except for occasional army vehicles.

We pulled off the road to have lunch in the shadow of the
Zugspitze. At least that hadn't changed, nor had the little chalets
on the lower slopes of the mountains. The return trip was a pleasant drive through Oberammeragau and delightful Bavarian back
country to Bad Tolz, and we reached Schliersee in time for dinner. No place in the world is quite like the mountain regions of
Bavaria and Austria, with their serene grandeur and peaceful aura.

That evening two intelligence officers, an American colonel and
a British major, dropped in to pick up a meal from us and spent
the night. They had just arrested the German commandant of the
Paris area, and were well stocked with rum and brandy from his
looted supply.

Dave finally left, as we expected (July 14). I would take over
command of the 1st HU and we would start the training program
for the Pacific on Monday. We expected some new medical offic-

ers, although the Medical Corps did not get home on the same
point ratio system that other officers and enlisted men did. Apparently, we were considered unexpendable!

The new job of commanding officer called for a promotion to
major and was, predictably, a headache—particularly during the
transfer of so many of the old enlisted men (85-pointers) and their
replacement by comparatively new men, who were unfamiliar with
this type of combat work and should have had some training. We
started an organized training program on Monday, July 15, and at
the same time moved, but not far, just transferring of the part of
the hospital still under tents into a building. We worked steadily
all day, interviewing new men, planning the new setup, and out-
lining the first couple of weeks of the training schedule.

Our new MAC (Medical Administrative Corps) officer, Phil
Evanoff, was a damn good man, which was lucky, because his job
in the unit was very important, particularly during a training period. He was an industrial chemist by profession, energetic, vigorous, and very capable, spoke several languages well, and was
unusually widely read and extremely intelligent. I couldn't have
asked for a better right arm.

The mail was always the high point of the day, but could also be
a source of irritation. Some moronic remarks on Russia by supposedly intelligent Americans that Blanche quoted didn't surprise
me too much, but my jaw dropped a little when I heard that some-
body believed the atrocity stories about Germany to be *propaganda.* My God! Dave was in a particularly sour mood towards
the world one night after reading a paper full of stories of strikes,
quotations by stupid congressmen, etc., topped off by a letter from
his wife that told him of an acquaintance of theirs on the home
front who wrote to Secretary Forrestal complaining that navy
planes had caused his wife to miscarry during a vacation on Nan-
tucket. On this front, we had French soldiers in our uniforms,

trucks, and equipment refusing gas to a passing American jeep, Russians refusing to take back their own citizens released from various concentration camps, Belgian miners causing a further reduction in already critically low coal output by striking as an objection to King Leopold, and DPs of all nationalities stealing anything they could lay their hands on from the troops who had liberated them and were trying to take care of and repatriate them. Very interesting world! I know what Blanche meant when she described in a letter "how emotionally wearing it could be to hear people in the streets whose idea of an interchange of opinion consisted of a tirade against Roosevelt, Russia, etc."

We were now into late July, six weeks after V-E Day. I was sure now that the war was really over in Europe—a general visiting one day and a team of 3rd Army inspectors the next. Regular garrison stuff! One of the best things about this type of mobile surgical unit was that, during combat, you were never bothered with inspections of any kind. Never during the months of combat did we see an inspector, and life was very pleasant. But now that everything had settled down to a peaceful, quiet, stable existence, they were flocking around in droves. A garrison existence is the ideal time for checking up on units, but there was no question that they would be the bane of our existence from this point on. It turned out not to be bad at all—the two majors involved were pleasant enough and happened to hit the hospital at a very dramatic point in the training schedule over which I had been sweating for some days, and they were duly impressed. If you snow inspectors at the first exposure, invariably they'll find that everything is beautiful for the rest of their tour, while conversely, if you let them get off to a bad start, nothing will be right from then on.

Macon and I were coming back to quarters after sending off the inspectors, "trailing clouds of smoke and glory," when a truckload of GIs drove slowly up the street cheering and shouting. Just ahead was a young lady on a bicycle parting company with a wrap-around dirndl skirt she was wearing. In front of the security guard headquarters, another group of GIs took up the cheering as the skirt finally lost its grip and trailed out behind the bicycle like a streamer. Suddenly realizing that she was all legs, the biker stopped abruptly and began frantically to readjust. By this time, the towns-people were hanging out the windows and grinning, GIs were offering helpful suggestions and advice, and the girl was rapidly turning a brilliant scarlet. The time and place couldn't have been more dramatically chosen by Gypsy Rose Lee. We decided she showed considerable promise as an ecdysiast.

As we moved ahead with our training program, one day was completely undistinguishable from one another, contributing to the universal feeling among men overseas of interminable monotony, the passage of time with no beginning and no end. Now, however, we were on a five-and-a-half-day training schedule, Monday morning to Saturday noon, and had no patients (except for minor overnight stays that required little attention). So from Saturday noon until Monday morning, we were free agents except for the rotating duty officers. I had been sweating over the training schedules for the eight different departments (Surgery and Central Supply, Pre- and Postop, X-ray, Laboratory and Pharmacy, Administration, Motor Pool, Utilities, and Supply) into which I divided the men for training. In addition, I organized a schedule of competitive sports for them with other units, as well as arranging for movies, a library, or getting boats for their use.

15

V-J Day

SCHLIERSEE, BAVARIA

May 24–August 16, 1945

By the end of July, the rumors about a possible Jap surrender had gained momentum. The Tokyo broadcast of July 26 was a climax, but personally, I didn't believe a word of it—I didn't believe that any surrender was impending, nor did any of the rest of us. Confirmed pessimists after our stretch in the ETO, we did concede cautiously that everything looked good for a fast finish.

It was a hectic and confused time. Each week's training schedule had to be made out, and lectures and innumerable incidents with German civilians coming in for treatment filled out the days. The Germans were supposed to go to their own doctors and hospitals, but they flocked in with all sorts of minor emergencies, and it was hard to turn anyone away, German or not.

Another Sunday went by, less peaceful than I might have thought or planned. Headquarters stole a couple of my best men, including my staff sergeant, which necessitated a complete shakeup in the unit all the way up and down the line, always a headache, as well as reorganizing the training schedule for the week. Phil

Evanoff and I worked over that for several hours and then decided we might as well make a day and night of it and started in on the various reports we had to have in at the end of the month. The damn paperwork, much of which was ignored in combat, was a bane of the peacetime army. At least it kept me busy and there was a certain amount of fun and interest in a command job, but my God, I should think that career officers in a peacetime army would go mad with all this stuff thrown at them year after year.

I thought of studying German while I was there, but it hardly seemed worthwhile when we had so little contact with the population. It seemed as though there should be plenty of time to learn a dozen languages, but it was surprising how the days disappeared. I never seemed to have as much free time in the day as I thought I would.

Churchill's overwhelming defeat in the election surprised us all, though we had noticed considerable social unrest. I wasn't at all sure he was the man to lead England into the peacetime reconstruction, but still, I felt sorry for him. I was irritated at what seemed to me the ingratitude of a people towards a man who had probably saved England and who unquestionably was a focal point of England's courage and dogged determination after Dunkerque. It must have hurt him badly even through his armor of exuberance and egocentricity. "The captains and the kings" seemed to be departing before the tumult was over.

Through a contact in the Signal Corps, we were getting a remarkable number of excellent training films, which the men enjoyed a lot—it was certainly pleasanter than sweating through eight hours of dry lectures, demonstrations, etc. The army had done a superb job in those films. One was a long documentary movie on China—a brief historical background and then a cinematic survey of recent events from Sun Yat Sen to the present. The shots were amassed from all sources—American, British, Chinese, and even captured Japanese film.

I went out to dinner with Frank Gamache, the army director of all the mines over a wide area of Bavaria. He had a magnificent house overlooking one end of the lake (his three enlisted men lived in one wing) with a stable of three horses, a seven-passenger car, a German cook, and a wine cellar. A tough life! The dinner was excellent—fried chicken, small roasted brown potatoes, delicious salad and dressing, and surprisingly good wines and brandy. Several other officers joined us and we enjoyed a very pleasant and congenial evening. I had almost forgotten how much I missed

"No comment!" W.V. McD. at Berghof in Bayerischzell.

good living. Not that there was anything seriously wrong with our own headquarters and food, but still, everything smacked of the army. It was hard to avoid it, except in an unusual case like Gamache's, where he had a more or less independent job almost disassociated from the regular routines of army living. I hardly envied him, however; I would rather spend a few months in a mudhole than face the prospect of a long stretch of occupation duty.

Tom Hamilton arrived from one of the other platoons to take Macon's place on the team. He was a very nice guy, quiet, pleasant, with a slow, almost drawling voice. Like Macon, he was thoroughly trained and an excellent surgeon. Along with all the rest of us, he was in the hot seat and made an amazing remark about coming to the 1st HU "staging area"! If you added up those who had left—Mike, Dean, Macon, Ken to the Pacific, Rafe and Dave back to the States—that's just about what it was, a very "elastic situation," to steal a bromide from the communiqués. I could see the steam rise whenever I sat down on the so-called hot seat, but I was far from alone in that. It was a universal feeling among all the doctors who were below the 90–100-point class, and even some who were higher. I had no objections to the Pacific as an ocean or as a theater, but after two years in the ETO, I most certainly wanted to see home before I saw it.

By the end of the first week in August, optimism about the Japanese war became increasingly prevalent and publicly expressed. Some of the brass hats made some exuberant statements, but I didn't notice that the exuberance filtered down to us small fry. Not that we were making any dire predictions about time or casualties, but it was a simple fact that when we were training for a war in which so many of our friends were participating, and when so many other friends were already on their way to the Pacific nothing suggested the end of the war on any given day. We all had an attitude of realistic fatalism, which we had to develop to prevent going mad with speculations and wishful thinking. We heard the radio announcement about the new atomic bomb. I am no physicist, but I knew enough about the work done with the cyclotron (much of which was medical) to realize what it might mean. In fact, we had occasionally speculated as to whether any type of atomic explosive would be developed to the point where it could be used in the war. The potentialities were stupendous, but nobody was indulging in any dreams that even widespread use of the atomic bomb would bring an immediate end to the war—although there was no question as to its value in shortening the period of fighting.

Schlier See, Bavaria, Wednesday, August 8, 1945

The news of Russia's entering into the war with Japan, coming on top of the fantastic tales of the development, use and effect of the atom bomb was too much for all of us and all the cautious restraint which we have been wearing as a veneer dropped off and we sat up half the night speculating on and discussing the future. I've always felt that it took the capture of territory to win a war and that the capture of territory meant that an infantry rifleman had tramped across it. Well, I'm not so sure now. It would almost seem that even the Japanese could not be steeped enough in fanaticism to want to carry on their suicidal war. My God, if the stories are true and I can see no reason to doubt them, there will be literally nothing left of the Japanese Islands in a few weeks or months. It's impossible to imagine they will continue the war but on the other hand, it's almost impossible for me to see how they would surrender at this stage or who would do the surrendering. It remains to be seen but I'm almost ready to say that it can't last much longer.

I was interested in the Pope's statement on the atomic bomb, but I'll admit to some irritation. I realize the difficult position in which he is placed since, in accordance with all the principles of Christ, he must be against war and killing in any form but what does he expect us to do? kill Japs slowly over a long period of time and prolong the misery and unhappiness of the whole world or finish the war off quickly even if it means employing such a deadly and inconceivably powerful weapon as this seems to be? Personally, I cannot distinguish much between methods of killing—I've seen as much suffering in tortured and maimed human flesh from light artillery or machine guns as from the heaviest of bombs and I can't quite see how anyone could advocate dragging out the war by killing slowly simply because of a new and incredibly powerful weapon has been classified as inhumane. If this bomb ends the war a few months sooner, as far as I'm concerned, it's the most humane discovery of the past six years.

Schlier See, Bavaria, Saturday, August 11, 1945

This is the first week of May all over again with the major exception that this time the war in question is on the other side of the world, and therefore doesn't immediately affect us here. Otherwise, however, it's much the same—the same uncertainty, rumors, counter rumors, the same sensation of an approaching inevitable end and the same hesitancy in believing anything but a fait accompli. Undoubtedly, this will drag on for several days just as the closing stages of the European war did. In the meantime, our training program for the Pacific runs along as if nothing was happening or would happen. Very stable thing, these training programs—even if the war ended by Monday, we would undoubtedly have to continue ours just as if there were still a climactic and undecided war going on. I suppose that this business of waiting throughout the day for each hourly AFN news broadcast will continue for an indefinite number of days—at least, no one can say it has been dull listening during this week what with the atomic bomb, Russia's entry into the war, Japan's offer to surrender and the subsequent interchanges of notes.

To get off this subject, the European radio is amusing these days with typical Americana flooding the ether. You would chuckle to turn to the Munich radiowave band, for instance, and hear the typical voice of a high pressure radio announcer ramble on about a musical program called "Luncheon in Munchen." They even have commercials now except that instead of plugging some "crispy, crunchy cracker" the insinuating voice urges soldiers to send their money home by PTA (Personal Transfer Account)—"The safest, quickest and surest!" I expect that the musical jingles of the Pepsi Cola variety will appear any day now.

August 13, 1945—Schlier See, Bavaria

Macon Leigh turned up this evening on a quick visit, bringing with him a member of his new unit, Bert Davis, who had been with the 30th Field for some time before I joined. . . . We sat around and talked away the whole evening which is no help to my letter writing plans. Macon was considerably buoyed up by the prospects of a surrender in the near future which, of course, will mean that he probably will not be heading for the Pacific and may, therefore, get home much sooner than he had thought when he left us some days ago. We exchanged news, had a few drinks, heard all the tales of his new unit and then listened to Bert's tales—he had been with a platoon of the 16th Field which had worked near us through the final drive into Germany. I am not sure whether or not I ever told you because of censorship, but they were captured shortly after the crossing of the Rhine and one of their doctors named Fondey, whom we had all known, was killed in the ambush. Even though it happened only a short distance from us and they were finally recaptured by elements of the 5th Division, we had never heard the full details so he had to go into his whole story at length. In the middle of the evening, I had to trot down to the hospital to see an admission with a broken ankle. This hospital is gradually filling up which is fine particularly if the war does end soon and our training program loses its raison d'être. Tonight, however, that prospect (that is, the Jap surrender) begins to look a little more dubious than it did 24 hours ago. I don't know. The Japanese maneuvering and phoney statements about when the terms were received have begun to give off a distinctly rank odor. While none of us have any clear ideas or theories about what is going on behind the scenes, I wouldn't trust any of them as far as I could kick a tractor with my bare feet. At any rate, I am not making any plans for relapsing into an immediate euphoric status. Not that there would be anything immediate whatever happens, but this morning we could almost hear the dove's wings flapping and catch the smell of tweeds and worsteds, whereas tonight the scenic backdrop of living is resuming the familiar color of olive drab.

The next few days were a replica of the period preceding V-E Day. What a diplomatic shambles! All evening we all hung onto the radio and listened to the various reports, which only added to the confusion. Whether all the delays and rumors were due to communication difficulty, internal strife within the Japanese government between the fanatical militarists and the pacifists, or just normal Japanese monkey business, I had no idea, but it was damn irritating. I was inclined to agree with Tom Hamilton, who thought we should have given them twenty-four hours in which to have their final reply back in Washington before beginning a concentrated blasting with naval guns, air attacks, and atomic bombs.

Regardless of the international shilly-shallying, we went ahead with the training program, which consisted of one group beginning to work with small arms on the firing range while most of the new men worked under a couple of old noncoms at tent pitching, i.e., setting up a mythical hospital under canvas in nearby fields. In ways it seemed unnecessary to go through all this backbreaking training on which depended to a great extent the efficiency and mobility of the outfit as a surgical unit. Still, the men were pretty good, diving in with remarkably little bitching and even with some enthusiasm. It was an anomalous situation but we couldn't very well throw out the program when it was still possible that the Japs might reject the terms and go on with a last-ditch fight. The firing, however, was hardly a chore, since it was one part of training that the men almost universally enjoyed, and it was important now because medics in the Pacific would be armed if they were far up in the lines, as we expected to be in those new MASH units. I had a chance to try out a small pocket gun and a beautiful Walther automatic that I had acquired along the line.

I couldn't stay long on the range, however, because we were rapidly becoming very busy at the hospital. In addition to a boy with a left renal stone whom we were observing, plus a room full

Patient being brought in from ambulance in Schliersee.

of respiratory infections (atypical pneumonia, tonsillitis, etc.), I operated on a boy who was shot in the left chest posteriorly with a 45. He was a nice boy (looked about sixteen) from a Ranger battalion and after he came out of the initial shock was delighted to be the subject of a photographic record of a case from start to finish. We took shots all along the line from the time he was unloaded from the ambulance through the preop X-ray and surgery until he was finally ensconced in postop quarters. The next day, when he felt better, he was very pleased at the prospect of having a record of his hospital career, even if he wasn't technically a war casualty and only represented an accidental shooting. I had picked up a new 35-mm camera and wished that I had had a good camera in England and had made a complete photographic record of the whole two years. I could have had some really great shots but would have missed many of them because of censorship—the regulations on cameras regarding what you could snap were very strict, particularly early in the game.

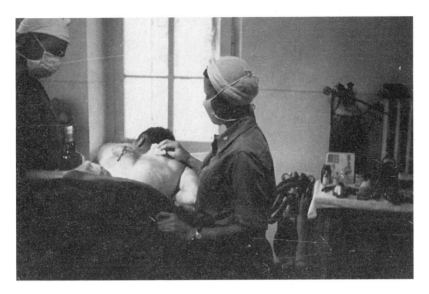

Lt. Spangler preparing the operating field.

The first HU hotel for "military transients" was still running at capacity. At first it was just weekends but then began to spread out through the week. The English and American intelligence officers were still there; Macon Leigh and Bert Davis were talked into staying longer, as was Colonel Sanford. Chester Myers, an ex-MAC, arrived, followed shortly by Sam Carlin, who had been with the 4th Aux and then went to a portable field hospital similar to the one to which Macon was assigned.

August 15, 1945—V-J Day—Schlier See, Bavaria

What can you say, dearest, about a day for which everyone has been waiting and praying but which took on through the years such a mythical form that even in reality it's difficult to grasp or believe. War has been for so long a part of our lives, in thinking, in actual experience and in every part of the daily routine from headlines to rationing, that the concept of a world at peace is something that will have to sink in slowly. All I knew when we heard the first official flash at 1:30 in the morning was that you and

I were together again even though we are still thousands of miles apart and might be for several months to come. It was different from the prospect of coming home to you for only a month or two which had existed up to the announcement. Without ever consciously thinking about it, I realized that as long as the war went on, it would never be wholly our life, even when we were together, just because of the fact that I had signed away a part of mine to war. Now, that's over, and we can live again for years and years and forever. Like the rest of the world, we've waited interminably, prayed, hoped, and wondered what this day would be like, doubting sometimes it could ever come in our youth. What it is like, I couldn't tell myself—it's living again, it is feeling life and foolishness in your veins; it is being able to look at the future without fatalism and to laugh without the conscious twinge that nothing could be very pleasant or amusing while men were being torn apart somewhere else in the most miserable existence imaginable. Even for a doctor whose life is a constant association with suffering, the first actual experience with war is a sickening thing. Probably the worst combination of all the horrors of war came last winter during the Bulge and the subsequent offensive through the Siegfried Line, when casualties were terribly high, fighting was constant and intense, the weather conditions under which the Infantry had to live and fight were awful and the replacements who streamed in continuously were only frightened kids. A high percentage of our admissions at that time had almost identical Army histories—18 years old, 6 months in the service, a few weeks or less on the line and then admitted to the hospital half frozen and ripped apart. For some of them, a wound didn't mean release but only a reprieve of a few weeks until they were back on the line again. Contrary to the movies and popular fiction, men did not evidence any horror or despair at crippling wounds—the experiences which they had been through were so bad that their initial reactions to being maimed were almost ones of relief because they knew that they were through with war for good; in fact, it was common talk about "million dollar wounds"—those that were incapacitating enough so they would be sent back to the States and eventually discharged. It is a helluva existence when the best which life has to offer us, as was the case with the infantry, is the prospect of a wound that would not be too crippling but which would be severe enough to get a man home. Thank God that none of them will have to go through that again this winter and I hope never again.

Until a few days ago, I didn't think that even the most confirmed optimist would have envisioned a world at peace this Summer. It's a real miracle and I thought it was very appropriate for the announcement to have it come while we were all awake to hear it. I think the actual date was August 14, wasn't it? When I finished writing last night, I sealed up your letter around midnight and then since the radio reports were getting hot, I stretched out with a book to wait. At about 1:30 came the sudden flash from the White House that the Jap note accepting the surrender terms had been received. Macon Leigh, Bert Davis, Sam Carlin (all overnight visitors from the newly formed portable field hospital), Tom Hamilton, Colonel Sanford and myself broke out bottles which we had been saving for the occasion and proceeded to drink and talk until about 5 A.M.—probably the most thoroughly relaxed drinking I've done in two years! For Macon and his group, it was particularly timely since they were "hot" and expected to leave for the Pacific at any moment. Quite a load off their minds! As for me, now that I'll never take this unit into combat, I'll be delighted to get home and out of the Army fast enough so that I'll exit as a Captain rather than wait even a day for the promotion to Major. There is no way of guessing how demobilization will be carried out now but I should guess that everything will be speeded up tremendously. I'll keep you posted even on rumors now since there is no longer the worry of raising your hopes only to have them dashed completely by a sudden trip to the Pacific. The only possible disappointment now would be that getting home was slower than expected. Not that I'll be any less frantic during the coming months but it will be different now—more of an impatience than the sense of grasping at a straw which the Army was holding out but might hold back at any minute. We have come a long way since Pearl Harbor and faster, I guess, than anyone would have dared to predict and while America can be proud of all of her accomplishments from production line down to the riflemen who did the work, it was the prayers and determination of thousands of wives and mothers which did more than anything else.

And so it ended—not with a whimper but with a bang! Rereading those last letters gave an interesting perspective on the endless philosophical discussion over the subsequent decades as to whether or not we should have "dropped the bomb." Having lived through the disasters of endless days of ground warfare with maimed and dead young men by the thousands, seen the results of attacks by both German and allied aircraft, sympathized with the miseries endured by thousands of civilians, and in particular, treated a small portion of the six million Jews subjected to the "final solution," my perspective on the effects and results of two atomic bombs becomes a little blurred.

It was fascinating to see the reactions of my compatriots to the atomic bomb and the end of the Japanese war. I cannot recall a single comment questioning the morality of the decision, nor do I remember any such commentary in magazines, journals, or newspapers. The general feeling we all had was that war was horrible from beginning to end, that men were being killed and civilians slaughtered, that there was nothing ennobling about war as such. We made no distinction between being drilled through the head with a rifle bullet, cut into pieces with shrapnel, burned to death in a tank, or blasted with an atomic bomb. The major objective of our lives was to end the war, and very little thought was given to the means used to accomplish that end.

Would it have been better to proceed with the invasion of Japan without the preliminary bombings and subsequent massive casualties? Can one balance the death of an individual from an atomic blast with death from an ordinary bomb, a shell fragment, or a machine-gun bullet?

Even today, I cannot provide any satisfactory answer for myself and I doubt if I will ever be able to, but perhaps we can learn something from an overview of all the varied horrors of war, and vow that we can somehow, someday, bring this madness to an end— a complete break with the history of the human race over several thousands of years.

16

The Occupation

REDEPLOYMENT AND HOME

August 16–December 25, 1945

Schlier See, Bavaria, August 19, 1945

Now that we are a few days beyond V-J Day, I thought I might give you a little fuller explanation of the redeployment program as it was planned after V-E Day. First of all, units were to be classified by the War Department with a specific number which was a clue to their future assignment—Class I units were to be Army of Occupation, Class IV units were to be sent home, broken up, and the men discharged. Class III were to be disbanded and Class II units were scheduled to join the forces in the Pacific but this class was further subdivided—IIA units were to go directly, IIB units were to go via the United States and have 30-day furloughs and TC (Strategic Reserve) were to return to the U.S. and remain there until some indefinite time when they would be called out to the Pacific. Under this system, 85-point men were to be taken from their respective outfits and assigned to the Class IV units, which obviously acted only as vehicles to get them home. We were IIB and the unit lost over half the total personnel by the shift of high-point enlisted men to IV units. Replacements for these men were from III and IV units—men who had less than 80 points. My God, what a shuffling and kicking around there was for a while. Now, we're all afraid that the kicking around will begin all over again on a lower point scale. I think that men and officers are almost unanimous in feeling they would rather remain with their present units rather than be bounced around regardless of whether staying with their unit meant they would be sent home a few weeks or even a couple of months later. Kicking around from one strange unit to another has always been the great horror of everyone in the Army. Now, of course, the other horror is the possible assignment in the Army of Occupation. I don't honestly think that is very likely for anyone except for very low-point men. Knowing the Army, however, particularly in the way they handle medical officers, I remain extremely wary, skeptical and ready to do violent battle with anyone up to the Surgeon General who might be harboring the idea of slipping me into the A of O. Now that the war is over, I no longer have any ideals, inhibitions or qualms and by God, I'll get home to you within the next few months if I have to develop a psychosis or build up a case for Court Martial to do it. My patriotism ended on V-J Day and as far as I'm concerned now, the Army can dig up plenty of doctors for the occupation from among those who have been overseas only a few months or not at all.

By late August, we were still in Schliersee. It seemed peculiar that I had been only forty miles from Munich for over seven weeks and hadn't seen the city. For one reason or another, I had been so tied down that, except for the trip to Innsbruck and Garmisch with Dave early in July, I hardly moved. On August 19, however, I finally broke loose and left for headquarters (and the Third HU). We went through the southern outskirts of Munich and I decided to put off sightseeing until the return trip.

Headquarters and the Third HU are set up near Greifenburg, a small town southwest of Munich, in a lonely rural setting. The buildings were said to have been a "girls' school," but there was something mysterious about it. It was a modern building, well equipped and furnished with furniture donated by Adolph himself. Nowhere was there any evidence of a library, classrooms, or any of the other appurtenances associated with a school. Local town gossip had it that this "school" was one of the many Nazi "baby factories" that were scattered throughout Germany, where "volunteer" frauleins were selected by the Gestapo with a view towards Nordic physiognomy and suitability for maternity. Each girl chosen was assigned a single room at one of the "schools" and when it was full, a quota of SS men on leave paid regular visits. Every girl had to agree on entry to leave her door unlocked and admit any of the SS men who chose to visit her—object, impregnation. A girl remained at the "school" until she was definitely pregnant. At this point, she was removed to another type of "home" where she remained through gestation, delivery, and convalescence. The offspring of these cold-blooded unions were destined to be brought up by the state, presumably to be future leaders of the Nazi party. Quite a system! It involved only a small number of girls, since it was a fairly recent brainstorm of some of the top Nazis and was in a very embryonic phase of development.

At any rate, there was only rumor, gossip, and circumstantial evidence to support the theory that the Third HU was in fact established in a former baby factory. Whatever it was, it made an excellent, comfortable small hospital. I transacted what business I had with the hospital adjutant, the colonel, and the supply officer, had lunch with them and a few other officers, and then started on the return trip. Tom Hamilton and I left early after lunch and had time to wander around Munich, so I took him on a tour of my old haunts—at least those which I could find or recognize! The city, once so gay and lively, was tragically smashed up—a somber shell with charred walls, acres of rubble, and piles of debris lining the streets. The area around the Bahnhof where the Loewenbrau Kellar had stood was thoroughly demolished and unrecognizable. The same was true of the hotel area where most of us had lived and where the American Express had stood. We couldn't even get through the rubble, which was still being cleared. Other sections were comparatively intact, particularly the large area including the Odeonsplatz, the Hofgarten, the Prinz Regenten Bad. Two of the three opera houses were damaged only slightly, but the Café Luitpold was little more than a bare shell, standing empty and forlorn with a chipped sign sagging down behind a heap of bricks and mortar. There were still spots where the relics of the Wittelsbach tradition, so comparable to that of Vienna, still remained. For me it was a rather sad and nostalgic afternoon. I had looked forward to returning to Munich, but except for a few ghostly remnants, the old Munich was gone forever. Little remained of the fascinating history and tradition of Bavaria and of the Wittelsbachs. The one bright spot was that the plaque in memory of the sixteen Nazi thugs killed in the 1920 Putsch had been torn down, and replaced by one carrying the names of the four policemen (members of the Landswehr) who had been killed in defeating the first Nazi uprising.

Schlier See, Bavaria, Sunday, August 25, 1945

As a day of rest, this particular Sunday has been a washout. I rolled out of bed fairly early to shave and from then on cases seemed to dribble in all day. Everything from a fractured wrist to a hysterical German woman with a two-year-old baby who supposedly had swallowed a deadly poisonous blackberry. They called it (the berry) Tollkirrchen but I haven't the vaguest idea of what the hell it was, so after slipping in a stomach tube, I burrowed around in various pharmaceutical and medical books on plants, drugs, etc. to find out what it was. It was determined that the poisonous element in the berry was belladonna (as in deadly nightshade) so I gave the baby the routine antidotes. Either the treatment worked or the baby had never swallowed the berry at all, because we sent her out in excellent shape after a period of observation. . . .

I decided to take a break and get out of here for the day so, after the usual routine of rounds were completed, I left in a jeep [for] . . .

the Chiemsee (just off the Autobahn to Salzberg) where Mad
Ludwig had built his most fantastic palace on an island in the
middle of the lake (Herrenchiemsee). . . . The palace itself is
modeled after the Trianon but while it was only partly finished, it
made Versailles look like the work of a very amateur megalomaniac.
I couldn't begin to describe it since every one of the completed
rooms was straight from the Arabian Nights, and the Hall of
Mirrors put its counterpart to shame. There were magnificent
floors inlaid with ebony or rosewood, the finest marble from every
country, huge chandeliers of crystal, Venetian glass and even one of
Meissen china, tapestries worked with gold and encrusted with
rubies and emeralds, tables with tops made completely of lapus
lazuli, magnificent pieces of Dresden, 3-dimensional ceiling
paintings, fascinating clocks of all varieties and a profusion of
paintings some of which were only fair but others by Fragonard,
Boucher, Franck, etc., were masterpieces . . . . It was hardly a cozy
little home but then, with his 18 other palaces scattered throughout
Bavaria, Ludwig only managed to spend 23 nights at Chiemsee so
he didn't benefit much from the millions of dollars which he
poured into the establishment. Bad as he was, he was still quite a
character and at least he left something behind at which future
generations could stare and wonder. You couldn't call it beautiful
since it was thoroughly garish and ornate but there was beauty
scattered throughout the building and the opulence and magnifi-
cence of his unfinished efforts (Ludwig himself designed the whole
building) was something worth seeing.

Frank Gamache, commanding officer of the engineering unit
which I described to you, has managed to corner four magnificent
horses, three blooded stallions and an excellent little pregnant
mare, and hired a groom to take care of them. A very tough life! At
any rate, it is great fun for me since it provides the opportunity of
having a break at regular intervals for excellent food and for riding
through this magnificent countryside so that we are planning on
going out every evening after dinner.

Obviously, once the war was a thing of the past, there was no
sense in keeping the men on a training program designed for war
in the Pacific just to make sure they were sufficiently occupied. It

was somewhat of a problem actually. You had to give them something to do and for a unit that had really worked in combat, the duties connected with demobilization hospital work were a pushover. We dug up a movie projector, a motor boat, and considerable athletic equipment and started an athletic program of intramural competition in the form of tournaments and outside competition with baseball teams of other units. Then we located music teachers through C.I.C. and began piano and violin lessons, brought in a German teacher in the morning and a French teacher in the afternoon to hold language classes, and apprenticed one man to the town photographer so that he could hold classes in photography and organize a photographic group with some enlargers, printing paper, and developer. In the evenings, we had movies, an occasional live show by troops of Bavarian entertainers, and took over a small cabaret on the lake where the men could go two nights a week. We brought in a small orchestra and got fairly good beer from a source in Augsburg, so they'd have some place to go for a change of scene and to sit and drink a few beers in fairly pleasant surroundings. There were regular trips once or twice a week for fifteen or twenty men at a time to various points of interest in Bavaria. All that, plus the ordinary medical and operating routine, was the life of an EM in a field hospital. It wasn't too bad and the men were busy enough not to become too bored, but like everyone else, they had only one fixed idea in mind—getting home. Everything else was just a matter of marking time.

I had a letter from our previous CO, Mike Mulligan, who had been promoted and given command of an evacuation hospital that was to be sent directly to the Pacific. The transport was in the Mediterranean on the way to the Suez Canal on V-J Day, whereupon it switched destinations and landed in Boston. It was ironic to think that if I had accepted Mike's offer to join him and head directly to the Pacific, I would have been home in Boston in late August instead of sitting in the foothills of the Alps.

Everyone in ETOUSA thought that the whole redeployment system was a mess—which to some degree it became, particularly when Congress and individual members began to get in the act. There was nothing simple about restructuring units with men and officers who had reasonably similar point averages and then arranging transport to ports of embarkation and thence to the United States for the formalities of discharge.

On October 19, 1945, we suddenly received orders to proceed to Pilsen, Czechoslovakia, which at least was a change of scene and provided some interesting further insights into the war. In the normal course of events, the American Army would have been in charge of practically all of Czechoslovakia; but the arrangements that had been made among the major powers were such that our troops were brought to an abrupt halt in Pilsen and remained there, even though reconnaissance units had gone as far as Prague long before the Russians were even approaching the city.

I had a field day in Pilsen. A group of us went to a football game at Marienbad between the 22nd Corps and the 4th Armored Division. They had a good field laid out on the outskirts of town, with wooden bleachers built down for each sideline. There was a good-sized crowd, perhaps four to five thousand, interspersed with Czech girls and often their families, so it was all very reminiscent on a small scale of a fall afternoon at the Harvard Stadium. There were even photographers from *Stars and Stripes* and *Yank* running up and down the sidelines with their cameras and little printed cards saying "Press" stuck in their overseas caps. A Red Cross doughnut-and-coffee wagon drove up and down during the half and a GI band added to the festivity.

Between the halves, a group of Russian Cossacks in their native costumes put on a horse show in an adjoining field, racing up and down doing all varieties of trick riding. They were damn good. A crowd of GIs formed a closely packed lane up and down which the Cossacks galloped. It was remarkable that no one was injured or killed, because following the usual custom of crowds, the Americans closed in more and more in an effort to see better until the galloping horses were brushing soldiers on both sides of the lane. The weather was good, so between the Cossacks and the football game, I used up a considerable amount of film.

The Bronze Star and Oak Leaf Cluster both came through, adding considerably to my point score. My only interest in them was the extra points they gave me. Conversely, I was trying to hold up a promotion to major, because the higher rank might require more points before repatriation. I had some ninety points but very few medical officers had been sent home with a total of less than one hundred. The system which was used for discharge of medical officers in the 3rd Army was entirely different from that used in the 7th Army or COM Z or any other group. The 3rd Army only released us as the army surgeon classified us as "available" for redeployment, which depended on the number of medical officers actually assigned to army units and on the replacements available.

Pilsen, Friday, October 26, 1945

A party last night wasn't very much except that it was interesting, if a little depressing, to hear an intelligent group of Czechs discussing their problems, personal and national. The main aftermath of the party is that I was persuaded to give a lecture and conduct a sort of forum for the Pilsen branch of the American Institute of Prague, which is a group of business and professional men who banded together in groups which meet twice a month with the purpose of furthering American–Czech relations and mutual understanding. It was originally formed long before the war, was obviously broken up during the German occupation, and re-formed as soon as the first American troops entered Czechoslovakia. The meeting today

lasted from 5 P.M. until almost midnight and was surprisingly
pleasant. They were a very intelligent group of men and all were
apparently extremely interested in American life, customs and
science. When we finally broke up, they presented me with a little
pin given to each lecturer at the Institute—my Czechoslovakian
decoration! I enjoyed it all much more than I thought I would last
night when I had the feeling I had been trapped into something.

The Czech money is being changed in valuation and a new
issue coming out so I took myself off to the finance office very early
in the morning since I felt it would probably resemble a run on the
bank. This changing of Czech money has been a helluva headache
for all the unit officers, myself included. Although I arrived at the
finance office at about 7:30 A.M., and well up in the line, I still
didn't get out until almost noon and feel as if I'd gone through a
small war. What will come of this new currency makes for interesting speculation. Although the new issue is valued at 2 cents to the
Kronen, instead of the previous 1 cent, we received an equal
exchange of new for old Kronen. Theoretically, that means that
each of us have doubled our money in dollars but for money
orders, etc. Finance is still using the old rate of one cent to the
Kronen, and we will be paid tomorrow at the same exchange.
Obviously that situation can't go on indefinitely with Army finance
and international exchange using a different basis but I can't
imagine they will let us make anything on the deal. How it will
work out, I don't know but it will be interesting to see.

The reason for this new issue was a move by the Czech Government to put an end to the black market which is rampant here as
well as everywhere else in Europe and also to combat inflation and
to spot those people who may have made money during the
German occupation. The Czechs have to turn in all their old
money to the banks and after today, it becomes valueless. Then
they are issued new money but are only allowed to withdraw a
minimal amount—the rest must remain in savings accounts for a
time, as yet unspecified. It's a pretty drastic move and will curtail
any large commercial operations but it should be quite effective in
achieving the purposes for which it was designed. Of course, with
the present division of Czechoslovakia into two zones, Russian and
American, Benes' Government has a helluva job achieving any
unified policy, and I doubt if either the Russians or Americans will

withdraw before the elections next Spring. From a strictly political point of view, this country is interesting because here is an independent nation where Russian communism and American democratic capitalism are meeting face to face, not only with ideologies, but with armies and influence. Like all of Europe, Czechoslovakia has swung to the left and communism is fairly strong (estimated 30% here in Pilsen) but my Czech acquaintances tell me that communism as such is much more popular in the United States zone than in Russian territory. The old story of the grass is always greener! Benes himself is, of course, a staunch democrat and very much pro U.S. and the popular rumor is that he postponed the general election from October until next Spring because he recognizes the trend away from out and out communism would increase during the Russian occupation. As you know, I'm far from a Russophobe, but the average Russian soldier doesn't make too good a political ambassador. American officers who have had much contact with them at the roadblocks and Czechs who travel back and forth between the zones, say that their habit of living off the country and their general attitude is not endearing them very much to the people. I don't believe any of the wild rape and murder rumors which circulate from time to time among Bolshevik-hating reactionaries, and I have never heard of a really authenticated case but there is no doubt that, except for the Guards divisions, the Russkie is a pretty unruly lad. I doubt if there are any more actual criminals than there are in our own army, but they do seem to indulge in promiscuous and continual looting here as well as in Germany. However, the Russians are people just the same as everyone else and except for lacking somewhat in the veneer of civilization because of their own very recent escape from serfdom, I don't think they differ very much fundamentally from any other race. At any rate, I'm damn sick and tired of idle prattle about war between the United States and Russia. The Germans, of course, would be delighted to see that eventuality but it's surprising how many people among our allied nations are terrified of the Russians and the communist bogey and accept a future U.S.-Russian war practically as a fait accompli. What a lot of stupidity! If they spent as much time trying to make democracy work as they do worrying about REDS, they need have no fear of communism extending beyond Russia. I am a little tired of the word itself, because actually, there isn't any such thing as communism existing in the world today unless it's in some remote Polynesian island which was overlooked in the Pacific war. What we need is a thorough vocabulary shakedown because I don't think anyone today knows what anyone else means in a conversation about fascism and communism, right and left, capitalism, socialism or whatnot—and that includes Laski and Wallace as well as McCormack and Bilbo.

The process of shifting men to various units consistent with their "point" score had begun for me with orders to proceed to the 67th Evacuation Hospital at Erlangen near Nuremberg, which interestingly enough, we had gone through during the invasion of Central Germany and Bavaria. There was no tremendous "rush" in completing the orders so I traveled leisurely to the West and arrived at Erlangen late in the afternoon of November 7. On checking in at headquarters, I found Chester Meyers, a MAC officer from the 30th Field Hospital, sitting behind the adjutant's desk. He organized everything for me, and I settled in with a number of old casual acquaintances to await further developments. The unit was not very active and the days were hardly inspiring but at least there were some surgical problems and surgical patients, which was a change from the moribund activities of the past month. In a way, I was glad to have had the chance to see how an evacuation hospital functioned—and even gladder that I never was assigned to one during the war. It was too dreary, immobile, routine, and uninteresting compared to our life with combat troops and auxiliary surgical teams, which I am convinced was the ideal job in a war for an active surgeon.

Finally, after two pleasant if unexciting weeks during which I had resigned myself to sweating out a month or so in this new environment, a TWX came down from USFET giving the army permission to send home excess medical officers with point scores above the high seventies. With the Bronze Star, Oak Leaf Cluster, Distinguished Unit Citation, and five Battle Stars, I was well into the eighties and was immediately transferred to the 90th Division on November 22 with orders to report in by midnight. After much frantic packing, streamlining, and mailing of excess baggage and footlockers, I took off on the long freezing jeep ride to the 90th Division at Weiden, Germany. From there it was a long train trip to Marseilles—perhaps four or five days with the condition of the railroads—so that we should arrive at the Port of Embarkation about November 30.

Our billets at Weiden were hardly comfortable, but who gave a damn at that point—we were going home! The few hours after our arrival were wild. The four of us who arrived on November 25 were the last officers to hit the division before the deadline, and we were racing around frantically being processed, stenciling our luggage, and doing all the thousand and one things that accompany an army overseas movement.

We finally boarded the train and after a miserable, stop-and-go, six-day ride, we finally debarked at the Calais Staging Area and settled into tents awaiting further orders. I harbored the illusion during the frigid train ride that it would be warm in southern France, but it was miserably uncomfortable. There was a shortage of doctors so I was handling a bunch of sad sacks with all varieties of crud.

Finally, on December 3, we were alerted and marched down to the docks at Marseilles. I remember looking around the harbor for some luxurious liner that would be taking us back to the States. As we lined up in battalion formation on the dock, we were actually looking over our ship—the M.S. *Cape Flattery*. She turned out to be a 1,600-ton motor ship, into which almost a thousand men were jammed. Shortly after passing the Straits of Gibraltar, one of the two engines on the motor ship gave out, leaving us staggering along through the Atlantic. We encountered a tremendous winter storm that did a great deal of damage to the *Queen Mary*, which was sailing from England at about the same time. This buffeted us around for several days. We were all continually seasick and the endless chow line was not very heavily occupied. The officers' quarters had a joint cabin where we sat around and played poker through most of the trip and spent the rest of the time stretched out in bunks reading and being sick. Finally, the sea quieted down. After more than two weeks crossing the Atlantic, in the early evening of December 24th we had our first view of the United States. On Christmas morning we sailed past the Statue of Liberty with the entire contingent lining the rails, cheering, laughing, crying, and gazing at that remarkable statue which had greeted so many of the ancestors of the troops in years past.

After landing, we went to Fort Dix very briefly, where I was able to call home. Then those from the New England area were put on troop trains to the Devens Separation Center. There were several days of processing but the army did evince a certain humanity and released us all on temporary leave, so on December 27, 1945, I was able to get a train into Boston and meet Blanche in the Ritz lobby. I spent most of the next few days going through the ritual of separation and entering terminal leave as a major, a promotion that fortunately had not come through in time to slow down my departure from the ETO. We revelled in the luxury of the Ritz, saw the family, painted the town, and on New Year's Eve had a marvelous reunion party with friends that went on until the very small hours of the morning.

Eventually I called the Massachusetts General Hospital to see what I should do in order to make formal application for resumption of residency training in surgery. To my astonishment, Ruth Meehan, the secretary in the surgical office, said, "Just a minute,

Dr. Churchill will speak with you." That was probably one of the most numbing experiences of my life. I recall stumbling and mumbling that I really didn't want to bother the professor and chief of surgery, when Dr. Churchill in his inimitable way interrupted to ask, "When would you like to start?" On April 1, 1946, a little over three years since I had left to go to Camp Edwards and thence to Great Britain, I returned to work as assistant resident on the West Surgical Service.

So ended the saga of ETOUSA in World War II, and a new life began. Blanche and I moved into our new apartment in Brookline, renewed our old friendships, grieved for our friends who had been killed—Perry Johnson, Angus MacDonnell, Bob Hurlbut, and others. But Oley Paul, Brad Millet, Crick Wight, Bob Bainbridge, Peter Allen, and many other old friends were back in town, so in every sense, it was both an end and a beginning.

References

Blumenson, M. *Patton: The Man Behind the Legend.* William Morrow Co., New York, 1985.

Churchill, W. S. *The Second World War.* (Vols. 4,5,6). Houghton Mifflin, Boston, 1948-1953.

Collins, L. and LaPierre, D. *Is Paris Burning?* Simon and Shuster, New York, 1965.

Gavin, J.M. *On to Berlin.* Viking Press, New York, 1978.

Manchester, W. *The Last Lion.* Little, Brown and Co., Boston, 1990.

MacDonald, C.B. *A Time For Trumpets: The Untold Story of the Battle of the Bulge.* William Morrow Co., New York, 1985

McDermott, W.V., M.D. "The Aftermath of Surrender." *Harvard Medical Alumni Bulletin,* Vol. 66, No. 4, Boston, 1993

Patterson, Joseph F., M.D. *Friends of the Line: Fifteen Friends in World War II.* Privately printed, 1995.

Ryan, Cornelius. *The Longest Day.* Simon and Shuster, New York, 1959

Ryan, Cornelius. *The Last Battle,* Popular Library, New York, 1965

Ryan, Cornelius. *On the Battle Field,* Popular Library, New York, 1970

Shirer, W.L. *Berlin Diary.* Alfred A. Knopf, New York, 1941

Shirer, W.L. *The Rise and Fall of the Third Reich.* Simon and Shuster, New York, 1965

Shirer, W.L. *The Collapse of the Third Republic.* Simon and Shuster, New York, 1969

Shirer, W.L. *The Nightmare Years: 1930-1940.* Little, Brown and Co., Boston, 1984

Wilmot, C. *The Struggle For Europe.* Harper Bros., New York, 1952.

Index

[327]

Typeset in Monotype Bulmer.
Printed on 60 lb. Supple Opaque.
Printed and bound at Thomson-Shore, Dexter, Michigan.
Design by Sarah F. Bauhan and William L. Bauhan